Working with Emotions

Responding to the challenges of difficult pupil
behaviour in schools

Working with Emotions

Difficult pupil behaviour presents a number of issues for teachers, parents and other children, as well as for the pupils themselves. Such behaviour can produce a range of emotions, and providing support in this context is far from simple.

This accessible and timely book examines how emotions can influence the provision and effectiveness of support to pupils with behavioural difficulties, and presents useful and practical ways of managing such challenges effectively. Key issues explored in this informative text include:

- the variety of ways to approach pupils' emotional issues;
- how the emotions of those receiving and providing support can best be addressed;
- the need for effective collaboration and a problem-solving culture;
- an examination of recent thinking on the emotional aspects of difficult behaviour.

Working with Emotions recognises the importance of addressing both child and adult emotions, and offers practical approaches and perspectives to all those involved with children whose behaviour gives cause for concern.

Following many years as a teacher, educational psychologist and LEA officer, **Peter Gray** now works as a freelance consultant to local and national government on policy and provision for Special Educational Needs.

Working with Emotions

Responding to the challenges of difficult pupil behaviour in schools

Edited by Peter Gray

Routledge
Taylor & Francis Group

LONDON AND NEW YORK

First published 2002 by RoutledgeFalmer

Published 2016 by Routledge
2 Park Square, Milton Park, Abingdon, Oxfordshire OX14 4RN
711 Third Avenue, New York, NY 10017

First issued in hardback 2016

Routledge is an imprint of the Taylor and Francis Group, an informa business

© 2002 Peter Gray

Typeset in 10/12 Monotype Sabon by Steven Gardiner Ltd

British Library Cataloguing in Publication Data
A catalogue record for this book is available from the British Library.

Library of Congress Cataloging-in-Publication Data
Working with emotions: responding to the challenge of difficult pupil behaviour in
schools / edited by Peter Gray.
    p. cm
Includes bibliographical references and indexes.
1. Problem children – Education. 2. Behaviour modification. 3. Emotions.
I. Gray, Peter, 1953–

LC4801 .W67 2002
371.93 – dc21

2001041830

ISBN 13: 978-1-138-15148-2 (hbk)
ISBN 13: 978-0-415-23769-7 (pbk)

Contents

Figures

Tables

Contributors

Peter Gray works as a freelance consultant to local and national government on policy and provision for pupils with special educational needs, including those with emotional and behavioural difficulties. He previously worked for many years as a teacher, university lecturer, educational psychologist, and LEA officer. He has a range of publications and is currently chair of the Policy Subcommittee of NASEN (the National Association for Special Educational Needs).

Gervase Leyden is Academic and Professional Tutor to the Educational Psychology training course at Nottingham University. He also works as an educational psychologist for Nottingham City Council. He is a trained occupational psychologist with a particular interest in the impact of schools as organisations on the safety and well-being of teachers. His other major research interest is Inclusive Education and he has travelled widely looking at good practice in this area.

Gerda Hanko works as an educational consultant and staff development tutor with schools, LEA support services and teacher training establishments. She is an Associate of the London University Institute of Education and a visiting Course Tutor. She has a number of publications aimed at promoting teachers' insight into emotional and social factors involved in learning and failure to learn and has been involved in training personal advisers for the new DfEE Connexions Project for disaffected 13–19-year-olds.

Tessa Sambrook is the parent of two teenagers, one of whom has complex special needs including speech and language, dyspraxia and hyperkinetic disorder. For the past 15 years she has worked to support parents through the educational maze, most recently with AFASIC (Association For All Speech-Impaired Children) as their Helpline and Policy Manager. She has represented parents at SEN Tribunals and, last year, was a member of the DfEE Speech and Language Therapy and SEN Code of Practice working groups.

Pauline Fell is an experienced teacher who has worked in a number of secondary and comprehensive schools in Solihull and Coventry. Since then, she has been actively involved in support roles, first as Team Coordinator of Warwickshire's Northern Area Education Support Service (Behaviour) and more recently as Learning Support Coordinator at Etone Community School. She has also had recent experience of managing a Pupil Referral Unit centre.

Bill Wahl is is a Chartered Counselling Psychologist as well as a Certified School Psychologist (USA). Having spent a number of years in England, working with difficult and challenging pupils in education settings, he is now employed as Staff Psychologist for the North Devon Health Care Trust.

Eddie McNamara works as a freelance educational psychologist and trainer. He has an active interest in cognitive behaviour therapy approaches, writing extensively on the subject and putting theory into practice through regular work with children in schools.

Rob Long is an educational psychologist who worked for a number of years as manager of one of Devon LEA's Primary Behaviour Support Teams as well as supporting secondary schools in reviewing their behaviour management policies and practice. Since then, he has worked nationally as a trainer and consultant. He has written extensively and is widely known for the accessible way in which he manages to help teachers and others understand and support pupils who faced emotional and behavioural challenges.

Adrian Faupel worked for many years as Associate Tutor to the Educational Psychology Training Course at Southampton University, where he continues to be involved in teaching and research. He also works for Southampton LEA, where he is significantly involved in the development of the Authority's Emotional Literacy programme.

Jey Monsen, Beverley Graham and R. J. (Sean) Cameron are all Associate Tutors to the Educational Psychology Training Course at University College, London. They are also employed as Senior Educational Psychologists, respectively, in Kent, Hackney and Surrey LEAs.

Hugh Williams is a Senior Educational Psychologist for Birmingham City Council. He trained as a secondary English and special needs teacher, and qualified as an Educational Psychologist in 1979. He has written articles on Precision Teaching, statementing and behaviour. He ran the New Outlooks project for Birmingham enquiring into provision and practice for children with emotional and behavioural difficulties between 1996 and 1998. It was this project which founded Framework for Intervention, for which he remains the development manager.

Amanda Daniels is also a Senior Educational Psychologist for Birmingham City Council. She taught in secondary schools before joining Coventry City Council as an Educational Psychologist in 1984. As part of the New Outlooks Project, she conducted the pilot of the Framework for Intervention in 1987 and has been the project manager ever since. Amanda has presented to conferences and interest groups around the UK.

Acknowledgements

A number of chapters in this book are based on seminars presented by contributors at a series of annual conferences organised over the last few years under the heading *New Directions in Behaviour Support*. An earlier volume: *Challenging Behaviour in Schools: Teacher Support, Practical Techniques and Policy Development*, edited by Peter Gray, Andy Miller and Jim Noakes, also published by Routledge, had a similar foundation. These conferences are designed to provide stimulation and support to people working across the UK in the behaviour support field.

I would like to take the opportunity to thank my fellow conference organisers over the years, Jim Noakes, Andy Miller, and those who have joined me more recently, Lynne Blount and Jamie Skeldon and, in Scotland, Michael McKean and Yvonne Wright. Thanks too to all those who have helped me during my life to address my own range of emotional challenges: my parents, friends and colleagues and, most of all, my wife Rachel and our three children.

Part I
Context

1 Working with difficult behaviour

The impact of emotions

Peter Gray

Fear and loathing in the nursery – how toddler rage is spreading through the nation

Such headlines are becoming increasingly common, even in the so-called 'respectable' newspapers. They seem to capture a mood in Britain that is inexorably drawn towards notions of a breakdown in society. Standards of children's behaviour in schools and elsewhere are seen to be deteriorating as family and societal values change and children are exposed to an increasing range of corrupting influences. Incidents such as the murders of Jamie Bulger, Damilola Taylor and of the Head Teacher, Philip Lawrence, which gained significant media coverage, only serve to confirm such beliefs.

Teaching unions in Britain have continued to argue that their members are experiencing considerable stress and hardship as a result of difficult pupils and unsupportive parents. There are an increasing number of cases where teachers are seeking compensation for physical or emotional damage that they attribute to their experience of difficult behaviour in schools.

At the same time, pupils and parents have also become more prepared to assert their rights and entitlements. There have been some high-profile cases where teachers and head teachers have been brought to court following allegations of physical or other assault by staff. The application of European law has also opened up the question of pupils and parents seeking compensation for unfair treatment that can be proved to have caused personal harm.

The emphasis on rights has raised the stakes in relation to tensions and conflicts that have always to some extent been present. And there are now very real issues about how to achieve a proper balance between the rights of pupils at risk of exclusion and their parents and the rights of teachers and the pupils with whom 'difficult pupils' are educated.

The government's Social Inclusion agenda has attempted to show that there are no 'winners' from unresolved difficulties at school. While permanent exclusion may shift the problem on elsewhere, those pupils who become marginalised from education affect all of us to some degree, whether in terms of their involvement in crime or other antisocial activity or in terms of their ability to make a longer term contribution to society.

Many politicians and commentators seek a resolution to this issue by arguing for more alternative provision for difficult pupils, away from the mainstream system, and the present government has invested additional funds to help create more such options. However, the costs of such provision make it unrealistic to expect that this will take all our problems away.

A key theme of this book is that problems can only be adequately addressed if there is a proper understanding of the *emotions* that are associated with difficult behaviour, not just for pupils but for the range of adults involved, whether they be teachers, parents, support workers, administrators or politicians. Emotions do not *excuse* difficult behaviour in children (or adults) but they do help to explain it. Any response needs to take on board and plan for emotional issues. They are part of the human condition. Understanding emotions is part of communication, and communication is ineffective if people's emotions are neglected or not properly understood.

The world of behaviour problems is characterised by blame. As problems become greater, there is an increased propensity for schools to blame parents, parents to blame schools, and both to blame the children. Support services and other agencies are not immune, either from being blamed for not producing instant solutions, or from finding inadequacies in others. And children are not always prepared to take responsibility for their own actions!

This book adopts a 'no blame' approach and rejects the more adversarial trends that have developed over the last 20 years. The contributors argue that behaviour, both in children and adults, is generally understandable, if not always easy to accept. This is not to imply that all behaviour has deep-seated emotional origins. Too much energy and time has been wasted over the years in trying to establish clear distinctions between pupils who are 'disruptive' (and therefore to blame as they are in control of their actions), 'disaffected' (school to blame for not providing a sufficiently relevant and interesting curriculum) and 'disturbed' (pupils not to blame, but potentially 'incurable'). Instead, the theme of the book is that all difficult behaviour has an emotional component, either in relation to the pupil whose behaviour is causing concern or the adults and other pupils who respond to it. Being aware of, understanding and planning for this component is an essential part of any intervention, whether this is at the level of the individual pupil, teacher or school, or at the level of local and national strategy.

The book is divided into several parts. The first of these sets out some of the broader context for understanding issues concerning difficult pupil behaviour. In Chapter 2, Gerv Leyden looks at the issue of violence. Teacher unions and others, both in Britain and elsewhere, have continued to express concern about increasing violence in schools. How accurate is their belief? Are schools really less safe environments than they were 20 or 30 years ago? The chapter sets out some of the myths and realities with regard to the theme of increasing violence and identifies ways in which violent incidents can best be prevented and avoided.

The second part focuses on *adult* emotions. Contributors provide an analysis of some of the issues faced by teachers, parents and others when difficult pupil behaviour is experienced. Gerda Hanko (Chapter 3) looks at the emotional experience of teaching and argues that helping teachers to understand pupil emotions gives them a better understanding and insight into their own positive and negative feelings. Tessa Sambrook and Peter Gray (Chapter 4) focus on issues for parents, who tend to be seen, unhelpfully, as 'always the problem' rather than 'part of the solution'. Pauline Fell (Chapter 5) looks at the relationship between teachers and those who attempt to support them in addressing problem behaviour.

The third part looks at *pupil* emotions. Rob Long (Chapter 8) argues that there has been an overemphasis on understanding pupil *behaviour* at the expense of a clear analysis of pupil *emotions*. He proposes an approach to assessment and intervention that takes account of both areas and the linkages between them. Bill Wahl (Chapter 6) focuses on the importance of developing an effective 'working alliance' between pupils and key adults. This requires an understanding of the way children's past experiences and associated emotions can affect the way in which they engage with those who are trying to help them. Eddie McNamara (Chapter 7) provides a more specific model for intervening with pupils with problem behaviour, based on a cognitive approach to assessing and working with pupil emotions. Finally, Adrian Faupel (Chapter 9) revisits the issue of violence, through examining the position of anger and aggression within a broader continuum of emotions.

The fourth part looks at some examples of supportive systems that help teachers and others in working with difficult pupil behaviour and which explicitly recognise the emotional issues this raises for adults and for pupils themselves. Jey Monsen and Beverley Graham (Chapter 10) point to the value of school-based teacher support groups as an effective means of solving problems cooperatively and positively in school. In Chapter 11, Jey Monsen and Sean Cameron describe the benefits of 'coaching' as a practical form of supervision and support. Hugh Williams and Amanda Daniels (Chapter 12) then outline the Birmingham Framework for Intervention model, which encourages teachers and schools not only to identify problems but also to think more clearly about ways in which they can help in addressing them.

In the final part, I look at the area of policy and provision for pupils with behaviour difficulties and show how this is affected by policy-makers' own emotions and sensitivities. The emotive (and political) character of the area makes it extremely difficult to develop and maintain coherent and consistent policy that can help address pupil and adult needs effectively. However, a number of steps could be taken to improve existing strategies and these are outlined.

The book does not espouse a specific theory about emotions and behaviour and is permissive of a range of models of analysis, from psychodynamic to behavioural. However, a unifying theme is that emotions are as much a part of the landscape in understanding the world of behaviour problems as the behaviour itself. In an era when emotions tend to be debarred from concepts of professionalism, we would argue that a professional response to resolving behaviour issues is only likely to be achieved if proper account is taken of both pupil emotions and our own.

2 Myths, fears and realities regarding pupil violence to teachers
Evidence from research

Gervase Leyden

Introduction

Concerns about violence in society have a long history. More recently, following union and media pressure, the focus has shifted to encompass workplace violence, particularly in the public sector where staff in hospitals, social services, housing and benefit agencies as well as schools have been the subject of violent attacks. The most up-to-date information we have about the nature and costs of workplace violence in the UK derives from the British Crime Survey for1997 (BCS 1999) which reports that:

- approximately a quarter of a million physical assaults at work resulted in actual physical injury (e.g. bruising, broken bones);
- in about 5,000 of the incidents the victim required an overnight stay in hospital;
- the majority of victims experienced distressing symptoms, including anger, fear and difficulty in sleeping;
- people who suffered violence at work were at a high risk of repeat victimisation (almost half of the assault victims suffered more than one incident in the year);
- the survey estimated 3.3 million working hours were lost each year because of violence, and the financial costs were around £62 million per year, potentially rising to £230 million taking into account potential compensation claims.

(HSE 1999)

In the education sector, teachers, parents and the general public were shocked by the murder of the headteacher of a comprehensive school in London, the frenzied machete attack by an intruder in a Wolverhampton infant school and the tragic murder of sixteen pupils and a teacher in Dunblane primary school. Although these incidents were primarily 'intruder violence', they served to draw the attention of parents, the public and media to the general problem of physical violence in schools, and culminated in a public enquiry chaired by Lord Cullen (DES/WO 1996) and a government-funded research investigation (Gill and Hearnshaw 1997).

This chapter takes the stance that pupil violence towards their teachers is an extreme example of challenging behaviour. In one author's account, it symbolises 'the most significant, disruptive and distressing expression of disaffection' (Parsons 1999). For teachers, violence presents a critical threat, not only to their personal safety and psychological well-being, but also to their professional motivation, self-belief and views about their role in the academic and pastoral development of young people.

In the following pages I will attempt to describe the nature and extent of pupil violence in schools and outline the steps individual teachers, schools and managers can take to create a safe learning environment for all who work and learn in them.

Social attitudes to violent and challenging behaviour by children

Attitudes towards and perceptions of violence are influenced by changing social and political values, and in turn influence the behaviour of individuals and groups in societies. Parsons (1999) claims that 'exclusions from school are direct consequences of socio-cultural arrangements' and points to the shift from humanitarian towards controlling and disciplinary attitudes in the latter years of the twentieth century. He comments that while most schools and teachers continue to value Personal and Social Education (PSE) alongside pupil-centred activities, the introduction of the National Curriculum, external accountability and the push for standards and basics 'has reduced the pastoral power of schools.'

Views about a 'golden age of education' or society tend to be accompanied by attitudes which construe children as being either 'angels or demons'. Such attributions are often enshrined in educational and legal procedures. Asquith and Cutting (1999) point to national differences underpinning the age at which children are held to be 'criminally responsible' for their actions, particularly in respect of serious offences such as violence and murder. They cite the abolitionist movements in the USA, which argue that young offenders should not be treated any more leniently than their adult counterparts. In their view, the focus should be on the crime, and not on the degree to which the offender is mature enough to take responsibility for what he or she has done.

While some believe that children who commit violent offences merit adult punishments within the framework of the law, there is no evidence that punishment is particularly successful in reducing the risk of reoffending in later life (Asquith and Cutting 1999).

The age of criminal responsibility varies greatly in European countries. For example, in Switzerland, this starts as young as 7 years of age. Belgium on the other hand does not consider young people as being criminally responsible until they are 18. Other countries lie between these two extremes. However, England, Wales and Scotland are much closer in this respect to Switzerland than to their other European neighbours. A 10-year-old child in England and Wales (and an 8-year-old in Scotland) who committed a seriously violent act would be held criminally responsible for his/her actions. In most other countries (e.g. France (13), Germany (14), Spain (16) and Poland (17)), this would happen at a much later age (see Asquith and Cutting 1999).

Incidence and definitions of violence in schools

A *historical perspective*

While myths of an idyllic 'golden age' of education persist, we have no reliable archive records to support this. In fact, there are examples of the reverse: such as the highly disciplinarian boarding schools in which pupils were the victims and staff were the assailants, either directly, through caning, or indirectly, through condoning institutionalised bullying. Smike, in the academy of Dotheboys Hall, would have been unimpressed to learn that he was living in an educational golden age!

There are examples too, in biographical accounts, of instances where students have risen violently against their oppressors. In 1793, Harrow students staged a rebellion which lasted for 3 weeks. Some 4 years later at Rugby, the boys blew the door off the headmaster's study and as a result troops were called in and the Riot Act read (Rock and Heidensohn 1969).

An illuminating account of the 1892 rebellion at Eton is provided by H. S. Tremenheere, a pupil at the time and subsequently a pioneering inspector of schools (Edmonds and Edmonds 1965). Tremenheere relates how '... the boys, nearly two hundred ... rose against the Authorities, took possession of the College, barricaded it unassailably, disregarded remonstrances, solicitations and threats of physical force, and only yielded when their demands were granted. Staff were held captive, the Constabulary mocked, and the Colonel of the Regiment threatened that "a good many heads would be broken"....'. Rhodes Boyson, a former headteacher and Minister of Education described his early teaching experience in a Lancashire secondary-modern school as 'a battle for survival compared with which periods in the war were like a holiday camp' (Boyson 1970). (For further oral and documentary accounts see Humphries 1995 and Pearson 1983.)

The role of the media

Writing in *The Times*, Robin Young reflected on his own part in a school mutiny, which took place at Winchester in 1957 following the death of a well-respected headmaster and the appointment of a senior chemistry teacher in his place. In Young's laconic account, 'Discipline rapidly foundered.' Students, largely from the school cadet force, armed themselves with Enfield-303 rifles, Bren guns, thunderflashes and live ammunition. A nearby RAF hut was commandeered as headquarters and the pupils took to the streets of Winchester (Young 1997). In contrast to recent sensationalist media portrayals of events at the Ridings and other schools, the Fleet Street press corps visiting the school were regaled with colourful interviews by gun-toting students, but no photographs or copy appeared in either the national or local press.

In contrast to Young's account, Peter Clark who took over at the Ridings school, a school achieving notoriety as the 'School from Hell' in the mid-1990s, described how the media contributed to the problems the school was facing. There was no doubt, in the words of the visiting Ofsted inspection team that the 'disorderly conduct of a significant minority of pupils continually disrupts many aspects of the school life' (Clark 1998). Clark described an incident when photographers persuaded two girls entering the school to 'flick us some Vs' – which they enthusiastically did. The resultant pictures captured headlines in the national press, and on prime-time television, imprinting in the national psyche an image of defiant, out-of-control youth. Clark records other events in which the media encouraged pupils to set off fireworks in the school grounds, invented accounts of pupils throwing cans of urine at teachers and promised payment to some pupils for their 'stories'. Clark concluded that the role of the media changed from 'merely reporting the incidents to being an intrinsic part of the problem.' (Clark, 1998). The school has since overcome its difficulties and is no longer experiencing serious weaknesses, nor requiring 'special measures.'

One major consequence of the 'demonising' of children by the media and politicians is to present difficulties for teachers and other workers in the field in maintaining a balanced focus on the educational needs of those children who undoubtedly pose challenging questions about the most effective ways of managing their behaviour. Violence in schools is a factual event. It is also a phenomenon which provokes strong emotions in us all. Attention on ways of minimising it and focusing on the needs and entitlements of teachers, pupils and others who work in schools is long overdue. However, it is equally true that alleviating violence in our schools first requires us to confront our own emotions and deeply held beliefs about the topic in order to arrive at a clear understanding of its incidence, nature and genesis.

Research evidence: methodology and definitional issues

Methodological problems have blighted research into violence against teachers, with the result that findings must be treated with caution and are difficult to generalise. Union surveys, while providing vivid case-study accounts, have generally sought information solely from their own member-ship, which may not reflect the views of all relevant staff. Terminology has remained a consistent problem, with no shared meaning of what constitutes a violent act; some studies including 'vandalism' within their definition of 'violence'. Other potentially useful surveys have suffered from sampling errors and low (or unreported) response rates. There is also an obvious risk that teachers may under-report violent incidents out of fear of being stigmatised or leaving themselves open to criticisms of poor pupil relationships or classroom management skills. The recent introduction in England of 'performance related pay', linked to an annual review of teachers' competencies, may add to this.

Finally, most of the data collection fails to recognise that violence in schools is an interpersonal process, influenced by the nature of the relationship between those involved and the setting and circumstances in which the violent episode occurs.

A majority of studies distinguish between physical violence (with or without a weapon) and verbal aggression or threats (e.g. ESAC 1990a). Verbal aggression may be distressing in itself and a signal of impending physical violence. The menace of verbal threats should not be underestimated, particularly when personalised towards the intended victim or members of her/his family: 'We know where you live. And where your kids go to school.'

More recent definitions include evidence of an *intent* to hurt in order to distinguish between accidental and deliberate harm (e.g. Elliott *et al.* 1998; Leather *et al.* 1999). Actions that are interpreted as 'good-natured' physical contact (e.g. playful pushing) with no intention of hurting, but which may accidentally do so, are now generally excluded (see the Appendices to the Elton Report (DES/WO 1989) for case studies of how teachers use 'intentionality' to determine whether or not they construe a physical encounter with pupils as violent).

Breakwell (1989) draws on the concept of 'tolerable aggression' to help explain teachers' appraisal of their interactions with pupils. Some form of 'jostling or horseplay' may be accepted as normal or tolerable; likewise staff involved in calming or restraining an infant tantrum may receive some uncontrolled physical contact. However, she suggests that the increasing professionalisation of teaching may have resulted in 'the frontier between the tolerable and intolerable being renegotiated.' As a result, teachers may now be more inclined to report as violent some incidents that previously might have been tolerated. This has implications when comparing response and incidence rates of violence in surveys and LEA records.

Teachers' own experiences or social background may also have an influence on what they perceive as a challenging or potentially violent situation. Weare cites Willis to make the point that the 'loud and jocular behaviour of working-class boys, which many teachers find disruptive, may well be behaviour that makes sense in other contexts, such as the street, the housing estate, the club or the workplace' (Weare 2000).

Violence, as an interactive event between two or more people, inevitably incorporates interpersonal elements and individual attributions, which influence understandings and accounts of what has occurred. While we are now able to record the incidence of violent behaviour in a more consistent and objective manner, we still lack the necessary research tools and data to provide us with a complete understanding of what happens between those involved, and how we can most effectively reduce the risk of violent behaviour.

Incidence of violence to teachers

Local authority records should provide a useful bank of information about the incidence of violence to teachers in our schools. The former Inner London Education Authority (ILEA) is one such source, but similar records across other authorities have not generally been maintained. The plea by The Health and Safety Commission (ESAC 1990a) for a national recording system of violence to teachers has remained largely unheard. Since the ILEA findings were published, most of what we know about the national picture of violence to teachers in the UK has emerged from the national surveys linked to the Elton Committee's work (DES/WO 1989) and the Scarman Centre investigation (Gill and Hearnshaw 1997). The major findings are summarised below.

(a) ILEA Records

Analysis of reported acts of violence to teachers.

- 535 violent incidents to teachers were reported.
- 0.23% reported violent incidents per mainstream school.
- 2.48% reported violent incidents per special school.
- 57% of the assailants were pupils.
- 5.5% of the assailants were intruders.
- 4% of the assailants were parents or other members of the family.
- A number of the returns were unclassifiable.

(Poyner and Warne 1988)

We know very little about the individuals involved, neither their gender/age, nor the nature of the relationship (past and present) between the teacher victim and pupil aggressor.

(b) The Elton Report

As part of its enquiry into school discipline and behaviour, the Elton Committee collected information about teachers' experience of violence during one designated week of the school year.

- Sample size: 2,500 secondary teachers (response rate 89%).
- Time span: one designated week.

- 15% of teachers reported verbal abuse.
- 1.7% of teachers reported physical aggression while teaching.
- 1.1% of teachers reported physical aggression during general school duties.

(DES/WO 1989)

(c) DfEE/Lamplugh Trust/Scarman Centre

Following the murder of Phillip Lawrence and other high-profile tragic incidents of violence to teachers in the 1990s, the DfEE and Suzy Lamplugh Trust commissioned the Scarman Centre to carry out a research study into personal safety in schools (Gill and Hearnshaw 1997). A major part of the study addressed violence to teachers, from whatever source. The survey generated responses from individual schools about their own experiences during the previous academic year. The recording criteria used by schools were vague and only a quarter said that they recorded all incidents of crime and nuisance.

- Time span: one academic year.
- Sample size: 2,303 schools (primary, secondary, special, PRUs) (response rate 58%).
- 12% of schools reported pupils carrying weapons on school premises during the period surveyed.

Assaults on teachers by pupils

- 16.1% of schools reported Level 1 violence from pupils (spitting, pushing).
- 18.7% of schools reported Level 2 violence from pupils (punching, kicking).
- 2.9% of schools reported Level 3 violence from pupils (assault with weapon, being stabbed, slashed)

Assaults on teachers from parents/outsiders

- 50% of schools reported verbal abuse from parents.
- 26.9% of schools reported verbal abuse from other outsiders.
- 2.7% of schools reported Level 1 violence.
- 2.4% of schools reported Level 2 violence.
- 1.1% of schools reported Level 3 violence.

(Gill and Hearnshaw 1997).

Violence to teachers: a summary

The findings from the above studies are consistent. The risk of actual physical violence to an individual teacher is low, but nevertheless each incident is a source of distress – in some instances tragically so – for those teachers concerned, their families and colleagues within the school. Risks are typically enhanced within some large, inner-city schools and within disadvantaged communities.

The incidence of 'lower level violence' (unwanted physical contact, verbal abuse) is a more frequent occurrence and source of chronic stress to teachers (Gill and Hearnshaw 1997; ESAC 1990b).

Not surprisingly, the major source of violence to teachers is pupils. Pupil violence represents as extreme example of pupil behaviour – not only threatening teachers' physical health and well-being, but also striking at the heart of their professional beliefs, confidence and self-regard. It is both a private and public event with repercussions not only for the teacher and his/her family but also for the school and neighbourhood community.

Where teachers were assaulted by outsiders, it was generally by ex-pupils, or by parents of pupils currently attending the school. 'Schools which suffer more types of crime were more likely to suffer more types of assault' (Gill and Hearnshaw 1997).

However, putting the above findings into a different perspective, an Ofsted survey of primary and secondary schools concluded 'Standards of (pupil) behaviour are satisfactory or better in most secondary schools and good in three out of four' (Ofsted 1993).

Understanding violent episodes

The incidence figures help to put school violence into perspective, but tell us little about the circumstances in which the incidents took place and the contributory factors. What do we know about violent episodes in schools?

With relatively few exceptions, violent incidents typically follow a five-phase cycle of behaviour. This cycle applies equally to the assailant and victim (Breakwell 1997). The five phases are 'trigger', 'escalation', 'crisis', 'recovery' and 'post-crisis depression'. As Breakwell points out, knowledge of this sequence allows teachers 'to predict better the development of violent incidents and understand their own reactions.' My own discussions with teachers confirm the applicability of this model to pupil–teacher violence in schools. It is worth noting that each stage of the model allows for a response from teacher or pupil, which can accelerate or calm the potential for violence. The social context is important. In some incidents, the aim may be to isolate the aggressor(s) or remove other pupils from the scene in order to ensure their safety, and prevent their playing a role in the escalation of the incident. Bystanders can also be enlisted in playing a constructive role in helping to defuse the incident (Gill and Hearnshaw 1997).

It is crucial to distinguish between acts of violence and personal fear of violence. While there may be unpredictable, apparently uncontrollable outbursts of challenging and violent behaviour, most 'day to day' acts are signalled and follow a relatively predictable sequence. Teachers need to recognise and manage their own feelings and responses in respect of teenage behaviour which may be boisterous and loud, but not necessarily violent – nor potentially so, unless mismanaged.

Initial and post-experience for teachers – and most other public-sector workers – should not only include an understanding of violence but also workshops on how to de-escalate, calm and control potentially violent encounters (see Leather *et al.* (1999) for a comprehensive account of strategies for monitoring, reducing and managing work-related violence).

Teacher and school factors

Few UK surveys have provided detailed information about the teachers who were the subjects of assault, although more attention has been directed to what they were doing at the time. The most detailed information in respect of teacher and school factors derives from a US study, *Safe Schools – Violent Schools* (NIE 1978).

In respect of school and neighbourhood factors, most surveys identify the enhanced risks of teaching in socially disadvantaged, inner-city areas and in secondary schools. Other surveys have also found higher risks for teachers in special schools and PRUs (NIE 1978; ESAC 1990a; Gill and Hearnshaw 1997; Elliott *et al.* 1998).

The findings from the USA in respect of the 'multiple victimisation' of teachers are cautionary, and require close attention in the UK. In the NIE survey, although the risks of attack were the same for male and female teachers, the risks of repeat 'victimisation' were particularly high for female secondary teachers in respect of rape: '. . . if a female teacher is attacked once in a two month period, the chances of also being raped in that period shoot up from less than 1 in 1000 to almost 1 in 10, more than a hundred fold increase in risk' (NIE 1978).

A number of studies have mapped out areas in schools where teachers feel most anxious about personal safety. Menacken *et al.* (1990) reported that less than 5% of Chicago teachers felt 'very safe' on the school grounds or car parks – and 20% of pupils also avoided the parking areas for fear of personal harm. The creation of 'no-go' areas in schools adds to the fear of violence, not only by making such areas threatening to teachers and pupils, but also through the message it conveys to other members of the school and neighbourhood community. We do not possess such a detailed breakdown in respect of UK figures, although Gill and Hearnshaw (1997) endorse the risks attendant to creating 'no-go' areas.

Critical activities for teachers

Survey findings identify a number of activities and locations within schools, which carry additional risks of violent encounters. Among the most prominent are:

- removing a pupil from the classroom;
- intervening in a fight between pupils;
- teaching/working in an isolated setting;
- dealing with angry parents/intruders;
- home visiting;
- working alone;
- evening working.

Pupil factors

As we have seen, pupils are the main source of violence to teachers. What do we know about the background of those children who commit violent and criminal acts? While no one negative factor is critical in the analysis of the children, there is general agreement on the significance and cumulative effect of:

- direct experience of physical/sexual abuse;
- experience of witnessing physical/sexual abuse within the family;
- punitive child-rearing practices;
- alcohol/drug abuse within the family;
- significant social disadvantage.

The lesson from the research is clear and perhaps best expressed by Asquith and Cutting (1999): 'Violence by children is inextricably linked to violence to them.'

Other factors, such as growing up in a violent, crime-ridden community (e.g. in some parts of the USA where there is easy access to and familiarity with guns) may also increase the young person's propensity to violence. This may be intensified in these schools where general levels of pupil behaviour are poor, and the quality of teaching is low. Nevertheless, we must remember that for pupils in high-crime communities, schools are still safer for them than are their own neighbourhoods (although in the USA this may not necessarily be the case for teachers; Menacken *et al.* 1990; Elliott *et al.* 1998). School, teacher and pupil dimensions are interactive, and there is much that schools can do to nurture development, improve pupil behaviour and minimise the risks of generally 'unruly' behaviour escalating into violence.

Work-related stress and school violence

Effects of violence on the individual

Whether or not there is any physical injury, the psychological effects on the victim of violence are well known. For some individuals, this may reveal itself as shock or disbelief. Once the reality of the event is recognised most people experience a range of distressing emotions. Brady (1999) describes how these may include feelings of disorientation and of being unable to think clearly or make decisions. It is not uncommon for victims to behave out of character by showing extremes of emotion, and becoming emotionally upset, or cool and withdrawn. Fear is a common initial response, followed by anger and often guilt. While one individual may appear to recover and resume work, others experience a loss of confidence in their own ability to deal with the situation or activity linked with the initial assault.

For teachers who have been victim of a pupil assault, a return to work inevitably involves renewed contact with pupils and the setting in which the violence occurred. Without support, some teachers may remain fearful of further contact with pupils and leave the profession. Breakwell (1997) describes the medium and longer term effects of experiencing physical violence, which may include post-traumatic stress disorder, and both she and Brady offer guidelines of how the individual – and the employer – can best handle this and assist the 'victim' in becoming a 'survivor'.

As we have seen from the above surveys, serious incidents of pupil violence may not be as prevalent as portrayed and the Gill and Hearnshaw (1997) research found that 'over 70 per cent of respondents felt that violence in schools was exaggerated by the media'. Averaging out responses conceals the diversity of experience across schools and we need to recognise that, for some schools and teachers, the experience of violence is very different. A national or regional recording system would help focus attention on the need to make some schools much safer places in which to teach and learn.

Fear of violence, and teacher stress

If violent and seriously challenging behaviour is not a major issue for most teachers, fear of violence certainly is (Gill and Hearnshaw 1997; Weare 2000). Nearly 40% of the schools in the Gill and Hearnshaw survey agreed with the statement 'Schools are no longer safe places'. Furthermore, and despite pupils being identified as the major *source* of violence, 70% of the schools rated 'outsiders' as the greater *threat*. There is also extensive evidence that when teachers are asked about the major sources of stress at work they cite the exhausting, day-to-day demands of teaching, the disruption of classes, excessive workload, external pressures and accountability plus externally imposed 'change upon change' (Wheldall and Merrett 1988; ESAC 1990a; Kyriacou 1996; Maden 1999). So violence *per se* is not necessarily the *major* concern that it is presented to be in the media and at union conferences, although classroom management problems, particularly in respect of 'difficult' pupils, continue to be a source of stress for many teachers (Galloway 1982; Dewe 1986).

There is general agreement on the high levels of work-related stress experienced by teachers. The distressing and disabling effects of stress may be compounded by the presence of a pupil with challenging behaviour, and is an argument for addressing stress in schools as part of any behavioural action programme.

The tension for the teacher in maintaining a professionally objective perspective when confronted by emotionally charged events is further fuelled when society looks to schools to resolve social concerns such as teenage pregnancy, parenting skills, drug misuse, underage drinking, violence and youth crime. It seems bizarre to place these expectations on teachers while simultaneously reducing the capacity of schools to fulfil their pastoral roles in order to fulfil academic targets.

Dewe (1985), in his studies of stress among teachers and other groups, distinguished between coping styles which focused on reducing the source of the stress, and those which dealt with the negative emotions experienced: 'Two thirds of people's efforts are directed at feeling better rather than dealing with the problem.' (Dewe 1986).

Some teachers' coping and survival strategies for severe job stressors, anxieties and fears take the form of 'disengagement' from their work. Disengagement involves withdrawing from the social and pastoral life of the school, thereby isolating oneself from students and colleagues – and the possibilities of social support they may provide. Breakwell uses the concept of 'incubation' to describe how an isolated person's fears and anxieties flourish in such circumstances. Such a negative cycle increases the vulnerability of the individual and diminishes the atmosphere of collegial support within the school.

How have we come to a situation where some teachers have low morale and are disenchanted with the professional vocation for which they trained? Weare links the erosion of teachers' professional autonomy – the degree to which they have control over their own work – as a major contributor to the 'remarkable rise in teacher stress levels' (Weare 2000). The link between job control and work related stress has been long established in health psychology across a number of occupations, including teaching. (Dewe 1986; Karasek and Thorel 1990).

There is also emerging evidence that 'job control' is associated with levels of coronary heart disease (CHD). Marmott and his colleagues at the Institute of Epidemiology, University College London found 'low (job) control to be involved in the process that links socio-economic status with coronary heart disease.' Weare (2000) has applied the concept of 'low job control' to teaching and cites 'the increased level of outside prescription, control and surveillance with which teachers are having to contend' as one possible explanation for low morale, absences from work and dropouts among the profession. Weare contends that teacher morale is unlikely to improve until the social and emotional health needs of the school are addressed.

Achieving this may seem a pipedream for those teaching in unsupportive or even hostile settings. However, workshops by Cox and his associates at the University of Nottingham with teachers drawn from a range of LEAs identified the psychological factors that contribute to the creation of the organisationally and psychologically 'healthy school'(Cox *et al.* 1989; Cox and Kuk 1991). The 'healthy school' is characterised by the subjective quality of its teaching and problem-solving environments balanced by its systems for promoting staff and organisational development. These dimensions are 'glued' together by the social, collegial aspect of the school community. The above model predicts teacher well-being, defined by lower self-reported levels of stress and ill health and increased morale, evidenced by a greater commitment to continuing to teach within the school. Preliminary work has produced promising results that can be translated into practice through school-based teacher workshops.

There is further encouraging evidence that young people's attitudes to school and teachers are not as bleak as many believe. Most pupils value their professional and informal contacts with staff. Maden draws on Barber's Keele University study to point out that 70% of pupils said they got on well with most or all of their teachers, valued opportunities for contact with teachers at lunchtime or after school and recognised the important role teachers play in supporting and developing their learning (Maden 1999).

Engaging constructively with the student peer group can be a source of support and professional affirmation for teachers as well as enhancing pupil learning. A number of collaborative learning strategies and 'inclusive tools' have been developed which enable teachers to create just such opportunities and foster relationships between pupils, and between pupils and their teachers (Leyden 1996). Weare also describes a number of similar strategies, including peer mediation and conflict resolution (Weare 2000) while there are promising developments from school community approaches, including Restorative Justice – which is a promising community approach to dealing with crime and restoring relationships. Collaborative and inclusive strategies such as these enlist the staff, the pupil and peer group as part of the school's problem-solving and community-building team.

The belief that long-term school improvement can be achieved solely through setting targets, without regard for the personal, professional and emotional needs of teachers, or the pastoral as well as the learning needs of pupils, is deeply flawed. Friedman, reviewing data on staff burnout, observes: "A school introducing hard driving, 'type A' organisational procedures in order to boost pupils' academic achievements at the expense of staff collegial support, does so at the expense of inducing stress and burnout among its teachers" (Friedman 1991).

Final comments

The more we can learn about the nature and genesis of violence in our schools, the more effective we can become in 'designing out' violence, fear and stress. There is no effective 'off the shelf' package for this, and each school must devise its own solutions to fit its own unique circumstances. However, the first step is for each school to carry out its own audit and involve staff and students in the creation of strategies for 'designing in' a safe and stress-free culture of learning and acceptance in our schools.

There are a number of Government sources and other publications to help guide the process in schools (ESAC 1990a; DfEE 1996a; DfEE 1996b. See also Leyden, 1999 for a description of planning an audit and school action plan). However, the overriding principle must be to create a safe and healthy school environment, not an educational fortress, a point endorsed by over 90% of the schools responding to the Gill and Hearnshaw survey.

School violence, and the fears it generates, is a global issue, not a prerogative of the USA nor a British disease. Among European countries, France and Germany have similar concerns, while UNESCO has commissioned a study of school violence in Jordan, Slovakia, Israel, Ethiopia and Latin America (Ohsako 1997). The evidence is that teachers teach best and students learn most effectively in safe, healthy schools, in which each member of the community has equal and full opportunities to participate and belong.

References

Asquith, S. and Cutting, E. (1999) 'Murder by children: Principles for a preventive strategy', in J. Tunstill (ed.) *Children and the State: Whose Problem?*, London: Cassell.

Boyson, R. (1970) 'Law and order in school', *The Spectator*, 28 February 1970, p. 270.

Brady, C. (1999) Surviving the incident. In: P. Leather, C. Brady, C. Lawrence, D. Beale and T. Cox (eds) *Work-related Violence: Assessment and Intervention*, London: Routledge.

Breakwell, G. (1989) *Facing Physical Violence*. Leicester: British Psychological Society.

Breakwell, G. (1997) *Coping with Aggressive Behaviour*, Leicester: British Psychological Society.

Clark, P. (1998) *Back From The Brink: Transforming the Ridings School and our children's education*, London: Metro Books.

Cox, T., Cox, S., Boot, N., Farnsworth, B., Walton, C. and Ferguson, E. (1989) *Teachers and Schools: A Study of Organisational Health and Stress*, Report to the National Union of Teachers, Centre of Organisational Health, Department of Psychology, University of Nottingham.

Cox, T., and Kuk, G. (1991) 'The healthiness of schools as organisations: teacher stress and health', paper given at International Congress on Stress, Anxiety and Emotional Disorders' University of Braga, Portugal.

DES/WO (1989) *Discipline in Schools*, report of the Committee of Enquiry chaired by Lord Elton (The Elton Report), London: HMSO.

Dewe, P. (1985). 'Coping with work stress: an investigation of teachers' action', *Research in Education* 33, 27–40.

Dewe, P. (1986) 'An investigation into the causes and consequences of teacher stress', *New Zealand Journal of Educational Studies* 21(2): 145–7.

DfEE (1996a) *Improving Security for Schools*, London: HMSO.

DfEE (1996b) *Report of the Working Group on School Safety*, London: HMSO.

Edmonds, E. L. and Edmonds, O. P. (1965) (eds) '*I was there.' The memoirs of H. S. Tremenheere*, Windsor: Shakespeare Head Press.

Educational Services Advisory Committee (ESAC) (1990a) *Violence to staff in the education sector, Health and Safety Commission*, London: HMSO.

Educational Services Advisory Committee (ESAC) (1990b) *Managing Occupational Stress: a Guide for Managers and Teachers in the Schools Sector*, Health and Safety Commission, London: HMSO.

Educational Services Advisory Committee (ESAC) (1990c) *Violence to Staff in the Education Sector*, Health and Safety Commission, London: HMSO. Reissued by HSE Books, Sudbury, Suffolk, August 1996.

Elliott, D. S., Hamburg, B. A. and Williams, K. R. (1998) *Violence in American Schools: A New Perspective*, Cambridge: Cambridge University Press.

Galloway, D. (1982) *Report on the 'Stress in Teaching Unit'*, Department of Education, Victoria University of Wellington, New Zealand Educational Institute.

Friedman, I. A. (1991) 'High and low burnout schools: Culture aspects of teacher burnout', *Journal of Educational Research* 84(6): 325–333.

Gill, M. and Hearnshaw, S. (1997) *Personal Safety and Violence in Schools*, Report commissioned by DfEE, Research Report No 21, Norwich: HMSO.

Health and Safety Executive (HSE) (1999) *Violence at Work: Findings from the British Crime Survey*, Norwich: HMSO.

Humphries, S. (1995) '*Hooligans or Rebels? An Oral History of Working-Class Childhood and Youth 1889–1939*', Oxford: Blackwell.

Karasek, R. and Thorel, T. (1990) *Healthy Work: Stress, Productivity, and the Reconstruction of Working Life*, New York: Basic Books.

Kyriacou, C. (1989) 'Teacher stress and burnout: An international review', in R. Riches and C. Morgan (eds) *Human Resource Management in Education*, Milton Keynes: Open University Press.

Kyriacou, C. (1996). Teacher stress: a review of some international comparisons. *Education Section Review*, 20(1): 17–20.

Lazarus, R. and Folkman, S. (1984) *Stress, Appraisal and Coping*. New York: Springer Verlag.

Leather P., Brady, C., Lawrence, C., Beale, D. and Cox, T. (1999) *Work-Related Violence: Assessment and Intervention*, London: Routledge.

Leyden, G. (1996) ' "Cheap labour" or "Neglected resource"? The role of the peer group and efficient, effective support for children with special needs', *Educational Psychology in Practice* 10(9): 49–55.

Leyden, G. (1999) 'Reducing violence to teachers in the workplace: Learning to make schools safe, In: P. Leather, C. Brady, C. Lawrence, D. Beale and T. Cox (eds) *Work-Related Violence: Assessment and Intervention*, London: Routledge.

Maden, M. (1999) 'The challenge of children in the educational system', in J. Tunstill (ed.) *Children and the State: Whose Problem?* London: Cassell.

Marmott, M. G., Bosma, H., Hemingway, H., Brunner, E. and Stansfield, S. (1997) 'Contribution of job control and other risk factors to social variations in heart disease incidence', *Lancet* 359: 235–9.

Menacken, J., Weldon, W. and Hurwitz, E. (1990) 'Community influences on school crime and violence', *Urban Education* **25**: 68–80.

National Institute for Education (NIE) (1978) *Safe Schools – Violent Schools*, report to Congress National Institute of Education, Vol I, Washington DC: US Government Printing Office.

Office for Standards in Education (Ofsted) (1993) *Achieving Good Behaviour in Schools*. London: HMSO.

Ohsako, T. (1997) *Violence at School: Global issues and interventions*. Paris: UNESCO.

Parsons, C. (1999) *Education, Exclusion and Citizenship*. London: Routledge.

Pearson, G. (1983) *Hooligan. A History of Respectable Fears*, Basingstoke: Macmillan.

Poyner, B. and Warne, C. (1988) *Preventing Violence to Staff*, Health and Safety Commission, London: HMSO.

Rock, P. and Heidensohn, F. (1969) 'New reflections on violence', in D. Martin, (ed.) *Anarchy and Culture*. London: Routledge, Kegan and Paul.

Smith, P. K. and Sharp, S. (1994) *School Bullying: Insights and Perspectives*, London: Routledge.

Tunstill, J. (1999) *Children and the State: Whose Problem?*, London: Cassell.

Weare, K (2000) *Promoting Mental, Emotional and Social Health: A Whole School Approach*, London: Routledge.

Willis, P. (1977) *Learning to Labour*, Aldershot: Gower.

Wheldhall, K. and Merrett, F. (1988) 'Which classroom behaviours do primary school teachers say they find most troublesome?' *Educational Review* **40**(1): 2–37.

Young, R. (1997) 'How the sixth form seized an armoury and shut a school', *The Times*, 24 January 1997.

Part II
Working with adult emotions

3 The emotional experience of teaching
A priority for professional development

Gerda Hanko

It is generally accepted that, to meet pupils' special emotional/behavioural and learning needs, it is essential that their teachers' needs are also addressed. What are these needs in the context of difficult pupil behaviour? Could addressing them be a task for continuing professional development?

There has been much debate about the inclusion of pupils who are difficult to teach in the ordinary classroom. On the one hand, some teacher and head teacher union representatives argue that teachers' (and other pupils') needs are best met by such pupils being removed to off-site or special school provision. On the other, some authors (e.g. Sebba and Sachdev 1997) argue that 'the experience of inclusive education can be a powerful basis for teacher development.' Typically, the emphasis in teacher support tends to be on developing knowledge, skills or appropriate attitudes. Little has been written about meeting teacher needs through the development of greater awareness of their own emotions as well as those of the children they teach. And yet emotional factors are key influences in both teaching and learning. This chapter explores how far improved insight about pupil emotions can affect teachers' own emotional experience and thereby influence their way of working with the most challenging pupils as well as all the others in their care.

Teachers' feelings about pupils: the challenge of both positive and negative emotions

Emotions influence all pupils' learning and need to be taken seriously by their teachers. Any school's learning environment will be affected by what teachers feel about their pupils. Teachers will have feelings about pupils the moment they meet them, feel hopeful or anxious about facing new classes, develop positive and negative feelings as they work with them. They enjoy transmitting knowledge and providing lifelong enabling experiences – which they know may, for many reasons, be harder to access for some pupils than for others. They feel frustrated, angry or despondent when their efforts appear not to reach those whose difficulties they note but may not always fully appreciate. The learning experience of all pupils, as that of their teachers, embraces a range of positive and negative feelings. They all challenge the 'responsive pedagogue' (Daniels 1996).

A fully responsive pedagogue endeavours to dynamically understand every pupil's learning progress (Elliott 2000). To be able to do so requires an understanding of both learning *and* teaching as an interactive emotional experience in all its complexity. As Warnock (1996) points out, however, legislation over the last two decades has seriously curtailed teachers' opportunities to attend to this dimension. Thus the discussion on 'challenging pupil behaviour' now relates almost exclusively to 'disaffection' rather than to sustaining the mental state of 'affection' which at some time in the pupils' lives, as use of the term suggests, will have preceded it.

Sustaining positive emotions about pupils and teaching

At first sight, experiencing *positive emotions* about teaching would appear to be without problems. Any teacher will derive pleasure and a sense of professional fulfilment from working with pupils who themselves enjoy the learning experience and who have set out with hope about what school may have to offer them. The challenge of experiencing such positive emotions will lie in sustaining them against a range of extraneous interferences.

Institutional, social and cultural constraints, educationally dysfunctional policies and specific individual needs arising from damaging experiences which teachers feel unable to 'put right', will all be severe tests of maintaining the pleasures of teaching creatively. A narrow focus on 'results' may engender dependence on extrinsic success and approval, fear of criticism, of being found wanting by authority, and both teaching and learning may lose their creative spark. Some pupils may then disappoint by developing an 'obedient to authority' or 'pleasing teacher' mentality (Hargreaves 1972; Milgram 1974). To others, teacher approval may look like preferential treatment and play havoc with the dynamics of the learning group. An apparent stereotyping of 'good' pupils ('this is excellent, exactly what I expected of Billy!'), if not guarded against, may produce disaffection and a range of problem behaviours in those who may feel less valued. In addition, those already troubled by experiences with non-caring or hostile adults outside school will have their anxieties confirmed by teachers who are seemingly unconcerned and who fail to make them feel cared about.

However, teachers may also manage to meet the needs, even of their disruptive pupils, without realising that they are doing so, feeling discouraged when the behaviour appears not to improve. Research (Quinton 1987) on the parenting abilities of young adults, who had been taken into care as children because of the damaging experiences inflicted by their parents, showed that, as parents themselves, they remembered such teachers with gratitude for not 'writing them off', for finding them 'worth bothering about' and for helping their self-esteem by letting them experience at least some success. When their former teachers were confronted with these findings, they well remembered how near they were to giving up on these 'difficult pupils', thinking they were 'not getting anywhere with them'. They were amazed about being remembered so positively.

Reducing negative emotions about pupils and teaching: promoting understanding of why children behave as they do

Clearly, these teachers would have felt less disheartened at the time, if they had been helped to understand why some pupils behave as they do. They might have realised that an outward façade may mask despair, loneliness and longing for recognition which some children may be unable to trust even when they meet it.

Feeling their competence under attack and their best efforts frustrated by unresponsive pupils who make them feel useless, teachers frequently begin to doubt the efficacy of their approach and waver between blaming themselves and blaming the pupils. Missing the emotional message behind the problem behaviour, they may handle the difficulties in terms of control rather than as pedagogical problems. They may resort to using fear, blame and shame as coping strategies which they may well despise themselves, but which allow them at least to 'keep going'. Engaging in a vicious interaction cycle, they may be dimly aware how they themselves add to their own and their pupils' difficulties. So despondency rises as they find it increasingly unbearable to see the damage they and the pupils appear to be causing each other in a deteriorating teaching and learning climate which they feel helpless to repair. Once overwhelmed by the complexity of uncontained emotions, however, it becomes more and more difficult to *think* professionally.

Teachers' feelings about using insight into emotional factors in the classroom

Many teachers have been introduced to the wealth of knowledge and understanding, developed worldwide, of how best to respond to the emotional, behavioural and learning needs of the many children affected by the damaging and traumatising experiences they have suffered at the hands of others. The practice of collaborative problem solving, for instance, has been found useful by numerous teachers in the UK (Hanko 1999), and was developed from Caplan's model of group consultation (Caplan 1970) with the workers of thousands of war orphans. He noticed that the children's distressing experiences were almost incapacitating the staff who seemed to internalise the powerful unmanageable feelings the children displayed. But when the staff were provided with support that helped them to understand this transference of feelings, this also helped them to contain their own distress, and they were then able to help these unhappy children.

Translating such information into their day-to-day role, most teachers seem to find no difficulty in accepting that children with problem behaviour (whether overtly displayed or masked in overcompliance or withdrawal) are likely to experience feelings they find difficult to bear. These feelings arise partly because of past damaging experiences and partly in response to a perceived threat in the present situation. As responsive professionals, teachers accept that they should attempt to understand these feelings.

Doubts frequently arise, however, about how they might as teachers apply such understanding. Comments like 'we are not trained that way', 'we are not psychiatrists, social workers, educational psychologists' demonstrate an underestimation of their importance as 'significant others' in their pupils' lives. There is a belief that you have to be a 'trained expert' to deal with issues like these.

Such views, however, can be quickly dispelled if teachers examine the effects of their negative feelings on their teaching. They may then recall how they felt like no longer bothering about a pupil who appeared to have a 'don't care' attitude or felt hopeless about a discouraged pupil who rejected their praise. Perhaps they did not understand his fear that responding to the teacher's praise might lure him into the risk of failing yet again (Hanko 1994); or they simply added their own anger to that of a pupil's. In all such cases they colluded with the feelings of the child, thereby confirming and reinforcing his early experience of negative adults.

Learning *not* to collude and noticing how quickly a child's behaviour may change when they change their own can appear quite miraculous, as is shown by the following example which one teacher presented for exploration by her joint problem-solving group (for further details see Hanko 1999: ch. 3).

She briefly described the situation she had been facing with one of her 10-year-olds earlier in the week. He had arrived at school in a state of extreme aggressiveness and anger which he directed at her. She described how she had managed to react to his angry façade not with anger of her own which she felt would only have made things worse. Instead, she tried to understand it as an outward sign of underlying distress. She told him how sorry she was that he was feeling so bad, and asked him whether there was something that had made him very sad, whereupon the boy started crying.

In the exploration that followed, her colleagues considered with her the factors that may have enabled her to react as she did and the ways in which her reactions may have been helping the boy. What insights, perhaps learnt in earlier explorations, had she been able to use, apparently quite intuitively, at the moment it mattered most? Their main suggestions were that:

- attacks like these come from unhappy children;
- the attack was not directed personally at this teacher who only stood in for all other adults who may have contributed to the child's unhappiness;

- she was 'containing' her own and the child's anger, something he had not yet learnt to do for himself;
- she had helped him to understand his feelings a bit better, such as the link between anger and anxiety;
- experiences like this would allow him to feel that he was, after all, capable of enlisting an important person's concern for him, perhaps beginning to see himself as someone worth caring about by a person significant in his life, rather than feeling 'written off'.

However, they were not deluding themselves into thinking that the boy's problems would now all be solved and that damaging past experiences can be 'deleted' from children's minds, simply by interactions with caring teachers. They had already been warned against this by a course which had introduced them to the basics of psychodynamic/ecosystemic understanding. At the same time, it was shown that features from behavioural approaches could also be accommodated. As has long been suggested (Hanko 1985; Miller 1996; Norwich 1996), teachers can, and need to, learn to work with 'multiple concepts'. As teachers themselves say, they are not psychologists nor psychotherapists, nor do they have any mandate for therapy. Teachers, can, however, be trained in 'therapeutic' teaching skills and learn, through learning-focused professional development initiatives, to respond more appropriately to children's emotional and social realities as they enhance their own learning-centred 'emotional competence' (DoH/ DfEE 1999).

Enhancing emotional awareness, learning and sharing skills through collaborative problem solving

There now exists a rich field of established practice geared to enhancing the capacities of professionals who endeavour, often in stressful circumstances, to meet the needs of pupils with emotional and behavioural difficulties. Such difficulties not only impede their learning but also challenge their teachers' effectiveness.

Such initiatives are based on the suggestion that what professionals need is a '*learning*' environment which accepts anxiety and uncertainty and promotes thinking and understanding' (Woodhouse and Pengelly 1991). They have been designed to demonstrate to teachers how much more they are able to help pupils who are difficult to teach if they learn how to share their collective expertise in consultative joint problem-solving groups.

As the example described above shows, the group found themselves to be reflective contributors to each other's professional expertise. They were achieving this not only by focusing on a specific child's problems as described by their colleague, but also by exploring these within a *problem-solving framework*. Consultative exploration skills were being used that were non-judgemental in nature. Staff were being trained in a process that promoted learning and that enabled them not just to focus on each case presented but also to extend their learning to other cases of concern. The approach is designed to help teachers proactively with future learning problems and is thus designed to be of immediate and of long-term use. Addressing anxieties, uncertainties and the range of teaching-impeding frustrations in such an insight-generating way highlights crucial dimensions of the learning process in general, relevant to pupils *and* teachers as professionals. It also adds to teachers' well-being.

Raising awareness in collaborative staff development groups

In order to promote insight into how emotional factors can stimulate or impede learning as well as teaching, it is important to raise awareness about the social dynamics of interaction between teachers and pupils. Teachers need to be aware that:

- emotional difficulties can lead to a range of problem behaviours (i.e. not just to misbehaviour);
- problem behaviour is likely to be a reaction to a situation the child perceives as difficult, triggering feelings s/he may find difficult to bear;
- such behaviour will be further influenced by a teacher's reaction to it; but
- the behaviour may become more 'manageable' if a sensitive professional response can unobtrusively convey some understanding of these underlying feelings, making them more 'bearable' (Winnicott 1965).

In the example, the teacher was able to contain her own feelings by thinking about the boy's (that he was not just 'feeling bad', but perhaps also 'feeling sad'). This also helped him to contain his feelings through a sense that his distress was 'being thought about' (Bion 1962). She thereby facilitated what Winnicott (1965) refers to as 'the spontaneous processes of self-repair'. She sensitively helped him to make sense of his distress (in the same way that, in early learning, a responsive primary caregiver provides a child with the 'secure base' (Bowlby 1988) from which to explore the world and 'learn without fear').

In this way her teaching became 'therapeutic' and was seen as an integral part of her professional remit as a *teacher*, at the same time facilitating a more 'secure base' for herself in which to '*teach without fear*'.

The special significance of Bowlby's attachment theory (1969, 1973, 1980) for teachers thus lies in the help it offers them to understand different patterns of children's responses to their teachers as they transfer their early attachment experiences in new settings (Barrett and Trevitt 1991). If early attachment has provided that secure base, a child is likely to approach new learning similarly at school; whereas insecure attachment may lead to avoidance, resistance, ambivalence, and lead to related feelings in a baffled teacher. If understood, these patterns can be mitigated through sensitively structured new learning by responsive teachers able to convey feelings of caring acceptance.

'Therapeutic' teaching may thus be summarised as understanding that:

- a pupil's current reactions and patterns of relationships may relate in part to important past experiences (such as being threatened, not feeling valued or accepted) which can be rekindled by a threat or fear perceived in the present;
- it is possible for past damaging experiences to be superseded by new reparative ones in an educational setting *if* a pupil is helped to perceive himself differently in relation to important others (e.g. being valued in a here-and-now learning group; Waddell 1998).

Teaching 'therapeutically' thus allows learning-impeded children, together with all others who benefit from their teachers' continuing professional growth, to feel newly valued as individuals and to succeed *socially* as well as *academically*.

Developing enabling skills in the collaborative setting

Collaborative exploration of the effects of emotional and social factors on children's learning inherently also involves *teachers* reflecting on their own learning. In addition to the awareness-raising and developmental work of people like Bowlby or Winnicott, those engaged in promoting teachers' insight into their pupils as learners also owe much to researchers like Bion (1961, 1962), Vygotsky (1978) and Schon (1983), who incorporated social/environmental influences into their theory of thinking.

Bion stressed both difference and complementarity between 'learning about' such issues (e.g. through educational theory) and 'being able to learn from the experience of the self in the group', as happens when professionals collaboratively explore essential dimensions of learning. Vygotsky showed how the individual (child or adult) contributes to his own learning through small group social interactions. During these, language employed *collaboratively* becomes a tool for thought and enhances learning. Meanwhile interpersonal experience is being transformed into intrapersonal competence. Schon's complementary terms of 'reflection in action' and 'reflection *on* action' are essential concepts in the field of consultative collaboration that aims at fostering insight into students and their teachers as learners. All these contributions are of relevance to those working in social institutions like schools, to parents and carers, and to the services and agencies involved.

Within schools, such ideas help teachers to attend to the affective/social dimension of learning as an integral part of their curricular work (e.g.

through Circle Time, Circles of Friends, Drama in Education). These approaches enable children to learn to support and empathise with each other in their difficulties, to experience each other as valued members of a group. Teachers have found that they derive similarly liberating benefits from professional development approaches that enable them to experience themselves as learners with supportive colleagues. Here they learn from, and contribute to, each other's experience, the experience of their pupils' parents and that of interagency staff who are now also expected to use their expertise in 'joined up' work (Hanko 1999). Personal advisers, now being trained in the new DfEE Connexions scheme (DfEE 2000) for disaffected 13- to 19-year-olds, are already finding their experience of collaborative problem solving of immediate value to themselves and to their clients.

How then, in Vygotsky's terms, does 'collaborative language become an enabling tool for thought so that interpersonal experience is transformed into intrapersonal competence' in the example described above? As detailed more extensively elsewhere (Hanko 1991, 1995, 1999), raising awareness about collaborative language skills implies consistent attention to how language 'works' in the process of joint problem exploration. Thus aided, reflective participants soon observe for themselves whether their consultative discourse takes their exploration further, increasing their 'intrapersonal competence', or whether it remains momentarily ineffective. Put briefly, these language skills can be listed as:

- The skill of *asking answerable questions* that are geared to widening insights about a pupil's needs and responding to them in the course of an ordinary working day. Questions need to be asked in a genuinely exploring, non-provocative and supportive way (e.g. 'could it be that ...?', 'I wonder if ...' and 'do you think ...?' rather than 'don't you ...?').
- The skill of discovering from the answers the teacher's *strengths* and, in the sharing process, building on these, accepting and supplementing the other's expertise with that of other participants rather than supplanting it.
- The skill of *generating problem-solving information* that can help to clarify the issues relevant to the situation being explored. This enables the presenter and his/her colleagues to find their own workable solutions (or part solutions) to the problem presented as well as to problems that may evolve in the future.

With a focus on the context of difficult pupil behaviour, a collaboratively supportive staff-development approach is capable of addressing the cognitive, affective and interactional dimensions of the learning process in general. In relation to a specific problem to be explored, information can be generated that helps to highlight its underlying issues. A better understanding of the emotional message behind the problem behaviour assists handling it as a pedagogical problem rather than merely as one of control, so that necessary control can become an aspect of the educational task. Interactionally, the negative feelings which problem behaviour tends to engender in teachers can be seen as a transference of the pupil's feelings. This can be used as a helpful source of information about the nature of these feelings, and the outward façade that masks a different part of the pupil's self, that wants to be found (Winnicott 1965). This has enabled many a despairing, disheartened, despondent teacher to look behind the displayed façade to find the child's 'teachable self', which is likely to become more reachable through the teacher's increased learning-related awareness.

Finally, we must think about colleagues who 'do not want to be helped', who, discouraged by years of relentlessly negative experiences, no longer believe that anything can possibly make a difference. In the context of children's learning, Canham (2000) calls this 'the tragedy of deprivation', suffered by the 'doubly deprived' (Henry 1974) whose early deprivations have trapped them in a vicious cycle of trying to protect themselves against new, potentially 'persecutory', contact. However, those engaged in collaboratively enhancing teachers' skills to address the emotional and social factors that shackle the progress of learning-refusing children, should not ignore the plight of similarly deprived professionals within and across schools and school services or indeed parents. Tutors of courses as discussed here should not find it impossible to include in such training at least an awareness that the child-related skills conveyed during the course may be redeployed to working with similarly rejecting fellow professionals, as well as helping seemingly hostile parents to recognise others as friends.

Conclusion

This chapter has focused on the collaborative exploration of teachers' emotional experience in the context of difficult pupil behaviour. By maximising their existing resources through discovering and building on each other's strengths, teachers can experience themselves as *learners* capable of further developing their interactive 'emotional competence' (DfEE/DoH 1999). They are thus enabled to further their pupils' progress. This alone should justify the chapter headline which suggested its content be seen as a priority for the professional development of teachers.

The suggestion now finds reinforcement in the important questions that are being asked by neuropsychologists and neurobiologists, relating to the impact of interpersonal emotional experience on the developing mind. Researchers such as Damasio (1994), Moore (2000), Schore (1994) and Siegel (1999), in line with many educators, not only point to the affective dimensions of cognitive development, but also strongly suggest that such links occur at every level of child and adult development, from caregiver–infant attachments to interpersonal relationships in adulthood. Could any other consideration be of greater importance for teachers?

References

Barrett, M. and Trevitt, J. (1991) *Attachment Behaviour and the Schoolchild*, London: Routledge.

Bion, W. (1961) *Experiences in Groups*, London: Tavistock.

Bion, W. (1962) *Learning from Experience*, London: Heinemann.

Bowlby, J. (1969, 1973, 1980) *Attachment and Loss*, **Vols I–III**, New York: Basic Books.

Bowlby, J. (1988) *'A Secure Base'. Clinical Applications of Attachment Theory*, London: Routledge.

Canham, H. (2000) ' "Where do babies come from?". What makes children want to learn?', *Educational Therapy and Therapeutic Teaching* **9**: 28–38.

Caplan, G. (1970) *The Theory and Practice of Mental Health Consultation*, New York: Basic Books.

Damasio, A.R. (1994) *Descartes' Error: Emotion, Reason and the Human Brain*, New York: Putnam.

Daniels, H. (1996) 'Back to basics', *British Journal of Special Education* **23**(4): 155–61.

Department for Education and Employment (DfEE) (2000) *Connexions: The Best Start in Life for Every Young Person*, London: DfEE.

Department for Education and Employment/Department of Health (DfEE/DOH) (1999) *Healthy Schools, Healthy Teachers*, London: DfEE/DoH.

Elliott, J. (2000) 'The psychological assessment of children with learning difficulties', *British Journal of Special Education* **27**(2): 59–66.

Elton Report (1989) *Discipline in Schools*, Department of Education and Science, London: HMSO.

Hanko, G. (1991) 'A school based in-service response to staff development', in G. Upton (ed.) *Staff Training and Special Educational Needs*, pp. 83–9. London. David Fulton.

Hanko, G. (1994) 'Discouraged children: When praise does not help', *British Journal of Special Education* **21**(4): 166–8.

Hanko, G. (1995, 1985) 'From staff support to staff development', *Special Needs in Ordinary Classrooms*, 3rd edn, London: David Fulton.

Hanko, G. (1999) *Increasing Competence through Collaborative Problem Solving: Using Insight into Social and Emotional Factors in Children's Learning*, London: David Fulton.

Hargreaves, D. H. (1972) *Interpersonal Relations and Education*, London: Routledge and Kegan Paul.

Henry, G. (1974) 'Doubly deprived', *Journal of Child Psychotherapy* **3**: 15–28.

Milgram, S. (1974) *Obedience to Authority*, London: Tavistock.

Miller, A. (1996) *Pupil Behaviour and Teacher Culture*, London: Cassell.

Moore, M. S. (2000) 'The impact of trauma on child developent: Implications for learning', *Educational Therapy and Therapeutic Teaching* **9**: 18–27.

Norwich, B. (1996) 'Special needs education or education for all? Connective specialisation and ideological impurity', *British Journal of Special Education* **23**(3): 100–103.

Quinton, D. (1987) 'The consequences of care', *Maladjustment and Therapeutic Education* **5**(2): 18–29.

Schon, P. (1983) *The Reflective Practitioner*, London: Temple Smith.

Schore, A. N. (1994) *The Neurobiology of Emotional Development*, Hillsdale, NJ, Lawrence Erlbaum.

Sebba, J. and Sachdev, D. (1997) *What works in Inclusive Education?*, Ilford: Barnado's Child Care Publications.

Siegel, D. J. (1999) *The Developing Mind: Towards a Neurobiology of Interpersonal Experience*, New York and London: The Guildford Press.

Vygotsky, I. (1978) *Mind in Society. The Development of Higher Psychological Processes*, Cambridge, MA: Harvard University Press.

Waddell, M. (1998) *Inside Lives*, London: Duckworth.

Warnock, M. (1996) 'Foreword' to Bennathan, M. and Boxall, M., *Effective Intervention in Primary Schools*, London: David Fulton.

Winnicott, D. (1965) *The Maturational Processes and the Facilitating Environment*, London: Hogarth.

Woodhouse, D. and Pengelly, P. (1991) *Anxiety and the Dynamics of Collaboration*, Aberdeen: Aberdeen University Press.

4 Recognising and working with parents' emotions

Tessa Sambrook and Peter Gray

Whether you are a parent, familial or professional carer of a child with emotional and behavioural difficulties, the challenges they present to you are significant. This chapter will outline some of the stresses that are placed upon parents and carers and how these influence their ability to engage with schools, services and service providers.

The chapter will then go on to look at what practitioners, schools and policy-makers may need to consider when seeking to support children, their parents/carers and other family members.

The causes of difficult behaviour

Difficult and challenging behaviour among children and young people, both at school and within society at large, has attracted an increasingly high profile over the years. This has given rise to intense speculation about causes, with the media, politicians and some teacher unions in particular suggesting a range of 'ills' which may have contributed to deteriorating standards of behaviour over time. Causes suggested are varied, including a breakdown in family and social values and the growth of 'counter-cultures', lower levels of parental care and commitment, the effects of new technology, greater stress and disturbance arising from lifestyle changes, biological factors linked to newly discovered syndromes or diet, as well as 'context-specific' factors such as disaffection with the curriculum currently on offer in schools.

Causation is typically presented far too simplistically, with behaviour attributed to one cause or another, depending on the particular fashion, political angle or news story. At best, in public debate, there is recognition that, for some individuals, particular factors may be more influential than others. However, even here, there tends to be overgeneralisation, with children often being grouped into different categories such as 'mad, bad or sad'.

In fact, research shows that behaviour difficulties are complex, with causes usually involving an interaction between personal characteristics and past and present experience. Too often, intervention is based on oversimplistic generalisation without careful analysis of particular factors that are contributing to the problems presented and faced by the individual causing concern.

In a recent paper about approaches to managing difficult pupil behaviour in schools (Gray 1998), one of the authors examines the relationship between emotional and behavioural difficulties and special educational needs and asks 'how can we be sure that school disciplinary measures take account of factors beyond the pupil's control?'. Despite recognition of behaviour difficulties as a form of special educational need (SEN) in the Government's SEN Code of Practice (DfE 1994), there is evidence that, during the 1990s, many pupils reached the stage of permanent exclusion without ever going through the relevant stages of assessment and intervention (Parsons *et al.* 1995). Yet our knowledge of the range and complexity of some behaviour problems would surely demand that, where these occur, we should be looking very carefully at the whole picture, not just at the behaviour but at the range of factors that might be contributing to it.

Parents' experience of difficult pupil behaviour

Parents come in all guises: the confident; the natural; the articulate; the shy; the diffident; the guilty; the insecure; the aggressive; those with money; those without; those with university degrees; those without; those with learning difficulties; those who have had loving homes; those who have known abuse; those who are at home; those who work. They also come from a range of different cultures. The common denominator is that they have children and in all but the most exceptional cases parents love and care about what happens to them.

Most parents do not set out to create problem children. However, most experience some problems at some stages of their child's development. In a minority of cases, such problems are long term. When difficulties occur, parents can experience a number of emotions: *anxiety* (particularly if they do not understand why the behaviour is happening), *shame* (that their child is behaving badly or strangely, in contrast to all other children who seem to be angels), *guilt* (that the behaviour may have been caused by something they have done or failed to do), *fear* (that things might not get better or might even get worse).

Many parents will already have experienced some degree of behaviour difficulty with their child before s/he starts school. It's part of what parenting is about! Parents will have adjusted their own approaches to dealing with that behaviour in a number of instinctive ways. They may have responded very firmly, or taken adaptive approaches to management and communication, or structured new routines for the child and family. Whatever they do, their actions will typically reflect their child's particular character, the particular features of their home and family/social environment as well as the societal constraints which demand a level of conformity that assumes an increasing level of importance, perhaps not previously encountered or consciously thought about. We all have views not only about the way we think our own children should be brought up but also other people's!

When children start school, most parents will see this as a major opportunity for them to learn new skills, both academic and social, as well as experiencing positive (and negative) influences from their peers. Some will hope that this new environment will overcome some of the difficult behaviour they may have encountered, perhaps offering a greater range of activity than parents themselves may have been able to provide. Others will fear that their children's vulnerability will not be adequately recognised in a context where there are so many competing demands and that this may lead to further escalation of difficulties.

Some parents may encounter concern about their child for the first time, as difficult behaviour develops in a new context that the child may find strange and challenging.

Parents' experience of partnership with schools

While much has been written about the value of partnership with parents (Wolfendale 1997; NASEN 2000), it is our experience that parents typically tend to feel (in their encounters with school staff) that they are somehow being blamed for their child's misdemeanours. Parents also often feel that they are expected to have an influence over behaviour that is taking place in a context over which they have little direct control (e.g. the classroom). Parents tend to be unfamiliar with the specific nature of classroom routines and teacher expectations and are not always in a good position to understand why difficult behaviour may be occurring. The frequent lack of a common understanding of the nature and reasons for problem behaviour, combined with the propensity of both parents and teachers to fear blame, can lead to difficult relationships that threaten the quality of partnership in action.

Another frequent area of parental concern is the degree to which schools and teachers are seen to take account of children's individual characteristics. These include academic skills and abilities, motivations and interests, emotional make-up and other personal or social features. A number of parents report that, in their view, children's behaviour difficulties in the school context can be created or exacerbated by lack of a differentiated response. Teachers, on the other hand, tend to argue that, with a wide diversity of pupils in any school or classroom (and current staffing levels), there are limits to the degree of individualisation that is possible.

A further issue raised by parents is the degree to which schools accurately estimate the contribution that parents themselves can make. There are dangers here of both under- and overestimation. Some teachers may feel that parents' contributions are unlikely to be effective when, in their view, such problems tend to have a family/home origin (see Croll and Moses 1985; Miller 1994). On the other hand, some parents have enough difficulty in coping and managing their day-to-day lives, let alone taking on problems in a context where they have even less control.

Parents' experience of support services and other agencies

When problems become more significant and support services and other agencies start to get involved, parents sometimes feel that they are living in a new land within their country. In this new land people speak a different kind of language; they often wear different clothes; their rules and customs are different. It is very difficult to find any guidebooks to help, and, because parents don't understand the system or the language, these people can appear to be very hostile.

After a period of involvement, parents may begin to learn the language and understand that they are being expected to engage in an activity for which there is no clear 'rule book'. Even if there is one (e.g. local education authority procedures for assessment and intervention with pupils with special educational needs), parents may find differences in the way in which the 'rules' are being interpreted.

Parents are expected to understand and engage with complex processes, but often feel ill equipped to do so. Not infrequently they find that they are batted from one person or provider to another as professionals (caught by the parameters of their own roles) try to help by suggesting new avenues for them to follow. Parents can find themselves on a loop road where the only junctions bring them back onto the same loop. Frustration reigns.

A key emotion here can be a sense of distrust, with a fear that services or agencies may have other agendas which are not being properly disclosed, or a sense of despair that services are seeking to find a way of passing on problems rather than working more actively with parents to address them.

The importance of communication

Parents come in many shapes and sizes with differing backgrounds and varying amounts of baggage that they have accumulated along the way. The common denominator for all these parents is that they are subject to varying levels of stress that affect their ability to engage with professionals and support their child. Rather than focusing on 'types' of parent, perhaps we need to look at the stressors parents have to deal with, then seek ways of reducing these tensions to promote more effective relationships, working towards the common goal of supporting the child.

Communication as a stressor

As we look around at society today, the need for humans to communicate has taken on a global importance that would have seemed impossible 50 years ago. Developments include mobile phones, television, radio, satellite links, the internet, e-mail, and these are just the technological advances. However, there have been a range of other developments in the way we convey meaning through spoken and written words. And that's the nub of it – language – we use so many different methods to communicate meaning. The sophistication to be found within the lexicon coupled with our ability to create new words or new meanings, alongside the other attributes of intonation, inflexion, metaphor, idiom, sarcasm, rhetoric, irony and body language lead to a wide range of ways of conveying and understanding meaning. It also creates substantial opportunities for *mis*understanding and differences in interpretation.

In her book *Working with Parents of Children with SEN*, Eileen Gascoigne examines the ability of parents (and, we would suggest, professionals) to misconstrue what is said to them. Coupled with parents' ongoing sense of insecurity and guilt when dealing with matters where their children are concerned, there seems to be an almost British ability to misinterpret both meaning and intention.

A common scenario is encountered at parents' consultation evenings where parent and professional are face to face with little time to really discuss or reflect on what is said. The teacher is trying to be objective and with time constraints to be businesslike. She says 'He never gives in his homework.' The parent hears 'Are you doing anything to help him get his homework in?!'; 'He seems to know a lot about Thomas the Tank Engine!', ('You're letting him watch too many videos!'); 'He's not picking up reading very quickly' ('She obviously thinks we don't have books in our house!').

Dealing honestly and objectively with even the little issues can present problems. Having sufficient time to build effective relationships with parents, so that these misunderstandings do not arise, requires both planning and commitment to working with parents.

When parents are invited to meetings there are often a number of professionals present. Each professional comes with their own background of training and status and within their role they will have a common language which is probably different to the language of others present. Let's take an example of an annual review meeting. Present are an SEN coordinator, the class teacher, an educational psychologist, a speech and language therapist, an LEA officer and the parents. It is most likely that each of those people will take away from that meeting different perceptions of what was said and what meaning was attributed to differing issues.

Having good communication skills and a command of jargon can make professionals feel powerful. However, this is immensely disempowering to parents and particularly for those who are less articulate or who have learning difficulties themselves. In times of competing demands for scarce resources it can be tempting to exploit power differentials.

Some families thrive on combative communication and environments. In one case where one of the authors was supporting a family it took her some time to realise that the normal style of discourse was full-flight debate even down to the menu for lunch! Not surprisingly the parents applied their style of communication to all those they came into contact with, with the result that almost all communication broke down after very little time. Had their child not had SEN this would probably never have been an issue, but it became an issue of some magnitude.

Where parents come from cultural backgrounds or where English is a second or even absent language the barriers become greater, the support mechanisms are more difficult to find. In some cultural traditions the role of women does not allow easy access to services and the cultural view of the male role may be at odds with views of service providers. Without adequate support mechanisms in place, communication is likely to break down.

In some instances the child may not be presenting behaviour problems, particularly at school. However, when the child gets home some sort of pressure release valve comes into play and the child explodes into demanding or challenging behaviour. In some cases the child will cause damage to property and at other times they will attack their parents and siblings causing actual bodily harm. The child often communicates distress in this way because s/he has no other means available. Other children express their difficulties in other ways such as wetting and soiling, becoming school refusers, shutting themselves away from contact, building imaginary worlds in which to live, talking out loud to themselves, etc. How do the parents deal with this? With a great deal of difficulty. There is a notion of stigma around parents who perceive themselves or are perceived as being unable to manage their children. Usually they will seek help through the school or GP, but mostly not until they are at crisis point. Often they are referred for 'family therapy' through the local clinical psychology service.

Recognising parents' feelings

As already mentioned, parents whose children have special educational needs or emotional and behavioural difficulties often feel they are being taken on a journey to alien and sometimes hostile territory. Their lives take a new and totally unexpected direction, for which there are few clear or accessible precedents. Parents' original aspirations may founder and they are often at a loss as to what their future expectations should be. Comparisons are made with friends, whose children seem to be following the 'normal' pathways and who seem to be able more easily to talk about successes. The experience of parents of children with learning or behaviour difficulties is different. There are fewer things to celebrate and more problems to report. Some people refer to this experience as 'grieving'. It is generally accepted (Byrne and Cunningham 1985) that such emotions among parents are not just a phase but recur, with different strength, at various stages of the child's development.

Each time parents meet a new kind of professional, they tend to be reminded of the differences between their child and others. And there are a lot of professionals that parents can meet! Here are a few of them:

Care assistants	Physiotherapists
Careers officers	Portage workers
Casework officers	Preschool teachers
Class teachers	Psychiatrists
Clinical psychologists	Respite providers
Consultant paediatricians	SEN coordinators
Counsellors	Social workers
Education welfare officers	Special needs managers
Educational psychologists	Specialist consultants
Further-education providers	Specialist teachers
Head teachers	Speech and language therapists
Health visitors	Subject teachers
Learning support assistants	Technicians
Occupational therapists	

Every time we meet one of these people, they will bring to that encounter differing levels of information, training and knowledge concerning the child and the family. News can be good; it can also be bad. But what happens every time for parents is that they are made to confront their child's difference again and again. The consequence is that parents are forever riding a roller coaster of emotion.

For some parents who move area, either by choice or force of circumstance, the breadth of communication may be even more extensive. Too often, the capacity of administrative systems to adjust to the needs of transient customers can be found wanting and parents may find themselves having to communicate yet again over issues that should be well known and already rehearsed.

The role of procedures

To try to systematize responses to concerns, professional agencies and services tend to operate through 'procedures' which may be represented by policies, protocols, forms, assessments, criteria, quality marks, etc. Parents seeking help from these services suddenly find that they too have to learn about these procedures and unfortunately there is little commonality between them. They discover that life takes on a new dimension of form filling, appointments, meetings, telephone conversations and deciphering different kinds of reports. These can present a number of practical difficulties for some families (particularly where it is difficult to get time off work or arrange alternative care to meet professional time-tables). In addition, each new contact provokes a new set of emotions. Something as simple even as having a conversation with the class teacher or caseworker takes on a new magnitude. It can be difficult to feel positive about engaging in such processes, especially when the parent feels the lesser partner.

Parents engaging with statutory SEN assessment procedures for the first time are frequently bewildered both by the process and what their expectations of outcomes should be. Professionals need to ensure proper understanding in order to facilitate effective partnership in the future.

Annual reviews and transition reviews can also cause parents significant levels of stress. Where parents are not provided beforehand with relevant information, they can feel unprepared and undervalued. Parents are often very self-critical and need the support of knowledgeable people around them. However, they need good-quality information and the opportunity to contribute, themselves, to a wider picture of the child's development and progress.

Preparation and training

It is a sad fact that most parents not only struggle to understand their children's difficulties but feel they are left to find out how to manage that situation alone. Professionals not only study for their profession, but they usually receive ongoing training and development. Few training opport-unities are available to parents. However, they are expected to ensure that their child receives an appropriate education, to support school work and implement programmes. The parent is unlikely to see the relevance of a programme or have the skills to support their children if they receive no training. Expecting the parent to suddenly acquire skills is not only unreasonable, but is likely to set up resistance, especially where parents may have difficulties themselves.

Training and preparation allow parents to develop a 'common language' with professionals that can serve to break down some of the barriers to communication outlined above. In some areas of special educational needs and disability, there are good arrangements for mutual support, through the voluntary sector or parent partnership schemes. Such arrangements appear to be less developed nationally for parents whose children experience behaviour difficulties that have no specialist label.

Ways forward

The sections above serve to highlight just how much stress is experienced by parents of children with behaviour difficulties. While some of this may be self-inflicted, it is generally unwelcome, and probably avoidable.

Policy

Policies on partnership with parents need to be developed at management level within schools, local education authorities and other statutory/voluntary agencies. These should be drawn up in partnership with parents and other relevant stakeholders. Policies are a start, but they need to be implemented and reviewed and appropriate opportunities provided for training and development.

NASEN's (National Association for Special Educational Needs) recent policy on partnership with parents provides a useful reference point (NASEN 2000). This was drawn up in consultation with a range of different people with an interest in special educational needs, including parents themselves. The key principles addressed in the policy are:

- a recognition of parental *rights*;
- clarity about associated *responsibilities*;
- parity in partnerships and *equivalent expertise* (Wolfendale 1992);
- empowerment;
- effective communication;
- understanding of the need for support;
- positive recognition of parental diversity.

To these could be added the need for confidentiality, training for parents and ensuring that the voice of the child is also heard.

Policy to practice

While the above elements help to direct thinking towards the construction of policy, parents are looking for practical approaches and services that help them to help their children. In this respect, parents want the following:

- to be listened to;
- to be believed;
- accurate information;
- clear and accessible information regarding formal processes;
- unambiguous reports, free of jargon;
- account to be taken of family pressures;
- to know that their views are respected and valued equally with other professionals;
- to have confidence in the professionals;
- independent support both generally and specifically in meetings;
- clear planning;
- training;
- safety nets for their children;
- swift responses to difficult situations/issues;

- accountability;
- honest relationships.

Obviously each school will have different starting points for developing their inclusion of and partnership with parents. Nevertheless, the future development of most policy and practice in schools will need to include parents in both the planning and consultation stages. Small steps that build confidence are often a good way to start. Simple measures such as:

- joint training opportunities, which help parents to see their own skills developed and acknowledged;
- encouraging parents to bring a 'best friend' to meetings and reviews;
- involving parents in the drawing up of individual education programmes/pastoral support plans;
- involving parents in homework clubs;
- exchanging regular informal information on day-to-day progress;
- encouraging social opportunities for parents with similar needs.

A key aim is to try and reduce the blame and stigma associated with emotional and behavioural difficulties and to 'set the scene' for more positive and collaborative working. In most cases where schools and parents encounter difficulties with pupil behaviour, it is suggested that working partnerships can be developed that take account of both parent and teacher perspectives (and feelings), allowing people to concentrate on understanding and resolving the problems experienced. However, perhaps inevitably, there are cases where feelings become more entrenched or where there is a breakdown in the relationship between parents and school. In these circumstances, emotions lead inexorably to blame and accusation. It is in these situations that support service personnel such as behaviour support teachers or educational psychologists can play a very important part. Miller (1996) describes in detail how behaviour difficulties can lead to 'boundaries and barricades' between home and school and how these boundaries and tensions can be resolved through effective joint consultation with both parents and teachers. This process is enhanced if parents are treated as equal partners and are enabled to understand the 'protocols' to which professionals are having to attend.

Concluding comments

The purpose of this chapter has not been to say that parents are the only ones with feelings or that these are always legitimate or rational. However, parents have a crucial role to play in both understanding and resolving behaviour difficulties. Their contribution can only be effectively realised if their perspectives and feelings are understood and valued. This does not imply that parents should be patronised or that one approach will suit all parents.

However, what is clear is that behaviour difficulties are stressful enough (for teachers, parents and for children themselves), without the additional stresses that can be created by misunderstandings and poor communication. The more we work to reduce these, for both parents and schools, the more likely we are to be able to work effectively together for the benefit of all our children.

References

Byrne, E. A. and Cunningham, C. C. (1985) 'The effects of mentally handicapped children on families – a conceptual review', *Journal of Child Psychology and Psychiatry and Allied Disciplines* **26**(6): 847–64.

Croll, P. and Moses, D. (1985) *One in Five: The Assessment and Incidence of Special Educational Needs*, London: Routledge and Kegan Paul.

DfE (Department for Education) (1994) *Code of Practice on the Identification and Assessment of Special Educational Needs*, London: HMSO.

Gascoigne, E. (1995) *Working with parents as partners in SEN*, London: David Fulton.

Gray, P. J. (1998) 'Following the patterns of behaviour', *Special! Autumn*, 20–1.

Miller, A. (1994) 'Parents and difficult behavour: Always the problem or part of the solution?', in P. Gray, A. Miller and J. Noakes (eds) *Challenging Behaviour in Schools*, London: Routledge.

Miller, A. (1996) *Pupil Behaviour and Teacher Culture*, London: Cassell.

NASEN (1999) *Exclusion from School*, Policy document issued 20 March 1999, Tamworth: NASEN.

NASEN (2000) *Partnership with Parents*, Policy document issued 4 March 2000, Tamworth: NASEN.

Parsons, C., Hailes, J., Howlett, K., Davies, A. and Driscoll, P. (1995) *National Survey of Local Education Authorities' Policies and Procedures for the Identification of, and Provision for, Children who Are Out of School by Reason of Exclusion or Otherwise*, Final report to the Department for Education, Canterbury: Christ Church College.

Wolfendale, S. (1992) *Involving parents in schools*, London: Cassell.

Wolfendale, S. (1997) (ed.) *Partnership with parents in action*, Tamworth: NASEN.

5 Overcoming barriers to successful support

An examination of issues for teachers and support workers

Pauline Fell

Introduction

Working with young people experiencing emotional and behavioural problems provides some of the toughest challenges in education for both teachers and those seeking to support them. The principles of inclusion and entitlement mean that there is considerable pressure on schools and local authorities to find ways of providing a full-time education for some pupils who can be very difficult to manage.

Many pupils with emotional or behavioural problems find it very difficult to develop positive social relationships with adults and peers. For these, school may provide an element of safety and stability as well as the chance to learn how to relate more successfully to a range of different people.

However, some pupils have difficulties that can get in the way of them benefiting from or contributing to the social systems as they currently operate in schools. There is a balance that needs to be drawn between meeting individual needs and providing social learning and inclusion for all. This challenge is a major issue for teachers and for those who seek to support them.

There has always been a level of tension between the role of those providing support and those receiving it (Gray *et al.* 1994). This continues to increase with every new pressure on an education system that is attempting to improve pupil attainments at all levels. There is much less scope for flexibility in the system to cope with the individual needs of challenging pupils. However, it is not just a question of external pressures. There are also a range of unhelpful beliefs that can have an influence when difficult behaviour occurs. These can be held by teachers, parents, pupils and support workers themselves and can impact on the provision of support for pupils in mainstream schools.

Unhelpful beliefs

Extensive research has been carried out in order to explain and analyse young people's behaviour and provide a theoretical perspective for understanding the challenging behaviours that some of them present in school. A range of models have been proposed which vary in their emphasis on within-child and environmental factors (Ayers *et al.* 1995). While environment is clearly an important influence, it is increasingly accepted that behaviour is affected by how children interpret and internalise their experience. This has influenced the development of cognitive behavioural approaches (McNamara, Chapter 7 in this book).

The Rational Emotional Behaviour Therapy approach (in particular Ellis 1962) has examined the role of beliefs and the effect of beliefs on cognition. Beliefs, both rational and irrational, influence the way in which people interpret their environment and the behaviour of others. Differences in beliefs affect the way in which similar situations are interpreted and the feelings that are invoked influence people's responses to situations. Ellis focuses on the 'shoulds', 'oughts' and 'musts' that operate and which affect individuals' beliefs and views about the behaviour of others. He considers these kinds of statements to be irrational and unhelpful in resolving personal and interpersonal problems.

Ellis's 'rational–emotive' theory is a useful model that helps us understand some of the barriers to problem solving. However, there are a range of other prejudices, expectations and inaccuracies in the interpretation of the behaviour of others, which affect the interactions between pupils, parents, teachers and support workers. This combination of influences can prevent effective collaborative working in the area of behaviour support. If we consider that in some ways adults function as children but are, generally, better able to control or at least mask their behaviour, feelings and emotions, it is easier to appreciate misunderstandings which occur when problems are examined from a different perspective.

Negotiation in these circumstances can be very difficult. However, it is necessary to examine the potential agendas, expectations, prejudices and unhelpful beliefs that can operate at adult level, in order to move forward and promote improvements in pupil behaviour. It is worth bearing in mind that there are no failures, just differing levels of success. The greatest barriers to effective joint working between schools and support services are a discrepancy in perception and a lack of understanding of the role of other professionals involved. It can be very difficult for schools and support workers to appreciate the pressure that each is under. The roles of all involved have changed, and are continuing to change very rapidly with greater accountability, monitoring and evaluation and the need to be cost effective. It is within this context of rapid change of practice and perspective that the whole area of support must be judged.

Teacher perspectives

When behaviour escalates to a level where teachers feel that support is needed, a whole range of concerns emerge. In secondary schools, someone specific usually has the responsibility of liaising with other staff and with external agencies. The problems presented may have built up over a considerable length of time or be at a sufficiently high level to need urgent action to avoid a permanent breakdown in the pupil's placement at the school. The link person is only one of a range of staff who may have direct involvement with the pupil. A large number of staff will have taught, supervised or had some responsibility for the pupil, and have been affected by his/her behaviour. A whole range of individual beliefs and interpretations may be operating which influence the beliefs and values of the school or organisation.

The key person making contact with the support worker is generally going to be either the special educational needs (SEN) coordinator or a pastoral leader in the school who has already had a high level of involvement with the pupil over a long period of time, possibly with only limited effect.

There is nothing that is more guaranteed to make our personal anxieties and insecurities surface than a pupil who challenges our fragile image as a figure of authority. School staff may therefore feel they must act as if they are in authority (Gordon 1996) in order to maintain the illusion of control. Their need to project this image may affect their perceptions of the motives of others.

By the time a support service is involved, schools may feel that all that can be done has been done and a wide range of strategies will have been employed. Most schools will have invested time and money, providing training for staff, writing policies and updating school systems, which promote and reward positive achievement. When a pupil presents challenging behaviour a wide range of strategies may have been employed:

- rewards offered;
- sanctions applied;
- problems discussed;
- perspectives of others explained;
- report systems used;
- parents contacted;
- time given.

The pupil may have been the subject of numerous discussions between staff at different levels. Discussions will have been held with the pupil's parents and the parents of other pupils who may feel that their own child's education is being affected. Having tried a number of strategies, the school or the teacher may ask for support, overtly to help them address the pupil's needs in a cooperative way. And yet, the support worker coming into this situation usually has to face a whole range of well-established teacher beliefs, which can get in the way of effective collaboration. These may include:

- I have already spent lots of time on this problem and *should* not have to deal with this any more;
- it *should* not be allowed to continue;
- there is nothing more anyone can do;
- this is not something that this school/staff *should* be expected to cope with;
- someone *ought* to take this child away!;
- if this child were not in school all our problems would disappear;
- there *must* be somewhere this child can go where the right help will be available for him/her;
- there *must* be people who are more expert than us who can help him/her;
- the child is deliberately trying to make me feel incompetent, inadequate or at fault;
- they *should* know I'm trying my best;
- my competence is going to be questioned by someone who doesn't understand my situation;
- people will think I do not care about this pupil;
- the parents do not care nor do they support us;
- the child hates me, hates school and cannot or will not change, so nothing can be done;
- I *ought* to be able to deal with all pupils in the same way (I *must* be incompetent if I cannot);
- 'people' and other pupils expect me to have all the answers (I *ought* to be able to deal with this without support and I cannot).

These distortions and unhelpful beliefs undermine the ability and willingness of teachers to work positively with the pupil. They can also inhibit the support worker's ability to help tackle the challenging behaviour presented in school.

Support perspectives

Any or all of these beliefs affect the way in which support workers and their role are perceived. However, support workers also have their own set of beliefs, which again may be personal as well as professional. These may include:

- I am expected and *should* be able to provide instant answers;
- they (teachers) *should* understand the constraints under which I operate;
- teachers/schools *should not* give up on pupils;
- schools *should* always listen to my advice;
- they want me to take the problem away – they *should* work with me;
- they are being deliberately difficult by expecting me to come up with a 'quick fix';

- the school *should* realise that I am busy too;
- the school system is too inflexible for me to work with – it is structured for the masses and will not accommodate this pupil;
- they expect me to be telepathic;
- they have a vested interest in my being unable to effect change;
- schools *ought* to understand how much time and effort I put in;
- I have years training and experience in this field and my input is still not appreciated or valued – it *should* be!;
- I am doing my best – people *ought* to appreciate that;
- I can't be expected to have all the answers and unreasonable demands are being made of me.

The pupil's perspective

There are many precipitating and maintaining factors which may influence a pupil's ability to improve his/her behaviour in school. Pupils themselves may have some unhelpful beliefs which affect their ability to respond to attempts to alleviate the situation. These may include:

- I *should not* be expected to do anything I do not want to do;
- if I didn't have to come to school everything would be OK – I *ought* to be able to do what I want instead;
- they *should* be able to control me – it's not my fault if they cannot;
- I am not capable of changing;
- I *must* be a bad person;
- no one cares about me;
- they do not like me;
- I can't do anything right;
- doing the right thing will feel uncomfortable and others will notice and ridicule me for it;
- when I try to make an effort, no one notices (they *should*!);
- if I do not try I cannot fail;
- I might need more help but admitting it to the teacher or the class would be disastrous.

Parents and a range of others (e.g. other agencies) also carry their own set of unhelpful beliefs into the dynamics.

Clearly, beliefs and expectations change as teachers, pupils, parents and support workers start to establish closer working relationships and experience some degree of success. However, some of these issues will re-emerge especially when new working relationships are being formed or when things appear to be going badly. It is a factor that in any case involving behaviour problems a considerable amount of time is needed to establish effective working relationships both with the clients and with professional colleagues.

Nor are beliefs the whole story. Some pupils may have difficulties with learning and be unable to access the curriculum in a wide range of lessons. They may have had or be experiencing a whole range of social, emotional or physical problems, which prevent them from giving the attention to learning that school expects. Poor social skills, low self-esteem and taught negative attitudes may have made their perception of school less than positive. Parents themselves may have had very negative school experiences or find the whole process of education irrelevant; in some cases the level of difficulty they themselves are experiencing puts their child's educational success very low on life's priority list. Professionals too can have their own periods of personal stress.

Managing our own behaviour can be extremely difficult but, within the context of school, for some young people, it can become impossible without a considerable amount of support, resources and expertise. Support services can be in the best position to have access to the resources, personnel and time that may help to promote more positive behaviour leading to improved learning for the pupil. But they cannot assume that the support relationship is a simple one.

A real issue is the time and speed with which improvements can be made and maintained. Change is likely to be relative and expectations have to be adjusted accordingly. It is the skill of the support worker as negotiator that is the key to really making a difference and providing a point of reference from which to measure progress.

It is essential that a supporter can challenge and deal with some of the possible barriers to change. Awareness of the hidden agendas and the potential for suspicion and confusion is vital to resolving these. Teachers need to feel as if they are valued and that there is a way of establishing and working towards a common goal without the need for conflict. On the other hand, support workers need to ensure that their work in school is cost effective (i.e. that the school perceives that any time spent has been beneficial). Credibility is always a real issue for people providing behaviour support (either internally within the school or as an external agency) and it is essential that a level of credibility is established early on in the relationships if progress is to be achieved and maintained.

Bridging the gap

We are inevitably affected by each other's behaviour. These externalised factors trigger our internal emotional responses through the mediation of our experiences and beliefs. They in turn affect how we behave. Adults need to be able to retain a rational understanding of feelings and beliefs in order to ensure that we communicate effectively. The support provider and the support receiver need to establish good working relationships that can be maintained over time if the needs of the pupils are to be the focus rather than time and energy being wasted on meeting personal needs and establishing superficial credibility. An objective outsider is often in the best position to promote positive relationships (e.g. between teachers and pupils, or teachers and parents; Miller 1996), which may have broken down as a result of an increasing sense of powerlessness.

It can be difficult to move forward. The first requirement is to ensure that lines of communication are kept open. It is important to be very careful in examining and analysing all the possible factors affecting the behaviour of others, but we also need to include an honest self-evaluation of our own feelings, beliefs and motives. One inherent problem is that the support provider and school-based staff may have different primary aims; the support provider is concerned with the individual pupil while the school is more often concerned with how the pupil fits into the school system and dynamics. There is always confusion about beliefs, feelings and expectations, but people do not necessarily articulate what they really feel, believe or expect and this makes negotiating very difficult (Karrass 1992).

Karrass suggests that the following competencies are prerequisites for effective negotiators:

- the ability to listen actively;
- the ability to reflect understanding of the other's viewpoint;
- patience and self-control;
- belief in your ability to reach a manageable solution;
- decisiveness;
- speed and clarity of thought;
- knowledge;
- intelligence;
- inter- and intrapersonal skills;
- verbal ability;
- honesty;
- integrity;
- status;
- the ability to motivate and enthuse others and engage their support for any action.

There are limits and boundaries in support work, which inform decisions about what is possible (out of a range of other actions). The most successful interventions are ones which have built in obsolescence (i.e. success is owned by the teachers and the pupil). If support is to be effective it needs to be phased out as rapidly as possible so that the usual systems within the school can be seen as adequate for meeting needs (and the support worker can turn his/her attention to more pressing problems). In order to effect change and use time effectively a support worker has rapidly to establish good working relationships with all involved.

It is important to bear in mind what the school wants from the relationship with the support provider. The reason for referral is often a last attempt to access resources, personnel and expertise. It may be that involvement of the service is the only way to effect removal of the problem, offload or share responsibility for a difficult pupil and perhaps even to gain 'permission' to act (e.g. exclude). The support worker can provide a means of communicating with parents or carers when relationships have broken down, have become fragile or acrimonious. It is likely that there is an unrealistic expectation about what is possible, available or acceptable as an intervention for a particular individual. The key person in the mainstream school is often responsible for a large number of pupils and will often feel s/he has not got the time or ideas to continue to attempt to meet the needs presented. They will feel that some sort of change has to happen quickly to show improvement if the pupil is to survive in the school long term.

However, the support worker also has needs in order to be able to work effectively. Any intervention relies on background and information about the individual, the context and behaviours occurring. Time is needed to analyse the following: factors which may be affecting the pupil; systems operating in the school; interventions that have been tried and data already collected. Effective, professional working relationships have to be established with all concerned which can promote positive outcomes for the pupil in the long term. These may involve carers, personal advisors, social workers, health workers, teachers, the pupil and other pupils. It is the support worker and the school key worker's ability to establish effective collaborative working that is the key to providing support in schools. In order to provide for the needs of challenging children, good communication and negotiation skills are essential.

In order to work effectively, unhelpful beliefs need to be acknowledged and challenged. Supporters need to remember that they have knowledge, skills and experience that can provide a fresh approach to refining and adapting existing systems which have been developed in school. When working with emotional and behavioural problems, it is all too easy for personnel to become emotionally involved. It is necessary to transcend such involvement in order to communicate effectively and ensure that the needs of the pupil remain the first priority for the adults involved. Establishing this 'shared vision and clarity of vision' (Lane 1990) is paramount.

Working effectively together as support provider and receiver

In order to achieve this the school needs to:

- Provide factual information with dates of all problems presented by the pupil.
- Provide evidence of any special educational needs experienced by the pupil and the action taken to address those needs such as Individual Education Plans.
- Provide copies of Pastoral Support Plans drawn up for the pupil.

- Provide clear records of parental involvement in planning for the pupil and evidence of regular consultation with parents.
- Provide clear records of what action has been taken by school staff to resolve difficulties prior to seeking external support.
- Be open to positive suggestions by the support provider of further interventions that could improve the situation for the pupil in school.

In order to achieve this, support workers need to:

- Ensure that relevant information is available to all involved. Problems have usually built up over time and careful documentation of difficulties (in performance terms) will save duplication.
- Investigate realistic options available for the pupil long term.
- Be open, honest and positive about what is acceptable and feasible. If necessary ensure that other personnel who are likely to affect the outcomes or operation of an intervention are consulted. It is not possible to work with a case if agreements reached are going to be overturned or challenged by another party. Any possible sources of conflict need to be identified and included in discussions.
- Allow sufficient but not excessive time for initial interviews. People need time to open up and usually give valuable information if careful questioning techniques are applied (that involve feedback and reflection). It is useful to agree an end time to prevent overrunning or having insufficient space for discussion.
- Show and expect respect as professionals. It is the pupil who is experiencing or presenting the problem and time spent in pursuing individual hidden agendas can only be counterproductive.
- Be honest but flexible and open-minded and prepared to discuss any idea fully. Creative conflict is a powerful tool if handled well.
- Be on time for meetings and try to prepare properly or provide information promised. Remember the five P's – Poor Planning Promotes Poor Performance.
- Ensure that you have read and have with you any documents needed.
- Reflect back what is being said so that all points of information are agreed at the outset in clear performance terms.
- Establish working relationships that are capable of being maintained over time.
- Have a clear idea of what is possible and be prepared to compromise and try out ideas.
- Demonstrate patience and self-control while being assertive and decisive.
- Maintain a belief that a positive outcome is possible but have contingency plans in case things do not work out as expected. Be prepared to break any interventions down into small manageable steps with frequent reviews.
- KISS – Keep It Short and Simple! Always set SMART targets for everyone included.

- Agree any intervention plans: this may involve compromising. Once an agreement is reached and a plan devised, ensure that it is followed.
- Always have a back-up plan (e.g. to ensure that the absence of a key member of staff does not affect the smooth running of the intervention agreed).
- Ensure that all rewards and sanctions are feasible and agreed by all concerned.
- Ensure that all actions or expectations are explained clearly to all involved and write them down for reference in a format everyone can follow.
- Set clear manageable deadlines for reviews and ensure that they are kept to and documented.
- Success or failure should be shared and blame avoided. Where responsibility is an issue then make any feedback to others positive and professional and accept any responsibility in the same way.
- No matter what the outcome in an individual case, the provider–receiver relationships established should be kept positive so that future collaborative working can be facilitated.
- Seek assertive win-win solutions to problems, which address issues. Challenge and an element of creative conflict may be a necessary stage in the process!
- Remember: support relationships are likely to be most effective where:

  (i)   schools see themselves as having ownership and responsibility for meeting the needs of all pupils whenever possible;
  (ii) support workers are there to provide effective advice and support to ensure that those pupils presenting challenging behaviour reach their potential and enable others to reach theirs;
  (iii) schools and support workers both share a belief that positive outcomes are possible.

In summary, the world of behavioural support is often characterised by unhelpful beliefs and expectations. They can undermine the confidence and professionalism of anyone involved in dealing with behaviour management. Retaining any individual's positive self-image and confidence is vital. However, in the area of behaviour support it is all too easy to allow our own needs and insecurities to become the focus and to spend a lot of time and negative energy in building up our own defences. If we are to be of benefit to ourselves and to those we seek to support then we need to retain as many helpful beliefs as possible.

References

Ayers, H., Clarke, D. and Murray, A. (1995) *Perspectives on Behaviour: A Practical Guide to Effective Interventions for Teachers*, London: David Fulton Publishers.

Cole, T., Visser, J. and Upton, G. (1998) *Effective Schooling for Pupils with Emotional and Behavioural Difficulties*, London: David Fulton Publishers.

Ellis, A. (1962) *Reason and Emotion in Psychotherapy*, New York: Lyle Stuart.

Fogel, J. L. and Long, R. (1997) *Spotlight on Special Educational Needs. Emotional and Behavioural Difficulties*, Tamworth: NASEN.Gordon, G. (1996) *Managing Challenging Children*, Nuneaton: Prime-Ed Publishing.

Gray, P., Miller, A. and Noakes, J. (1994) *Challenging Behaviour in Schools Teacher Support, Practical Techniques and Policy Development*, London: Routledge.

Karrass, C. (1992) *The Negotiating Game* (rev. edn), New York: Harper Business.

Lane D. A. (1990) *The Impossible Child*, Stoke-on-Trent: Trentham Books Limited.

Miller, A. (1996) *Pupil Behaviour and Teacher Culture*, London: Cassell.

Morse, P. and Ivey, A. (1996) *Communication and Conflict Resolution in the Schools*, California, Corwin Press Inc.

Whetton, D., Cameron, K., and Woods, M. (1991) *Effective Conflict Management*, Hammersmith: Harper Collins.

Part III
Working with pupil emotions

6 The adult–child working alliance
From conflict to collaboration

Bill Wahl

'It's the relationship that heals,
the relationship that heals,
the relationship that heals-
my professional rosary.'
                    Irvin Yalom (1989)

The purpose of this chapter is the exploration of the relationship that exists between a professional (e.g. teacher, classroom assistant, psychologist, social worker, etc.) and a child with emotional and behavioural difficulties. The tone will at times be philosophical but the reader will also be offered pragmatic suggestions designed to strengthen the adult–child working relationship and to support a child's growth process. The chapter is written for adults having a significant ongoing relationship with a challenging child or for those who act in a consultant role to parents or to other professionals.

Labels, technique and the working alliance

There is no shortage of *diagnostic labels* for children with emotional and behavioural problems. Psychiatrists and clinical psychologists often use DSM IV (The Diagnostic and Statistical Manual of Mental Disorders, 4th edn) categories such as 'conduct disorder', 'oppositional defiant disorder' or 'attention deficit/hyperactivity disorder' (ADHD) (American Psychiatric Association, 1994). British educational psychologists and other educators make reference to children with 'emotional and behavioural difficulties'. When I worked in America as a school psychologist we had a different label for each of the three states I was employed in. There is also no short supply of information concerning specific *techniques*, as any trip to a well-stocked university library illustrates.

While I don't doubt that there is value in diagnostic categories and technique, the emphasis placed on these areas often appears to overshadow consideration of the *quality of the adult–child relationship*. And yet, the most powerful diagnostic tools and technical expertise may amount to little if one does not know how to forge a relationship with a child. Various interventions can work well if grounded in a solid relationship, while potentially powerful interventions are unlikely to be effective in the absence of such a relationship (Clarkson 1995).

For the purpose of discussion, the adult–child relationship can be distinguished from technique. This 'relationship' has gone by different names in the literature, including 'the therapeutic bond' (Orlinsky *et al.* 1994) and 'the working alliance' (Clarkson 1995). Technique is what we do to intervene, whereas the quality of the relationship is the context within which we intervene. Technique is perhaps like the seed we plant whereas the relationship is analogous to earth, sunshine and water. No seed will grow without good earth, sunshine and water, just as no technique can be effective in the absence of a relatively solid relationship or bond. In practice, of course, technique and the quality of the relationship intermingle. A reasonably strong relationship is the ground for effective technical intervention, while choosing well thought-out interventions is likely to support the strength of the relationship.

The fields of clinical/counselling psychology, counselling and psychotherapy learned the importance of the quality of the working alliance the hard way. Over the last 100 years (but particularly between the 1960s and 1980s), researchers conducted several thousand studies aimed at answering the question, 'What model of therapy (or technique) works best?' (Barkham 1996). Despite the huge expenditure of time, money and energy involved, the answer which emerged was that technically different therapies result in similar outcomes (Norcross and Goldfried 1992; Elkin 1995; Seligman 1995; Parry and Richardson 1996; Shapiro 1996). However, amidst this competitive fervour to see which model of therapy 'wins', another finding was slowly but very definitely emerging: the quality of the *working alliance* was found to be strongly predictive of positive therapeutic outcome (Lambert 1992; Orlinsky *et al.* 1994). In fact, after conducting a large review of relevant psychotherapy research, Lambert *et al.* (1986) concluded that the particular therapeutic model or technique used is not nearly as important in predicting success as is the quality of the relationship or bond.

Characteristics of a fertile working alliance

Children with emotional, social and behavioural difficulties always experience problems *in relationship* to others, which gives me cause to wonder if the term 'relationship difficulties' is perhaps a more apt descriptor than labels which simply list mostly behavioural symptoms. It is my experience that forming a reasonably healthy working alliance with such children is often the hardest and yet most essential task we face. Freud's discovery and illustration of the 'compulsion to repeat' (1962) perhaps goes a long way in explaining why it is so difficult to establish a solid working relationship with children who have relationship difficulties. Freud felt that if a child has learned to protect themselves or get their needs met through aggression, resistance, negative attention-seeking, dishonesty, withdrawal or sexualised behaviour, they will feel 'compelled to repeat' such behaviours in ongoing or new relationships.

Such behaviours are clearly unlikely to support a collaborative and productive working alliance, so a central problem facing us goes something like this: '*How can we develop a working relationship whereby the child can feel free to drop a resistant and closed stance and begin to collaborate?*' The particular technique or intervention we might apply is of secondary importance to this question because virtually no intervention is likely to be effective in the absence of a reasonably solid adult–child working alliance. In those instances where I have been, despite my efforts, unsuccessful in helping a particular child, I have also been unable to engage with the child, to get beyond the child's felt need to push me away or hurt me.

In my experience, no particular group has a monopoly on the ability to form a productive working alliance. I have known classroom assistants and non-professionals who are very talented in this respect and highly qualified and experienced individuals who are not. What follows (Table 6.1) is an outline of characteristics that seem to coincide with or support productive working alliances. This list of characteristics is applicable not only to adult-child alliances but to alliances we may have with almost anyone (including parents, colleagues and others).

While these characteristics are presented here in an ideal form, it is important to set realistic expectations for ourselves in terms of what quality of working alliance is possible. As a rule, the more disturbed the child we are working with, the more realistic our goals should be. I once worked with an 8-year-old who was so disturbed that the only way he would engage with me at all was if I quietly read picture books about boats to him. That was after months of work, and virtually any other attempts at engagement resulted in aggression or withdrawal.

Children with relationship difficulties, by definition, do not easily engage in positive working alliances with adults, and yet it is crucial that we strive to create reasonably productive working relationships. This explains why working with such children necessarily poses such an intellectual and emotional challenge. Before we consider various means of developing stronger working alliances, let us briefly look at some ways in which the adult–child working alliance can go wrong.

When the adult–child alliance goes wrong

Over the past 11 years I have had the privilege of spending thousands of hours in hundreds of classrooms in the USA and Britain, an opportunity which has allowed me to observe many teachers dealing with challenging pupil behaviour. Some teachers are more effective in building productive relationships with children which mitigate against behavioural difficulties,

Table 6.1 Characteristics of fertile working alliances

Characteristic	Description
Trust, safety	The child believes they will not be hurt or let down by the adult and the adult feels reasonably psychologically/ physically safe.
Openness, expressiveness	There is an ongoing and productive exchange (verbal, non-verbal or physical) between the adult and child.
Bond*	The relationship matters or is meaningful to both adult and child.
Reciprocal attunement*	The adult and child are on the same 'wavelength' and are not at cross-purposes. Similar to Rogers' (1951) idea of empathy.
Reciprocal affirmation*	Verbally, non-verbally or physically the child and adult are able to express liking or affection for one another. Similar to Rogers' idea of unconditional positive regard.
Motivation for and commitment to change*	Child and adult experience a desire for things to be better/different and a willingness to continue the relationship despite difficulties or ruptures.
Collaboration, cooperation, engagement	Child and adult are working as a team.
Consistency of arrangements*	The child believes that the adult will 'follow through' and believes in what the adult says. Similar to Rogers' idea of congruence.
Expectation of change	The adult and child believe that change is possible. Similar to Yalom's (1985) idea of 'instillation of hope'.
Clarity of roles and procedures*	The child and adult are clear about expectations, responsibilities and processes.
Maintenance of boundaries	There exists a clear and achievable means of containing the child, where necessary.

* Adapted from the meta-analytic review of Orlinsky *et al.* (1994).

whereas other teachers seem to consistently fall into 'the ten traps' (see Table 6.2). Teachers who consistently fall into these traps often get caught in seemingly inescapable circumstances of conflict, particularly with children with relationship difficulties. Such conflict cannot last for long before the adult and child grow to dislike and project blame onto each other. While the descriptions in Table 6.2 were created with classroom circumstances in mind, the various traps can also occur between children and their caretakers or non-teaching professionals.

Table 6.2 Problems in adult–child alliances: the ten traps

Trap	Description	Predicatable child response
1. Nagging	Adults repetitively express their needs in a manner which has little or no meaning to the child	Child 'tunes out' adult.
2. Shouting	Loud nagging. The dynamics are similar – only the volume has changed.	The child eventually 'tunes out' the adult.
3. Public verbal reprimand	A form of punishment that relies on social shaming.	Child may appear repentant during and just following reprimand, but the behaviour is likely to recur due to resentment, lowered self-esteem, negative labelling and possibly a desire to 'get even'.
4. Groundless threatening	Usually an 'off the cuff' threat, which the adult cannot follow through on.	Child's behaviour usually recurs as the child senses the adult cannot or will not follow through.
5. Vague promises	A promise of a reward that is unclear.	Child's poor behaviour often recurs because they are unclear of what is expected of them or believe they will be rewarded despite their behaviour.
6. Character attacks	A form of punishment that is focused on the child's *person*, rather than his/her behaviour.	Poor behaviour often recurs due to labelling, lowered self-esteem and possibly a desire to get even'.
7. Pointless ignoring	Ignoring poor behaviour when there exist sources of reinforcement other than the adult.	Poor behaviour recurs or even escalates.
8. Blaming or accusing	The strong insistence that the child has behaved poorly.	Child projects blame either privately or socially.
9. Inconsistent responding	Responding to a child's behaviour in unpredictable ways.	Poor behaviour continues as the child develops a 'gambling mentality'.
10. Physical punishment	Spanking, hitting, grabbing, etc.	Child engages in poor behaviour in instances where they believe they will not get caught. No internalisation of wrongdoing or learning of appropriate behaviour.

Teachers can often get away with using the traps in their relationships with many children, but children with relationship difficulties seem particularly immune to such unsophisticated approaches. In the United States we refer to the sports team playing locally as having the 'home field advantage', because they are familiar with the circumstances of their playing field and their home audience. Children with relationship difficulties are usually well acquainted with conflict relationships and have often habituated to the ten traps over time. Circumstances of conflict and the use of the ten traps are like playing on the child's home field.

The traps do not encourage the establishment of an adult–child working alliance that is collaborative. This is because the traps overfocus on the adult as authority figure and fail to offer an opportunity for the mutual exploration of the needs of adult and child.

The ten traps are also ineffective in the long term and often leave adults feeling guilty and exhausted: guilty because adults realise on some level that they are contributing to lowered self-esteem, and exhausted because the traps require continual repetition – they do a poor job of changing the child's behaviour. So why are the traps so popular? The traps are deceptive because, first, they often offer the adult instant relief and, second, they frequently appear to work in the short term. When an adult nags, shouts or reprimands, the adult is often able to vent some uncomfortable emotions (e.g. frustration) and the child may stop the unwanted behaviour or engage in the desired behaviour. However, changes in the child's behaviour tend to be short term for several reasons. First, the traps all rely on the adult exercising their authority over the child in order to coerce the child into meeting the adult's needs. There is something about the human spirit which finds coercion fundamentally offensive, and children are not exempt from this condition. Second, the traps do not attempt to tap into the child's capacity (however limited in development) to empathise with others. As such, the traps do not encourage the child to develop an internal sense of control over their behaviour (i.e. a social conscience). Note that it is the development of a conscience that enables individuals eventually to act in authentically empathic ways. Third, the traps in no way allow the child to discover alternative and healthier means of getting their needs met. Fourth, the traps model or teach children that the best way to get their needs met is to find ways of coercing or tricking others.

The alternatives to the traps are numerous. Some are seen in the form of formal therapeutic, educational or behavioural interventions that are easily found in the literature. But other alternatives are seen in the countless, informal behaviours of sensitive adults who are simply using good judgement. In the next section, we will look at seven approaches designed to offer adults means of productively engaging with children having relationship difficulties.

Strengthening the working alliance: practice considerations

What follows are not really 'techniques' in the commonly understood meaning of this word. Instead, these suggestions are more like 'ways of being' with a child which, with a bit of luck, will encourage the development of stronger, healthier and more productive adult–child working alliances. These suggestions have been drawn from my own experience and the experiences of colleagues, as well as from relevant literature. I should mention that every adult–child relationship is unique and whereas some suggestions may make sense, others will perhaps feel wrong when considering a particular relationship. I would encourage the reader to trust in their judgement concerning the application of the following ideas.

1 Learning the 'transference dance' on offer and refusing to do 'your steps'

Before a child ever met you they had numerous relationships through which they learned certain habitual coping strategies designed to get their needs met or to protect them from real or imagined threats. You are just another adult so they are likely to transfer these strategies onto you and are fully expecting you to play a certain role.

In the real world of dance each partner has a role, whether the dance is the cha-cha, the rumba or a waltz. Children with relationship problems each have a dance or dances that they know and they expect you, as one of many partners, to keep your end up. The variations in such dances are numerous, but here are some examples, as seen from the child's perspective:

- I have disturbing or annoying behaviours and you pay attention to me;
- I have challenging or rejecting behaviour and you reject or hurt me;
- I throw a tantrum and you let me have my way;
- I withdraw from you and you leave me alone;
- I withdraw from you and you work harder.

Some dances are on a more disturbed level such as:

- I act provocatively and you sexually or physically abuse me.

Just because the dances may seem irrational does not make them any less real. On some level, the dance makes perfect sense to the child doing the dancing. Also, while the above representation may suggest that children are quite consciously aware of the dance they are doing, this is often not the case as many children are simply acting out of habit.

Continuity and familiarity, however upsetting, may feel more comfortable to children than entering into new forms of relationship to adults. But herein lies the challenge for us. Once we have learned the dance, the goal is to help the child learn that you are not going to reject, hurt, give into their wishes or whatever your part of the dance is meant to be. This is often frustrating for children and they may continue to try to get you to do the dance steps they imagine you are meant to do, so it may take some time. However, if the child learns, for example, that you will not reject or hurt them no matter what their behaviour, the child may come to understand that their habitual means of coping are no longer necessary. When this happens, you may have provided the child with a 'reparative relationship' (Clarkson 1995), or a relationship which introduces the child to new ways of being with others.

2   Understanding 'payoffs'

From the perspective of many adults, a child's challenging behaviour is about causing problems for others. However, from the child's perspective (conscious or unconscious) their behaviour is about solving a problem. In order to understand how the child's behaviour is attempting to solve a problem, we need to understand what sorts of 'payoffs' usually accrue from such behaviour. Table 6.3 illustrates typical payoffs that frequently result from common behavioural problems.

Often, adults scuttle the working alliance with a child because they merely try to get the child to stop unwanted behaviours. The child resists in most instances because the behaviour is simply too important to them. However, if the adult is able to understand the payoffs that are linked with particular behaviours, they are in a position to help the child solve their problem or meet their needs through healthier means. For example, if a child displays aggression in order to obtain a feeling of control or importance, what can we do to enable the child to feel in control or important? If a child seeks negative attention, can we help the child learn and to seek attention in healthier ways?

Table 6.3 Payoffs from typical behaviour problems

Typical behaviours	Common payoffs
Aggression (verbal or physical)	Control, protection, avoidance, conflict, preferences obtained, catharsis.
Non-compliance	Preferences obtained, attention, conflict.
Negative attention seeking	Attention, social recognition or acceptance, conflict.
Tantrums, emotional 'blow-ups'	Catharsis, avoidance, preferences obtained.

3 The beauty of having a plan (or knowing why I'm doing what I'm doing)

Having in place a well thought-out approach to helping a child can offer consistency/security to the child, and security as well for the adult. Often, I see teachers and other educators 'winging-it' or *responding* to difficult circumstances whenever they arise. A plan is *proactive* and *preventative* in nature and offers adults a means of gauging whether they are on the right track. Plans can be meaningfully amended, whereas 'winging it' is like playing darts in the dark. There is also considerable evidence that helpers (in whatever form) are significantly more effective when they are perceived as 'sure of themselves' and 'credible' (Orlinsky *et al.* 1994). Children sense when we don't know what we are doing and feel 'held' when they believe we do.

Different forms of intervention serve different purposes, though they are not necessarily better or worse in relationship to one another. It is important to collaborate with a child on a form of intervention which is meaningful to both parties. A simple model (perhaps overly simple) shows that children need essentially three things from adults: *structure and encouragement*, because offering children structure/encouragement helps them to feel secure; *nurture*, because nurturing helps a child to value themselves (i.e. self-esteem); and *teaching of interpersonal skills*, because this provides a base of knowledge which allows children to cope successfully and develop rewarding relationships. Not surprisingly, these three areas are mirrored by the three most well-known models of child support: behaviour modification (structuring), use of counselling skills (nurturing) and social skills training or instruction (teaching) (Table 6.4).

Of course, these forms of intervention are not the only means of helping, but considering the particular needs of a child helps us develop a plan. I often ask myself, is the issue primarily a structure deficit, nurturance deficit or skill deficit? The answer often helps me develop an approach for engaging with the child (or children). Also, experience tells us that these approaches have their uses as well as blind spots. Behaviour modification can be used in many contexts and circumstance (Hoghughi 1988) and is often the fastest

Table 6.4 The nature of the adult-child relationship in different forms of intervention

Behaviour modification	*Counselling*
Adult provides: structure/encouragement	Adult provides: nurture
Child receives: security	Child receives: self-esteem

Social skills instruction
Adult provides: interpersonal teaching
Child receives: interpersonal knowledge

way to support dramatic changes in a child's behaviour; however, it may not reach 'deeper issues' or directly teach needed skills. Counselling skills can be experienced as supportive and offer opportunities for insight (Kazdin 1994), but often have less dramatic effects on behaviour. Social skills instruction (formal or informal) is perhaps the best way to directly teach new skills (Goldstein 1988), but often is time intensive and not as dramatic as behaviour modification.

The adult–child working alliance not only requires potent interventions for directly promoting growth, but also requires a means of effectively containing or placing boundaries around the child's behaviour. We do a child with more serious behaviour problems no service by allowing their disturbing behaviour to continue. Containing this behaviour is the area I most see neglected by school staff. Frequently, they have no plan to refer to when children placed themselves or others in danger or seriously disrupts learning. A plan is often required with a structured 'back-up system' for those times when front-line staff lose control of a child. With a plan, which is agreed to and contracted, a means of response can be implemented in a consistent manner. This provides staff (and the child) with the security of a having a structured response available which adults know can be followed through. Back-up systems can include other staff members being called to the room, removal of the child from the classroom or even asking a parent to pick up the child for the remainder of the day. Schools also seem to have a poor understanding of physical management and much more training for staff is needed in this area.

4   *Going beyond your 'role' with the child*

Children seem to have an acute sense of what is expected of the adults who teach or help them. One trick I have had up my sleeve for quite some time now is to surprise the child by going beyond this prescribed role. For example, in my work as a member of a behaviour support team I sometimes spontaneously call the school of a child I am working with and tell the secretary I would like to have a chat with the particular child, assuming it's OK to interrupt him or her. When the rather bemused child answers the phone I might say something like, 'Hi David, I was just thinking about you and wondering how things are going for you at the moment'. The discussion rarely goes into any depth, but the simple act of taking 3 minutes to call is often experienced as therapeutic for the child. Alternatively, I might mail the child a note. Teachers or support staff often feel that if they treat a particular child in a special way, they are being unfair or that the child will reject their efforts. However, children with relationship difficulties rarely find ways of reaching out to us, so it behoves us to find clever ways to enlist their engagement.

5 Intervening at the appropriate level

Building strong working alliances also means intervening with an appropriate level of intensity. I once met with school staff who discussed a
particular 8-year-old boy's behavioural difficulties. The child was physically
hurting other children on a daily basis, refusing to follow directions 'most of
the time' and running off school grounds about two to three times a week.
When I asked how the staff were working with the child I discovered that
their input was limited to attempting to talk with the child during or
following one of his 'episodes' (an approach which was not working). I
have also worked with a case that involved two social workers, an outreach
worker, a psychologist, a GP and a full-time classroom assistant – a set of
circumstances that seemed to be creating an unproductive overkill.

Here is a rule of thumb to consider: provide the smallest level of
intervention necessary to achieve desired ends (O'Connell 1998). This is
not only therapeutically sound but economical as well – after all, most of us
work within environments having limited resources. The challenge is to
provide an intensity of intervention consistent with the level of presenting
needs. Clarkson (1996) describes three levels of presenting need (i.e. danger,
conflict/confusion and deficit), and I have developed a format (see Table 6.5)
which relates this model to the context of supporting children with relationship difficulties.

Table 6.5 Matching interventions to levels of presenting need

Level of presenting need	Representative behaviours/issues (examples)	Level appropriate responses (examples)
Danger	Physical aggression, self-harm, running away from staff or school grounds.	Parent involvement, physical management, back-up procedures, referral to other professionals, behaviour modification.
Conflict/confusion	Negative attention seeking, non-compliance.	Behaviour modification, social skills instruction, counselling skills, curriculum modification.
Deficit	Low self-esteem, socially excluded, social skill deficits, withdrawn behaviour, fear of failure.	Counselling skills, social skills instruction, one-to-one meetings with child, modification of expectations, peer pairing.

6   Read Thomas Gordon

Until the early 1970s, behavioural and psychoanalytic models of helping were largely what was on offer in terms of supporting children with relationship difficulties. Using many skills borrowed from humanistic counselling, Thomas Gordon taught parents and teachers how to have a sensitive, collaborative and creative problem-solving dialogue with a child. For educators and other professionals who wish to learn the skills of intervening with children through dialogue and creating stronger working alliances, Gordon is essential reading. Recommended books are *Teacher Effectiveness Training* (1974) and *Parent Effectiveness Training* (1970).

7   The advantages of meeting privately with children

When I worked as a school psychologist in the USA, I used to meet one to one with many children who had relationship difficulties, mostly for the purpose of performing a psychoeducational assessment. Children described as disruptive, non-compliant or aggressive in the classroom ... were most often polite, respectful and helpful in the context of our meetings. Why was this? Was there some wonderful quality about me that brought out such behaviour in these children? Hardly. What made the difference was the context of the meeting. Within the classroom setting, children are often motivated to entice their teachers or other adults into conflict-laden relationships. However, meeting with a child individually offers opportunities for engagement and alliance building which may not be possible in a public context. Teachers and other helpers are often reluctant to meet with a child one to one, citing time constraints as the major impediment. However, I often point out that a small investment of time in one to one meetings can result in large gains.

I am here suggesting one-to-one meetings as a *preventative* and *proactive* intervention. This may seem obvious, but I find that when educators meet with challenging children it most likely takes the form of a *response* to behavioural difficulties that have recently occurred. The content of such meetings often involves a 'telling off' and may take place within earshot of other children or adults.

My suggestion is that the teacher hold a regularly scheduled and brief meeting (perhaps once a day to once weekly for between 5 and 15 minutes). The teacher should ensure that they will not be interrupted and might begin such meetings by giving the child an opportunity to express themselves (e.g. 'Well David, I just wanted to check in with you to see how you felt things were going'). Often children will have a difficult time offering information and it may be necessary to ask more pointed questions or express your observations. Such a meeting is also a good context for offering praise or sensitively expressing your concerns or feelings or collaborating on/reviewing behaviour-management approaches you may be using. Even when children are unable to engage in much dialogue, the simple act of reaching out in this manner is often experienced as therapeutic.

References

American Psychiatric Association (1994) *The Diagnostic and Statistical Manual of Mental Disorders*, 4th edn, Washington, DC: APA.

Barkham, M. (1996) 'Quantitative research on psychotherapeutic interventions: Methodological issues and substantive findings across three research generations', in R. Woolfe and W. Dryden (eds) *Handbook of Counselling Psychology*, London: Sage.

Clarkson, P. (1995) *The Therapeutic Relationship*, London: Whurr.

Clarkson, P. (1996) Personal communication to the author during training at Physis, London.

Elkin, I. (1995) 'The NIMH treatment of depression collaborative research programme: Major results and clinical implications', *Changes* **13**(3): 178–85.

Freud, S. (1962) *New Introductory Lectures on Psychoanalysis*. New York: Penguin.

Goldstein, A. P. (1988) *The Prepare Curriculum: Teaching Prosocial Competencies*, Champaign, Illinois: Research Press.

Gordon, T. (1970) *P.E.T. Parent Effectiveness Training: The Tested New Way to Raise Responsible Children*, New York: Plume.

Gordon, T. (1974) *T.E.T.: Teacher Effectiveness Training*. New York: Peter H. Wyden.

Hoghughi, M. (1988) *Treating Problem Children: Issues, Methods and Practice*, London: Sage.

Kazdin, A. E. (1994) 'Psychotherapy for children and adolescents', in A. E. Bergin and S. L. Garfield (eds) *Handbook of Psychotherapy and Behaviour Change*, (4th edn) New York: John Wiley & Sons.

Lambert, M. J. (1992) 'Psychotherapy outcome research: Implications for integrative and eclectic therapists', in J. C. Norcross and M. R. Goldfried (eds) *Handbook of Psychotherapy Integration*, New York: Basic Books.

Lambert, M. J., Shapiro, D. A. and Bergin, A. E. (1986) 'The effectiveness of psychotherapy', in S. L. Garfield and A. E. Bergin (eds) *Handbook of Psychotherapy and Behaviour Change*, 3rd edn, New York: Wiley.

Norcross, J. C. and Goldfried, M. R. (1992) *Handbook of Psychotherapy Integration*. New York: Basic Books.

O'Connell, B. (1998) *Solution-Focused Therapy*, London: Sage.

Orlinsky, D. E., Grawe, K. and Parks, B. K. (1994) 'Process and outcome in Psychotherapy – noch einmal', in A. E. Bergin and S. L. Garfield (eds) *Handbook of Psychotherapy and Behaviour Change*, 4th edn, New York: John Wiley and Sons.

Parry, G. and Richardson, A. (1996) *NHS Psychotherapeutic Services in England*, London: Department of Health.

Rogers, C. R. (1951) *Client-Centered Therapy*, Boston: Houghton Mifflin.

Seligman, M. E. P. (1995) 'The effectiveness of psychotherapy', *American Psychologist* **50**(12): 965–74.

Shapiro, D. A. (1996) Forward to *What Works for Whom? A Critical Review of Psychotherapy Research*, A. Roth and P. Fonagay, New York: The Guilford Press.

Yalom, I. D. (1985) *The Theory and Practice of Group Psychotherapy*, 3rd edn, New York: Basic Books.

Yalom, I. D. (1989) *Love's Executioner and Other Tales of Psychotherapy*. London: Penguin.

7 Motivational interviewing and cognitive intervention

Eddie McNamara

I'm bad ... I want to behave but I can't
(Tony, 10 years of age)

Tony is a pupil at a residential special school for pupils experiencing emotional and behavioural difficulties (EBD). When referred to me, he was on the verge of permanent exclusion because of 'violent and aggressive behaviour'. He had already been excluded from the school on a fixed-term basis on three separate occasions. He had attended the school for over 2 years, but his behaviour had not changed – and had perhaps even deteriorated.

The school had in place a Pupil Management System based on 'points'. The number of points earned by each pupil in each week were used to allocate the pupil to a band – bands ranged from Band 6, the lowest, to Band 1, the highest. The points were awarded to pupils on a lesson-by-lesson basis and also in out-of-school situations depending on their behaviour towards other pupils and staff and for their academic effort and achievement. Bands dictated access to rewards and there was also a 'fine' system in place.

Tony had been exposed to this management system for some time. The school had been rigorous in applying the system. However, it was clear that such externally imposed environmental management approaches (a behavioural regime) had been ineffective in resolving his behavioural difficulties.

The purpose of describing Tony's situation is to illustrate the limitations of focusing solely on pupil behaviour and the need for a wider conceptual analysis and formulation of problems so that more effective intervention strategies can be generated.

The assessment methodology used to arrive at a formulation will be described later in this chapter. However, at this stage, it is worth reflecting on Tony's own formulation. He had a negative self-image, '*I'm bad*', and believed that he could not change his situation ('*I can't (change my behaviour)*'). Tony wasn't trying to change his behaviour as he believed that he was '*bad*' and that he couldn't change.

In this kind of situation, any effective intervention has to address two major obstacles. These can be defined as (i) the person's lack of motivation to change and (ii) their belief that they couldn't change, even if they tried. This second aspect (beliefs about one's capability of achieving something) is known as *self-efficacy* and is an important determinant of whether a person will attempt to tackle a problem.

This chapter address the two problems described above. The issue of eliciting motivation is addressed by describing the theory and practice of motivational interviewing. The second issue – how to change one's beliefs about oneself – is considered through reference to the rationale underlying the practice of cognitive therapy. Cognitive therapy is the term used to describe the theory and practice of helping people change their beliefs about themselves and their situation in order to promote self-change.

Motivational interviewing

The practice of motivational interviewing (MI) evolved from a consideration of a model of therapeutic change (Prochaska and DiClemente 1982). This model proposed a six- stage process (see Figure 7.1). Clients progress from

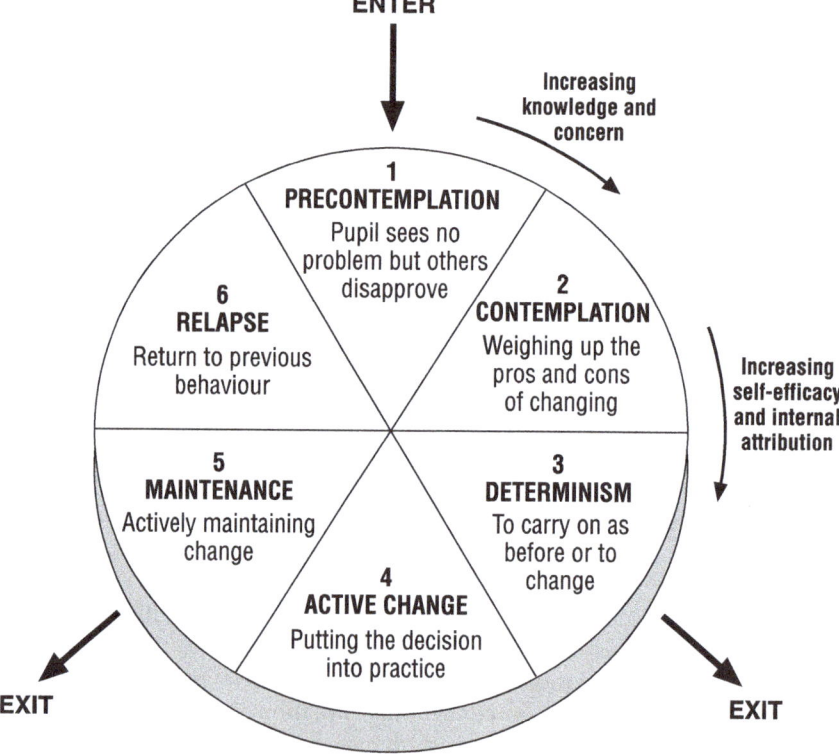

Figure 7.1 Facilitating movement through the stages of change.

an initial stage at which they do not accept that a problem situation exists – and therefore do not feel a need to address it or engage in a process of change – to a fifth stage at which change is achieved (i.e. the problem is addressed successfully and therapeutic change ceases). A sixth stage, relapse, is included to accommodate the reality that clients sometimes do not maintain successful change at their first attempt.

In order to effect change successfully, we have to facilitate client movement through the stages of change from Stage 1 through to Stage 5. The six stages of the model are briefly described below, followed by a brief description of the goals of MI and the techniques used to achieve these.

The stages of change

Stage 1   Precontemplative stage

It is self-evident that a person who does not see that s/he has a problem will not be committed to do anything about 'the problem'. This is the situation that exists at the precontemplative stage. To acknowledge that we have a problem can often lead to a loss of *self-esteem*, uncomfortable *feelings of concern*, lowered feelings of *self-efficacy* (the belief of being able to cope) and to feelings that we are not in control of our own situation (*external attribution*).

The precontemplative stage is characterised by statements such as '*I haven't got any problems*', '*It's the teachers, they pick on me*' and '*Everybody messes about*'.

Uncomfortable feelings of worthlessness and incompetence can be a threat to the person's self-image. Many people 'protect' their self-image by either denying that a problem exists (thus avoiding threats to self-esteem) or by locating the 'cause' of the problem outside themselves (external attribution) (e.g. to unreasonable teachers).

The higher a person's self-esteem the less difficult it is for them to accept that they may have a problem. Consequently, three of the aims of motivational interviewing are:

1   *to promote pupils' self-esteem* – and thus enhance the possibility of the person accepting and acknowledging the negative information about themselves and/or their situation;
2   *to promote knowledge* (elicit information) about the 'problem' situation; and
3   *to promote concern* about the situation.

Success in achieving these three aims enhances the probability that the pupil will move from the precontemplative stage to the next stage, contemplation. The contemplative stage is characterised by statements that acknowledge the possibility that a problem exists. (e.g. *'Sometimes I behave well'*, *'Yes, I would like to keep out of trouble'*.

The pupil is more likely to decide in the first place that a problem exists if s/he has:

1   *knowledge of the problem*; and
2   *concern about the problem.*

Achieving these outcomes are the first two objectives of motivational interviewing.

Stage 2   Contemplative stage

The contemplative stage is characterised by statements indicating acknowledgement of the possibility that a problem may exist (e.g. *'Sometimes I behave well'*, *'Yes, I would like to keep out of trouble'*). Implicit in the first statement is the information *'... and sometimes I don't behave well'* while implicit in the second statement is the information ... *'I get into trouble'*. It is at this stage that the pupil is able to consider the fact that a problem may exist and to think of ways to respond to it.

Promoting knowledge and concern facilitates movement from Stage 1 to Stage 2. However, enabling the pupil to acquire greater knowledge about the problem and to experience concern does not necessarily ensure that the pupil will decide to do something about it. Movement from Stage 2 to Stage 3 (a decision to change) requires that the pupil:

1   believes that the contributory factors to the problem situation can be influenced (i.e. *internally attributes the contributory factors*); and
2   feels and believes that s/he is capable of successfully tackling the problem (i.e. *has feelings of self-efficacy*).

Achieving these two outcomes are the second two objectives of MI.

The overriding objective of these aims is to produce *cognitive dissonance* within the pupil. The teacher/counsellor is trying to facilitate a move from a situation in which the pupil is not questioning his/her behaviour, attitude or contribution to a situation in which the pupil *does* ask questions about himself or herself in these areas. By promoting the aims listed above, the pupil is more likely to acknowledge the desirability of change: the cognitive dissonance can be first acknowledged and then 'resolved' by making a commitment to change. This position needs to be established in order to move to Stage 3.

Stage 3   Determinism Stage

This involves a transition from the contemplative stage to either a decision to address the problem or to exit from the model (by deciding that change is not needed). The determinism stage represents the key decision-making process.

Dr Henck van Bilsen, who has developed motivational interviewing over the last two decades in the area of addictive adult behaviours (particularly using hard drugs, alcohol abuse and gambling), views the process as '*helping the client make wise decisions*' (Van Bilsen 1991). In other words, the counsellor is not engaged in a possibly unethical exercise of coercing or '*conning*' the client, but helping him/her to generate the fullest possible information on which to make decisions about the desirability or otherwise of behaviour change.

Stage 4   Active change stage

Stage 4 consists of identifying and putting into practice strategies for achieving the change. Once the pupil reaches the stage of active change, then s/he has '*passed through*' the motivational interviewing gateway and entered the realms of the self-management of change. In this stage the relationship between teacher/counsellor and pupil is very much like that of a coach and player: they are engaged in a *collaborative* exercise to identify and implement strategies for change.

The actual strategies used to effect change can range from behavioural contracts through self-management techniques to cognitive-behavioural management strategies (see McNamara 1996(a), 1996(b) and Fox 2001).

Stage 5   Maintenance

This stage is known as maintenance – a stage in which the desired behaviour change has been achieved and the programme (i.e. intervention strategies) has been withdrawn.

Stage 6   Relapse

This stage is included to reflect a 'phenomenon of the human condition' (i.e. that not all change will be sustained). Teachers should not be surprised if youngsters are committed, make decisions to change achieve, change and then relapse. It is not uncommon for adults in smoking-cessation pro-grammes to relapse on three or four occasions before stopping smoking for good. This fact is equally applicable to changes in pupil behaviour. When a relapse occurs, we should avoid the conclusion '*motivational interviewing doesn't work*' – for the task then is to re-enter the stages-of-change model at the appropriate stage and to use the experience of prior success to achieve more long-lasting improvements.

The techniques of motivational interviewing

The techniques of motivational interviewing involve both *active listening* and *selective active listening*. By using active listening techniques the teacher/counsellor can elicit from the pupil a range of statements concerning the problem situation (McNamara 1998). These techniques involve judiciously reflecting back only those components of the pupil's utterances which are indicative of concern about the situation, contain information about it or which indicate an internal attributional style and feelings of self-efficacy.

The techniques of MI can be considered an amalgam of humanistic, Rogerian and behavioural counselling. The humanistic component is made up of an *unconditional positive regard* for the client – value judgements about the client as a person are not made. The Rogerian component takes the form of 'semi' non-directive counselling (the Rogerian method in its pure form involves totally non-directive counselling – the counsellor follows the direction of the client). By reflecting back the client's own utterances the counsellor uses the client's statements, observations and feelings to elicit further statements, observations and feelings. Thus the counsellor joins the client on the client's 'journey'.

The behavioural component of MI is used to modify the Rogerian component so that the approach becomes more guided. This is achieved by the use of selective active listening. Before describing the characteristics of selective active listening, the process of active listening is described. This is a core component of most counselling approaches.

Active listening

Active listening has both non-verbal and verbal dimensions. It involves communicating to the client that what s/he says is of interest, relevance, importance and worth listening to (i.e. is valued).

The non-verbal behaviours that communicate this include eye contact, facial expression and posture. For example, if the counsellor sits back, arms folded and intermittently looks at the clock on the office wall then this would not constitute active listening: active listening would include eye contact, leaning towards the client and nodding to give the client non-verbal feedback that the therapist is following, understanding and sympathetic to what the client is saying.

The verbal manifestations of active listening include accurate reflections, summaries and structuring the client's utterances.

Examples of verbal active listening

(a)   Reflections

These can consist of parroting/repeating, rewording or paraphrasing.

I) PARROTING/REPEATING

This involves simply repeating the exact words used by the client:

PUPIL: I nearly always do my homework.
COUNSELLOR: You nearly always do your homework.

It is important that this reflection is not received by the client as a question – for the client may then respond with a 'yes' or a 'no', consequently closing down rather than opening up the exploration of a problem area. The counsellor guards against allowing a reflection to slip into a question by slightly lowering rather than raising the tone of voice at the end of the reflection. This technique should not be overused as its repetitive use may irritate the client.

At this point the counsellor may be tempted to ask direct questions to elicit information about specifics (e.g. *'Tell me the homework you get each night and tell me which homeworks you usually do and those you don't?'*). This temptation should be resisted: the time to ask direct questions is at the determination stage (i.e. after the client has made a decision to change): the client can then be asked direct questions as part of a collaborative procedure to agree a programme for self-change. The strategy used at this stage to elicit further information and concern about the problem is *selective active listening* (see p. 83).

Direct questions should be kept to a minimum at this point in the counselling process. The problem with direct questions is that they may (i) allow the client to respond with a '*Yes*' or '*No*' and consequently close down the area of enquiry and (ii) elicit resistance from the client (personal disclosures at an early stage of the interview may be threatening to the client and not support a move towards the four key objectives of motivational interviewing).

(II) REWORDING

This technique involves restating the client's utterances using different words and synonyms: it is particularly useful when the client uses colloquial terms:

PUPIL: I threw a rubber at the teacher and it hit him on the side of the head … it was wicked.
TEACHER: You hit the teacher on the head with a rubber and you now realise that it was a bad thing to do. *(NB statement not question).*
PUPIL: No … it was great … it was a good laugh … everyone was laughing their heads off.

In this case the pupil was not using the dictionary meaning of the word 'wicked' but a colloquial meaning indicating 'enjoyable and amusing'. This is the main purpose of using rewording – for it helps to establish that the client and counsellor both mean the same things by the words used.

The use of rewording also avoids the potential of irritating the client by the over-use of parroting.

(III) PARAPHRASING

This response goes beyond merely attempting to reflect back exactly what is said (parroting/rewording) and towards establishing agreement about the content of what is said. The counsellor attempts to establish the intention and underlying meaning of the client's words. In a sense it can be seen as a reflective response with a hypothesis testing function:

PUPIL: I'm thinking about leaving the gang.
COUNSELLOR: You want to stop getting into trouble and leaving the gang will help *(again statement not question)*.
PUPIL: I'm not sure.

(b)   Summaries

This strategy consists of the counsellor drawing together utterances of the client into a neat, succinct summary. The summary allows the client to agree, disagree, modify, develop or correct the counsellor's version. After five or six pupil–counsellor interactions the counsellor might summarise as follows.

COUNSELLOR: As I understand it, you have been excluded from school on three occasions. If you are excluded again, it will be a permanent exclusion. At first when I asked you how you felt about this you said 'I'm not arsed'. Later you said you are worried about it because it is unlikely that you will get a place in another school.
PUPIL: Yes.

A summary can be used by the counsellor to elicit from the client further information, concern and possibly commitment to action:

COUNSELLOR: Not following teachers instructions in class and then arguing with the teacher when asked to leave the classroom has led to you being excluded three times and the next exclusion may be permanent ... and you do not want to be permanently excluded ... what conclusion do you draw from this?
PUPIL: I'd better make sure I don't get excluded.

(c)   Structuring

Frequently in a counselling situation the client responds to the counsellor's prompts with further information. This can provide the counsellor with further opportunities to help the client generate more information about his/her situation. Ultimately, these may lead to the development of concern on the part of the client. However, information presented usually needs structuring to enhance its potential to generate this concern:

COUNSELLOR: Tell me more.

PUPIL: I'm not going to apologise to that dickhead.

COUNSELLOR: You are not going to apologise to the headteacher.

PUPIL: No, even if I'm out of school for another 2 weeks.

COUNSELLOR: You're not concerned about missing school.

PUPIL: My GCSE exams start in 3 weeks and he's (the headteacher) not letting me back in for revision lessons.

COUNSELLOR: You're worried about missing your revision lessons.

PUPIL: Yes ... You need five C-level GCSEs to get into the Sixth Form College.

COUNSELLOR: Let's see if I've got it right. You want to go to the Sixth Form College and you need at least five C-level GCSEs to get there. If you don't resolve your difficulty with the headmaster you will be unable to attend revision lessons. If you don't go to revision lessons there's less chance of you getting five C-level GCSEs.

PUPIL: Yes.

COUNSELLOR: What conclusion do you draw from my summary of what you've said?

PUPIL: I don't know really ... well I suppose I'd better try and get back into school for the revision lessons.

Selective active listening

The behavioural component of MI is the crucial strategic strategy used to facilitate client movement from the precontemplative stage through the contemplative stage to the determination (decision to change) stage.

The phrase 'active listening' is prefaced by the descriptor 'selective' because the counsellor selectively reflects back to the client the aspects of what the client says that facilitate achievement of the four primary goals of MI being achieved. Essentially, attention is given to when the client is:

1   making explicit specific information about the problem (which may enhance the client's knowledge);
2   expressing concern about the problem;
3   showing feelings of enhanced self-efficacy;

4   providing indications of internal attribution (i.e. that s/he contributes to the problem and has a role in changing it).

Here is a practical example:

(i) Specific information about the problem

PUPIL: Michael's always messing around that's why I hit him.
TEACHER/COUNSELLOR: You hit Michael – *a selective reflection.*
PUPIL: He's always getting on my nerves so I punched him.
TEACHER/COUNSELLOR: You punched Michael – *a selective reflection.*
PUPIL: Yes, and now I'm suspended.

The teacher/counsellor only reflected back to the pupil those parts of the pupil's utterances that were leading to the nature of the pupil's unacceptable behaviour being made explicit. Consequently the parts of the utterances that did not facilitate this were ignored (i.e. '*Michael's always messing around ...*' and '*He's always getting on my nerves*'. Thus by being selective in what was reflected back to the pupil the teacher/ counsellor elicited the nature of the problem behaviour and its consequences from the pupil.

(ii) Eliciting concern

PUPIL: Yes, and now I'm suspended.
TEACHER/COUNSELLOR: You punched Michael and as a result you have been suspended.
PUPIL: Yes, I shouldn't have lost my temper.
TEACHER/COUNSELLOR: You lost your temper.
PUPIL: I try to control it but sometimes I can't.
TEACHER/COUNSELLOR: Sometimes you can't control your temper.
PUPIL: Yes, that's what gets me into trouble.

In this continuation of the MI interview the pupil is moved from a description of a specific incident (punching Michael) to (i) the identification of a more general problem, losing his temper, and to (ii) an expression of concern about this general problem. The technique of selective active listening is seen in the teacher/counsellor reflecting back 'You lost your temper' but not 'You shouldn't have' and reflecting back 'Sometimes you can't control your temper' but not 'You should try to control it'.

(iii) Promoting feelings of enhanced self-efficacy

PUPIL: I've always done awful in exams except for science.
TEACHER/COUNSELLOR: You've done well in science.

The teacher/counsellor's selective reflection emphasises a positive pupil achievement. 'I've always done awful in exams' (the negative component of the pupil's utterance) is ignored. Emphasising the positive aspect facilitates feelings of self-efficacy.

(iv) Promoting an internal attribution bias

The above interaction continued as follows:

PUPIL: Only because I like science and I revised.
TEACHER/COUNSELLOR: So when you revise you can do well in exams.

The teacher/counsellor's response selectively promotes an internal attribution of causality (i.e. 'when you revise you can do well in exams'). He is reinforcing the contribution that the pupil makes to outcomes.

Summary

MI can be viewed as a synthesis of Rogerian and behavioural counselling to the extent that *non-directive* strategies are used to elicit a range of client utterances. These utterances are then responded to using behavioural counselling strategies (selective active listening) to facilitate the client moving in the direction of the goals of MI.

Tony (continued)

In the light of the above account of motivational interviewing, let us return to Tony's situation. He had a negative self-image '*I'm bad*': in addition, he expressed feelings of low self-efficacy '*I want to but I can't*'. Based on this statement, and others in the assessment/interview, it could be concluded that Tony was at the *precontemplative* stage of the stages-of-change model.

Miller and Rollnick (1991) grouped the many and diverse reasons why a person might be in the precontemplative stage under four headings – precontemplators could be *reluctant, resigned, rationalising* or *rebellious*.

In terms of these four common reasons for clients being at the precontemplative stage, Tony could be described as a '*resigned*' precontemplator. This is the term given to those people who appeared to have given up the possibility of change and are resigned to the status quo. They sometimes feel overwhelmed by the problem. They either don't want to even think about it, or feel it is too late to do anything. This may follow unsuccessful attempts to tackle the problem in the past.

Tony's negative self-mage '*I'm bad*' was obstructive to effecting change – for there is a strong tendency for people to behave in a manner which is consistent with their self-image. In the light of this formulation of Tony's difficulties, a crude approach to contingency management of behaviour through rewards and sanctions (as had been adopted by the school) would seem inappropriate. Of more relevance to Tony's situation were the negative thoughts that he held about himself and his situation. These kinds of obstacles to change are most appropriately addressed by using *cognitive* techniques.

Cognitive interventions

People function within three modalities, *thinking, feeling* and *behaving*. There is an assumed interdependency of functioning within these three modalities – to the extent that it is generally accepted that effecting change in one modality of functioning may effect change in one or both of the other modalities (see Figure 7.2). For example, if a school-phobic child undergoes a successful systematic desensitisation programme (i.e. gradually achieves the behaviour changes necessary to re-establish school attendance), it is likely that s/he will think more positively about school (a cognitive change) and feel more comfortable in school (an affect/emotional change). However, it is difficult to predict the exact relationship between collateral changes that may occur when change is effected in one modality of functioning. Thus if a school phobic child is successfully desensitised, the likelihood of mainte-nance (i.e. continued school attendance) after the programme has been withdrawn, is enhanced if collateral changes in cognition and affect have also been achieved. Conversely, if little or no change has been effected in these two modalities of functioning, then supportive collateral change to

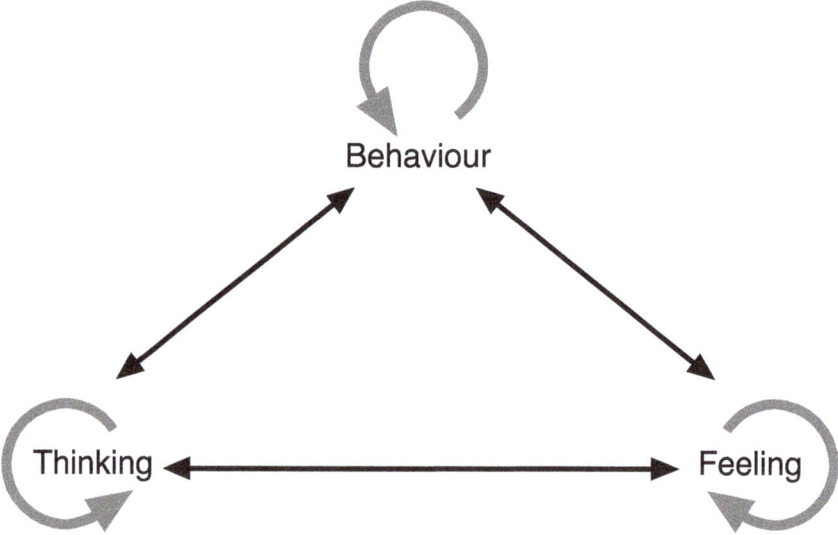

Figure 7.2 The interactional relationship between thinking, feeling and behaving.

help maintain new behaviour patterns will not be evident and consequently relapse is more likely.

In contrast to traditional behaviour therapists, whose primary focus for change is in the behaviour domain, cognitive therapists focus primarily on the *cognitive* domain. Cognitive therapists believe that as *dysfunctional thinking* contributes to *dysfunctional behaviour*, the most effective and appropriate intervention focus is on changing the thinking, as opposed to primarily addressing the behaviour this generates.

With reference to the model presented in Figure 7.2, the thoughts that can contribute to maladaptive behaviours are often described as *automatic thoughts*. The term 'automatic thoughts' is used to describe the phenomena by which the thoughts are generated without reflection or consideration. Thus, for example, when a student is presented with a series of mathematical problems the automatic thought might be '*I can't do these*' or '*I'm no good at maths*'. Such automatic thoughts are not helpful to the pupil addressing the mathematical problems successfully; they are not supportive of appropriate '*mathematical*' behaviour.

A further example would be a student who is reluctant to participate orally in a French lesson – either not responding when invited or mumbling at an almost inaudible level. This pupil's automatic thoughts might be '*I can't speak French*' or '*Everybody's going to laugh at me if I try this*'.

It can be seen that negative automatic thoughts are situation-specific – they reflect a negative view about a particular situation. However, the theoretical model underlying cognitive therapy postulates that automatic thoughts (both positive and negative) are generated from *underlying core beliefs* or *schemata*. Thus, the negative automatic thoughts with regard to mathematics described above, though situation-specific, may be generated from the more general core belief '*I'm no good at schoolwork*' or '*I'm stupid*' or '*There's no point in trying 'cos I never get things right*'. This model is illustrated in Figure 7.3.

The teachers trying to elicit successful performances from the two students described above are 'swimming against the tide' as such performances

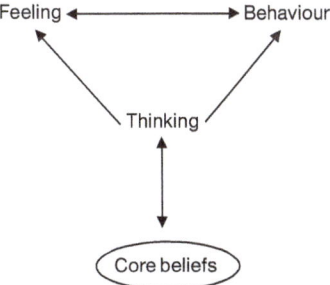

Figure 7.3 Core beliefs generate automatic thoughts.

would be contrary to their core beliefs and automatic thoughts. Cognitive therapists assert that the most successful intervention in such cases is achieved by affecting change in core beliefs so that the required behaviour change is more easily affected. This can be achieved by either substituting a positive core belief for a negative core belief (e.g. '*I can do schoolwork*' for '*I can't do schoolwork*') or, as is more usual, the replacement of an absolute negative core belief by a qualified positive core belief (e.g. instead of '*I'm never any good*' – an absolute negative core belief – the pupil is encouraged to think '*Sometimes I behave well*' – (a 'partially positive' one). Such changes can be helpful in facilitating motivation and goal setting; thus, the student might accept a goal such as '*I could try to behave well more of the time*'.

The theory of cognitive therapy refers to changes in core beliefs as *changes at the underlying level*, while changes in automatic thoughts are referred to as *changes at the surface level*. In terms of interventions a major strategy to effect changes both in negative automatic thoughts and negative core beliefs is to help the pupil to collect evidence that refutes these. While examples used in the preceding paragraphs relate to academic behaviour, the same considerations are also relevant to the affective (emotional) domains. For example, a core belief may be '*I am unlovable*': this will contribute to withdrawn/depressive behaviour – and may even promote aggressive acts. If such a core belief can be changed to '*I am lovable*' or '*I can be lovable some of the time*' then this may produce a more relaxed individual who allows him/herself to get closer to people.

Where do core beliefs come from?

Greenberger and Padesky (1995) put forward the view that early development of core beliefs/schemata probably coincide with language development – for the young child probably uses language to organise experiences. For example, from particular experiences children may make generalisations. If a dog barks and growls and attempts to bite a child, the experience may generalise to '*dogs are dangerous and should be avoided*'. If, on the other hand, a dog wags his tail, presents as playful and accepts a pat on the head, the child may generalise the experience to '*dogs are friendly and can be played with*'. However, the authors go on to point out that with experience, and as a child grows older, absolute simplistic rules and beliefs become more flexible and adaptive. For example, the two contradictory beliefs described above (which promote contradictory behaviours) can be integrated to a more flexible adaptive belief such as '*some dogs are dangerous and should be avoided and some dogs are friendly and can be approached*'. The behavioural conclusion that can be drawn from such an adaptive belief is that '*I will avoid dogs that snarl and growl and approach dogs that wag their tail and present as playful*'. It is when absolute beliefs (which in the majority of children become more flexible and 'adaptable' over time) are inaccurate and remain fixed that dysfunctional behaviours may result.

Greenberger and Padesky (1995) hold the view that absolute beliefs may remain fixed if they develop from very traumatic circumstances, or if consistent early life experiences convince the child that such beliefs are always true even as the child grows older. This may be particularly the case in the area of child abuse. Many children come to the conclusion that they, and not the adult perpetrator, are responsible for the abuse. The reasons for such dysfunctional beliefs will vary. For instance, it may be that the child's belief that s/he was being punished for 'badness' was less threatening than believing that an adult close to them was 'bad' (for children need to believe that adults are 'good' so as to feel safe and secure). However, the same authors go on to point out that other types of early childhood experience can result in dysfunctional core beliefs. For example, an able young sibling may always be in the shadow of an even more able older sibling. Consequently, despite being successful, their success never matches or exceeds that of the elder sibling. The belief may develop that '*I am inadequate/worthless*' because in his/her own mind no accomplishment is worthwhile unless it is the absolute best (i.e. superior to the elder sibling's achievements).

When adults enter into cognitive therapy and long-standing dysfunctional core beliefs are identified, it may take months to modify effectively or substitute these. They have usually been consolidated over many years, having generated outcomes that are self-confirmatory. In contrast, children's core beliefs, because they are not so long-standing, are more amenable to modification and change. Kendall, who pioneered cognitive–behavioural approaches with children, put forward a linear descriptive model to illustrate the process of consolidation of core beliefs (Kendall 1988) (see Figure 7.4). I adapted (McNamara 1994) this model to that of a looped feedback model (see Figure 7.5) in order to illustrate:

a   how the negative outcome consolidates a negative bias in the information processing mechanism;

b   how intervention can be focused on change in the information processing (so as to produce less dysfunctional products, i.e. *more helpful core beliefs*) and/or evaluating the product in a more positive light (thereby *modifying the existing core belief*).

Greenberg and Padesky (1995) use a *scaling approach* to help the client move from absolute negative core beliefs to partially positive ones. For example, the client's absolute negative core belief may be '*nobody loves me*': at the time of intervention the client believes this absolutely and therefore considers it to be 100% true. A significant element of the intervention is helping the client to seek/identify and then record evidence that is contrary to this core belief. The client is then asked to re-evaluate its accuracy: as

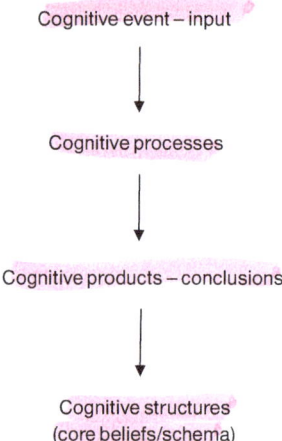

Figure 7.4 Kendall's linear model of core belief (schema) consolidation.

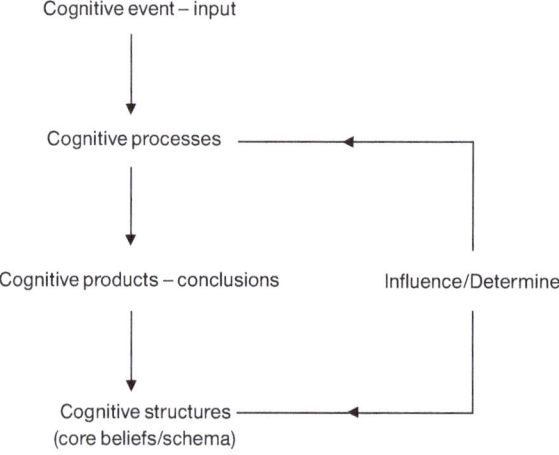

Figure 7.5 Core belief/schema consolidation – feedback model (McNamara, 1994).

evidence is now available that the core belief is not always true, it therefore cannot be rated as 100% true. The successful collection of contrary evidence can be used to facilitate the client developing a modified or even new belief. For example, the absolute negative belief '*nobody loves me*' can be modified to a less negative core belief '*some people love me*'; at the same time, the rating of the 'truth' of the initial core belief may change from 100 to 85%. The collection of further evidence to refute the core belief may result in its truth rating being further reduced, perhaps from 85 to 60%. In parallel with this, the client may be invited to review the core belief '*some people love me*' and consider a move to an even more positive core belief '*quite a lot of people love me*'.

Once a modified core belief is identified and accepted by the client, the intervention imperative is to help the client collect further evidence (or, less preferably, to provide evidence to the client) in order that the modified, more positive/less negative core belief is consolidated and strengthened.

The identification, articulation and awareness of the modified or new core belief is essential. It makes the client more sensitive to information that is consistent with this belief, which will help to consolidate this. It also facilitates memory storage (and retrieval) of this supporting information.

Cognitive interventions with children

Children are different from adults in many ways. With regard to cognitive development, children have a less extensive life experience and therefore negative core beliefs and schemata are generally less consolidated and therefore less rigid than those of adults. Thus, whereas adult cognitive therapists often focus on changing core beliefs with a view to facilitating changes in negative dysfunctional automatic thoughts, I am developing intervention strategies with children that work in the 'reverse' direction (i.e. changing negative automatic thoughts and then facilitating reflection on more positive automatic thoughts in order to 'refute' negative core beliefs).

The rationale behind this approach is that if the child can be 'taught' to acquire positive automatic thoughts, then two consequences are possible. First, a positive automatic thought will enhance the likelihood of positive behaviour change being achieved (i.e. that behaviour is consistent with the thought acquired). Second, the evidence generated by this change can be used to help the child to reflect further – reflection which can be focused on modifying or changing dysfunctional, absolute core beliefs about him/herself.

Tony – assessment and intervention in practice

Tony's situation has been described at the beginning of this chapter. In summary, 'traditional' behavioural approaches had been ineffective in effecting change in his behaviour and he was at risk of permanent exclusion from a residential school for EBD pupils because of violent and aggressive behaviour. The assessment revealed that he had developed a negative self-image and was not motivated to change his behaviour – he was identified as a 'resigned precontemplator'.

Assessment

A psychoeducational assessment was carried out to identify if learning/educational difficulties were contributing to Tony's overall maladaptive responses to the education situation. Tony was assessed to be of average intellectual ability and experienced very mild specific learning difficulties of a dyslexic nature – difficulties which were known to his teachers and addressed in an appropriate and supportive fashion.

With adults, cognitive pre-intervention assessments are often carried out through a combination of 'clinical interviews' and questionnaire/self-report techniques. Similar strategies can be used with children – although young children are often less aware/ accurate/reflective with regard to problem situations. Moreover, some children do not have the language skills necessary to communicate effectively. My preferred assessment model is to ask the pupil to complete a number of sentence completion blanks (SCBs), either providing a written response or an oral one if literacy and/or motivational difficulties prevent the pupil from writing things down. The SCBs used tend to be:

1   school/incentive/punishment orientated (e.g. '*The three things that I like about school . . .*');
2   open-ended with an affective bias (e.g. '*I love . . ./I hate . . . , my greatest wish . . ./my greatest fear . . .*');
3   an assessment of strengths (e.g. '*One thing others like about me . . . .*

Early indications are that pupils' responses to items relating to the 'assessment of strengths' can provide very informative information. In particular, when a pupil is reluctant to make a positive self-statement, this is strong evidence for a powerful negative core belief. For example, one of my clients responded to the item 'One thing others like about me is . . .' with '*Nothing . . . no one likes me . . . I always let people down*'. In Tony's case, the following responses were significant as they shed light on his belief system and on beliefs which were obstructive to him developing more positive and adaptive patterns of behaviour:

*   I hate . . . '*me (because I'm always bad at school)*';
*   when I was younger. . . '*I was bad*';
*   at bedtime . . . '*I think (about trying to be good – but I can't be good)*';
*   I can't . . . '*be good in class*'.

These responses, particularly his comment about thinking at bedtime, indicate that he was at the precontemplative stage/contemplative stage interface in the stages-of-change model: furthermore, they indicated that he was a 'resigned' contemplator (i.e. he had given up on the possibility of change). This assessment is supported by his response to the cue 'I can't . . .', which was '*. . . be good in class*'.

A follow-up question was put to Tony, namely 'Would you like some help so that you can be (good in class)?' to which Tony responded '*Yes*'.

Intervention

There were three aspects to this. First, a staff briefing was held that described the rationale behind the proposed intervention strategy. This was as follows:

Staff briefing: Tony Smith
Tony has a strong negative self-image with regard to his behaviour (i.e. he sees himself as badly behaved). This negative self-image is an obstacle to helping Tony improve his behaviour.

Formulation
- How a person sees himself is his self-image.
- How a person evaluates his self-image determines his self-esteem.
- A positive evaluation results in high self-esteem.
- A negative evaluation results in low self-esteem.

People generally behave in ways that are in agreement with their self-image/self-esteem. Therefore an indirect way of helping pupils improve their behaviour is to help them change the way they see themselves. Children develop a negative self-image by engaging in thinking styles which exaggerate their 'problem' behaviour and minimise their 'good' behaviour. These 'thinking styles' are often referred to as 'cognitive distortions'.

Second, the following strategy was adopted by the author for use in his weekly meetings with Tony.

1 Elicit from as many significant adults as possible up to three positive statements about Tony – eight adults (teachers, support assistants and residential care staff) each contributed three positive statements. Write these on cards.
2 Have the contributors' names in an array in front of Tony.
3 Have him repeat (or read independently if he can) each positive statement and attempt to attribute it to an adult. If attribution is correct, say 'Well done' and place the card in front of the appropriate name. If incorrect, have Tony repeat (or read again) the positive statement and again attempt to attribute. Repeat process until he successfully attributes. A record of responses is kept on an appropriate record form.
4 Repeat this activity on a regular basis – at least weekly – preferably more frequently until he attributes all the positive statements to the correct source.

5   Keep repeating this activity until Tony sorts very quickly: this enhances the likelihood that the positive self-statements are embedded in long-term memory and can be elicited automatically.
6   'New' or different positive statements can be introduced and others dropped out: Judgements should be made as to what to 'keep in' and 'add' such that an increasing range of positives is 'in the pool'.
7   All positive statements made by Tony about himself are recorded and he is encouraged to reflect upon them; the statements were then included in the above exercise.

Within the Code of Practice (DFEE, 1994) pupils are required to have Individual Education Programmes – they are sometimes referred to as Individual Behaviour Programmes when the focus is on behaviour and emotion. The strategy devised for Tony was drawn up and presented in such a way that it could be accommodated within an Individual Educational Programme (see Table 7.1).

Evaluation

Ten individual sessions, totalling 6 hours were given to Tony. The sessions ranged in length of time from 1.5 hours to 15 minutes – with subsequent short intermittent 'booster sessions'. The following improvements have occurred:

a   *Exclusions:* from January to December 1999, three exclusions; from January to July 2000, zero exclusions.
b   *Points band:* The school operates a system from Band 6 (lowest) to Band 1 (highest). In the last two terms of 1999, Tony averaged a weekly band of 4.5. In the most recent two terms, Tony averaged a weekly band of 3.0. In the same period the percentage of Band 2 weeks rose from 13 to 56% (with Band 2 achieved in 36% of weeks during the spring term 2000, increasing to 75% in the summer).
c   A special-support assistant kept a record of Tony's lesson-by-lesson behaviour. This revealed far more 'problem-free days'. In addition, when incidents have occurred they have been less intense and of shorter duration.
d   Tony's sentence-completion responses at the time of assessment were put to Tony 6 months later and he was asked to review them. The responses from both occasions are listed in Table 7.2.

Summary

A review of Tony's 3 years at the residential school for children with emotional and behavioural difficulties reveals that, for 2.5 years, attempts were made to meet his needs within a behavioural regime: these attempts

Table 7.1 Part of Tony's Individual Educational (Behavioural) Programme

Short-term objectives	Interventions
1. Verbalise and increase awareness of negative self-statements.	i Confront and reframe the negative self-statement(s). ii Assist Tony in becoming aware of how to express his negative feelings about himself.* iii Be alert to opportunities to give positive feedback to Tony to promote his self-esteem.
2. Decrease the frequency of negative self-descriptive statements.	i Ask Tony to make regular positive self-statements about himself and record it on a chart or in a diary. ii Assist Tony in developing positive self-talk as a way of boosting his self-confidence and a more positive self-image.
3. Identify positive traits and talents about himself.	i Appropriate strategies from those described above. Develop with Tony a list of affirmations (positive self-statements) and have Tony read them aloud three or more times per day – until Tony knows them off by heart (i.e. automatically).
* In particular, facilitate Tony moving away from 'black and white' statements about himself (e.g. I am 'good' or I am 'bad'.	Encourage Tony to make 'shades of grey' judgements (e.g. 'I behave well some of the time and not so well some of the time').

The target to be aimed for is 'to behave well more of the time' and consequently 'not so well' less of the time. This approach will also help Tony make the distinction between the person and the behaviour (i.e. it is the behaviour that is 'good' or 'bad', not the person.

were manifestly unsuccessful. In the 6-month period described in this study the focus of intervention was changed to Tony's thinking (i.e. a cognitive intervention). Tony's behaviour was improved through changes in his thinking about himself (self-image) and about his ability to change his behaviour (self-efficacy).

This case study illustrates the increased effectiveness of intervention achieved by extending the behavioural model of intervention to a cognitive–behavioural model (i.e. by addressing the thoughts and feelings of the pupils as well as their behaviour).

Table 7.2 Pre- and post-intervention responses to sentence-completion blank cues

	Assessment (December 1999)	7 months on (August 2000)
One thing I do very well is	*being naughty*	*not sure*
I regret	*being naughty*	*not sure*
At bedtime	*I think about trying to be good but I can't*	*I think I can be good*
I feel	*OK*	*great*
I can't	*be good in class*	*false* (i.e. statement/belief made at time of assessment)
My nerves	*are horrible*	*are better*
My mind	*is not bad and not good*	*is better*
The future	*is bad for me*	*is good*
Sometimes	*I am good*	*I am good most of the time*
I hate	*me*	*I am good now*
At school	*(it is) bad*	*(it is) good*
The only trouble is	*school*	*none*
I wish	*I was good*	*(I was) even better*
My greatest worry is	*school*	*not school*

References

DfE (Department for Education) (1994) Code of Practice on the Identification and Assessment of Special Education Needs.

Fox, M. (2001) *The Theory and Practice of Cognitive-Behavioural Management*, Merseyside: PBM.

Greenberger, D. and Padesky, C. A. (1995) *Mind Over Mood: Change How You Feel by Changing the Way You Think*, The Guilford Press: London.

Kendall, P, (1988) Cognitive Behaviour Management of Anxiety Disorders in Children. Paper presented at the European Cognitive Behaviour Therapy Conference: Edinburgh, Scotland.

Miller, W. R. and Rollnick, S. (eds) (1991) *Motivational Interviewing: Preparing People to Change*, New York: The Guildford Press.

McNamara, E. (1994) 'The concept of motivation: An applied psychologist's perspective', *Education and Child Psychology* 11(2): 6–15.

McNamara, E. (1996a) *The Theory and Practice of Behaviour Contracts*, Merseyside: PBM.

McNamara, E. (1996b) *The Theory and Practice of Pupil Self-Management*, Merseyside: PBM.

McNamara, E. (1998) *The Theory and Practice of Motivational Interviewing*, Merseyside: PBM.

Prochaska, J. O. and DiClemente, C. C. (1982) *The Transtheoretical Approach: Crossing Traditional Boundaries of Therapy*, Homewood, IL: Dowe Jones/Irwin.

Van Bilsen, H. (1991) 'Motivational interviewing: perspectives from the Netherlands, with particular emphasis on heroin-dependent clients', in W. R. Miller and S. Rollnick (eds) (1991) *Motivational Interviewing: Preparing People to Change*, New York: The Guildford Press.

8 The 'E' in EBD

Rob Long

Introduction

This chapter argues that there has been too much emphasis over recent years on understanding *behaviour* rather than adequately appraising the significance of pupil emotions. There is no doubt that an understanding of how behaviour can be modified has helped us work successfully with challenging behaviour. Yet there is much more to pupils' difficulties than just inappropriate behavioural patterns.

Back to the future

A good place to begin this 'emotional' journey is to briefly consider our own development. Each one of us comes to the world with an existing range of emotional responses. The most obvious ones are fear, sadness, anger, joy and curiosity. These are the primary emotions. Culturally, we have found some emotions more difficult than others to accept and manage. It is not unfair to describe us as being dominated by a 'neck up' approach; we have a history of preferring to deal with matters rationally. The Victorians set the stage for the denial of emotions having any significant role; they were to be controlled at all costs. Thankfully Darwin and Freud laid the foundation for effectively challenging such a view.

However, many of us are still socialised to deal openly with only a narrow range of emotions. Many of us find anger an extremely difficult emotion to manage, similarly loss. Our own families will have encouraged us to show only those emotions that our parents were comfortable with. Similarly we learn a range of values and attitudes that shape our future experiences. It is a truism to say that we enter tomorrow with yesterday's eyes. We have no choice. But when we are working with children whose emotional needs are central to their behavioural difficulties, we need to be more aware of this. Given that many people still see negative emotions as reflecting poor self-control and indiscipline it is hardly surprising that the solution can be punishment. However, too often we seek to blame rather than understand children's behaviour. The result is that when we are faced with children with emotional and behavioural difficulties the safest way of making sense can be to focus on their behaviour. The E in EBD (emotional and behavioural difficulties) has consequently been poorly understood.

Self-awareness

Each of us carries emotional ideals. These are memories from our early childhood that influence our first impressions of other people. Most of us are aware of finding some children easier to like than others. There are some that seem to raise our hackles more than others. Two children may misbehave similarly but we find one easier to like than another (the 'likeable rogue' syndrome). The child that triggers our negative reactions is the one that, for irrational reasons, has triggered negative memories. As these negative emotions are released they in turn trigger the 'fight or flight' reaction. This reaction causes us to experience stress as the energy made available for flight or fight is not used. If children are motivated to gain control over adults, then every time they cause the adult to lose control, they have gained control. So the need for some degree of self-awareness is essential when supporting troubled children; we cannot ignore our role, and an understanding of our own emotions is paramount.

There are many ways of making sense of how adults and children behave. Some involve models that clearly focus on behaviour, and use the law of effect as a central principle. Others emphasise the way in which we interpret and make sense of the world from a cognitive perspective. To fully understand the difficulties of children identified as having emotional and behavioural difficulties, we need a model of emotions that provides us with practical suggestions to improve the way in which we can support them in school.

It is perhaps worth emphasising that this approach complements rather than replaces the positive-behaviour management systems employed by most schools. Behaviour is always a management issue. How we as adults respond to children's behaviour influences how they behave. Even before children enter school we need to have definite ways for promoting positive behaviour. We should not wait and see if there are any problems. But in the best managed class there are likely to be a small number of children whose life experiences have led to them developing ways of coping that will not always be positive within the school context. If we are to successfully include these children, and not just contain them, we need to understand their emotional world, as much as the learning context.

Making sense of emotions

At the surface level, we are all different from each other: we look different, have different habits and different likes and dislikes. These differences make it interesting to meet new people. But what is it that motivates these differences? It is the interaction between our emotions, our beliefs and the context in which we develop. Emotions give our lives colour and meaning. Without emotions there would be no problems or difficulties because we would not care. Can you imagine trying to make a decision if you didn't care about the outcome? Our preferences come from our likes and dislikes, the emotions. We are often concerned with the lack of motivation some students have towards their work. But motivation is the surface issue. It is emotions that drive us into action. Motivation masquerades as an explanation when it is the emotions that truly determine our behaviour. For example, a lack of motivation may stem from a 'fear of failure'.

Being human we all have basic emotional needs, the key ones that concern us are the need:

- to belong;
- to be safe;
- to be valued;
- to be in control.

These needs are common to both staff and students. Many of us will see the similarity between these and Maslow's hierarchy of needs, which remains a useful model to understand how our inner emotional world drives our behaviour (Maslow 1970). The problem behaviours we observe in many children stem from the way in which they seek to achieve these core emotional needs. What is a solution to them can often be a problem to us. Because we have been so dominated by objective, scientific methods of understanding human behaviour we have tended to stop after an analysis has been made of the surface behaviour. We can readily accept that behaviour is functional in that it serves to meet specific needs. If we use emotional needs as our starting point then we can make sense of behaviour in terms of the emotional needs that are being met. In other words, emotions are functional and cause specific behaviours that enable those needs to be addressed.

This can best be seen if we recognise that a child's will to survive adverse life experiences will lead them to develop behaviours that achieve this goal. These behaviours can become problems when either taken to extremes or displayed in different settings. For example, if children are being parented by adults who depend heavily on alcohol and/or drugs, then they are likely to be erratic in their behaviours. They may at times be euphoric and at others suspicious, hostile and paranoid. To cope under such conditions such children may become excessively perfectionist. They may try to avoid the need for their parents to correct them by being perfect all the time. When this pattern of coping or resiliency is brought into school it is less successful. Such pupils may now find completing any work difficult as they fear the consequences of being wrong. Children who face emotional and behavioural difficulties more often than not come to our attention because of their less-than-appropriate ways of meeting their needs. What is a strength in one context becomes a weakness in another.

Similarly a child who is being parented in a hostile manner may become extremely aggressive as a way of coping. Anger is a natural response we each have when our goals are blocked or frustrated. The anger provides the energy and the motivational drive to overcome such blocks. However, it can also be used to prevent social bonding and attachment. To be attached to a carer who is overtly hostile in their parenting style is clearly life threatening to the child. Such maltreated children can adopt hostility as a means of survival. But when they face learning challenges and the everyday frustrations of normal school life they respond with aggressiveness as a natural response to any social or learning challenge. There are always compelling reasons that explain the behavioural difficulties that some children present in school.

Even passive withdrawal and helplessness can be understood as a child's learned way of coping with adverse circumstances. Fear leads to children adopting submissive posture, reduced eye contact or tearfulness. Assuming a passive position and crying act as cues of helplessness and submission, which serve to block further acts of aggression.

Using our understanding of emotions the challenge should be for us to develop a model that:

1   relates specific behaviour patterns to specific emotional needs;
2   suggests management techniques to support these emotional needs more positively;
3   indicates competencies that would enable a child to better meet their emotional needs;
4   provides methods for achieving change compatible with educational values.

It is important to stress that such a model cannot be a quick-fix recipe guide for children with emotional and behavioural difficulties. It can only offer a framework for school staff to make informed hypotheses for those children who are clearly distressed and facing failure and perhaps at risk of exclusion. The observed data that will have been collected on such children can be used to generate a plan of action that accepts a child's inner emotional needs as valid and requiring support as much as their behavioural and learning needs.

In seeking to understand why children behave as they do, we can be driven to find a model of linear causality. That is to say that whenever *x* happens, it is because of *y*. For example:

Aggressive behaviour indicates a child's lack of control .
Refusal to attempt new work indicates low self-value.

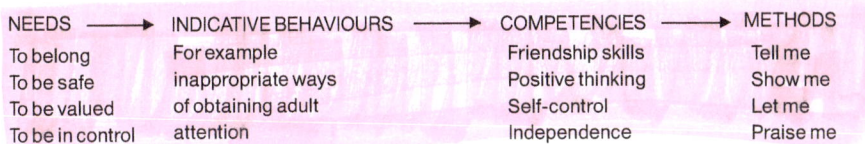

NEEDS →	INDICATIVE BEHAVIOURS →	COMPETENCIES →	METHODS
To belong	For example	Friendship skills	Tell me
To be safe	inappropriate ways	Positive thinking	Show me
To be valued	of obtaining adult	Self-control	Let me
To be in control	attention	Independence	Praise me

Figure 8.1 Model for linking needs to intervention approaches.

Imagine three children who are all displaying outbursts of aggressive behaviour in class. There could quite plausibly be a different explanation for each. One may have learning difficulties and be using his/her anger to relieve frustration and avoid the work that is perceived as being too difficult. Another may be experiencing some form of abuse at home. Another may live in a subculture where aggressive behaviour is condoned and seen to produce positive outcomes. We are looking to make informed interpretations of problem behaviour to help us better support children who are as much troubled as troublesome. Without a model we will persist with reactive strategies that will emerge from a sense of frustration and helplessness in not knowing what to do for the best. But with an understanding of emotions we will be better equipped to generate creative interventions in school as well as to share some common assumptions when we meet in multi-agency case conferences to develop complementary support programmes for some of our most troubled pupils. The model shown in Figure 8.1 reflects this approach.

The indicative behaviours suggest the core need that the pupil is trying to meet. Because of negative emotional experiences, the way in which they seek to do this is less than appropriate in the school setting. Our task is to detail those competencies that the pupil either does not have or is not using which would enable them to meet their needs more positively. Within the school context we can design intervention programmes that reflect an educational bias (i.e. we will 'teach' the pupil why such behaviours are inappropriate). We can then show them other pupils using competencies that enable them to get their needs met. We can break these competencies down and allow the pupil to practise them. We can feed back on their successful progress.

This model stresses the need for children to be supported in developing those competencies that will enable them to meet their emotional needs in more appropriate ways. It is not theories that we apply to children but the techniques that the theory suggests. An immediate criticism of a model such as this is that it oversimplifies complex situations. Children's behaviour will often be motivated by some, if not all, of these basic needs. While this is true, to seek for the all-encompassing theory remains an illusory goal. Don't winners break impossible tasks down into small manageable ones, while losers take small manageable tasks and add them together to make them impossible? Because we can never be absolutely certain that our hypothesis is correct, we should aim to make small interventions and observe any effect. To invest a lot of time and resources in grand intervention plans is a sure recipe for disappointment and frustration.

Learning as an emotional experience

We have focused so far on how negative emotions can lead to behavioural difficulties in school. We need also to appreciate that learners interact with their context. Their behaviour only makes sense when we understand the context in which it happens. Learning involves a child taking a risk. There is always the risk of failure, whether real or imagined. Confidence is required to enable learners to make this leap. We are asking them to use some of their emotional energy to expand the boundaries of their mind. However, troubled children have less free energy, and, as we have seen, their goal is often to protect themselves. Consequently much of their troublesome behaviour is in fact their attempt to avoid engaging with situations that are perceived as threatening to them (see Chapter 9 by Adrian Faupel in this book). In fact, much of the disruptive behaviour can be better understood when it is seen as being driven by internal emotional drives. As a child becomes more emotionally defensive, it is not uncommon for them to become increasingly egocentric in an attempt to protect their remaining self-esteem. Children with emotional and behavioural difficulties typically have poor self-esteem. They can often have negative relationships with key adults, poor peer relationships, a low academic success and poor role models at home.

If we accept that new learning experiences can be potentially distressing to these children, then some of their behaviours can be reinterpreted as being indicators of stress reactions. For example:

Pupil behaviour	*Stress indicator*
Odd noises and babyish behaviour	Regressive behaviour
Fighting and squabbling	Displacement activity
Distractible and poor concentration	Low tolerance to frustration

Emotional needs

Using the core emotional needs, we can now make sense of some of the troublesome behaviour so frequently faced in classrooms.

1   Emotional goal: the need to belong

The emotional attachment that children develop to their carer has both biological and social functions. For the infant, safety stems from being close to their 'secure base' (Ainsworth 1967). When an infant feels anxious or fearful, being close to his/her carer reduces these feelings. Children need to be able to separate from their carers in familiar surroundings to enable them to develop independence. However, if a child's carer is unresponsive, hostile or anxious towards a child, then, rather than the child separating from the carer, the need for attachment is increased. The more a child is rejected the more s/he seeks attachment.

Problem/Mistaken behaviours

- attention-seeking behaviour;
- shouting out;
- interrupting others;
- not listening to instructions;
- making noises;
- out of seat;
- no equipment.

Competencies needed

- listening and following instructions;
- asking for help;
- waiting in turn;
- putting hand up.

Intervention strategies

- make time for one-to-one attention;
- value their efforts;
- give them encouragement;
- use quiet reminders;
- use logical consequences;
- a pay back system for inappropriate time taken.

2   Emotional goal: the need to be safe

Safety is a basic need of all children. Some, if they have experienced hostile or ambivalent parenting, can develop feelings of apprehension and inadequacy. This can result in withdrawn and passive behaviour. Such behaviour can result in adults treating the child like a victim and constantly 'coming to the rescue'. This can in effect reinforce the child's inadequate behaviour. The typical behaviours of passivity and little eye contact can also serve to reduce the chance of attack by others, thereby increasing the child's sense of safety.

Problem/Mistaken behaviours

- withdrawn behaviour;
- fearful of new situations;

- poor friendship-making skills;
- attitudes of helplessness.

Competencies needed

- friendship-making skills;
- ability to trust others.

Intervention strategies

- one-to-one time with adult;
- review progress regularly;
- recognise and manage negative emotions.

3   Emotional goal: the need for control

The drive to master and control our world is a fundamental need. Many theorists have seen this as a core component for successful development. Piaget spoke of a child's needs to master their world and Adler saw the 'inferiority complex' as a key driving force. The need for control becomes a problem when it exists in a vacuum, and control is to be achieved at all costs.

Problem/Mistaken behaviours

- defiant;
- confrontational;
- argumentative;
- domineering.

Competencies needed

- impulse control;
- recognise feelings;
- empathic awareness.

Intervention strategies

- problem-solving skills;
- positions of responsibility;
- negotiation skills;
- stress management;
- impulse-control techniques.

4   Emotional goal: the need to be valued

Being social animals, we each have a strong need for approval from group members. It is through belonging to different groups that our social identity is shaped. To be approved of is to be valued and for children much of their early learning can be linked to the desire to be valued through pleasing others.

Problem/Mistaken behaviours

- passive;
- withdrawn;
- little involvement;
- 'I can't do it' attitude.

Competencies needed

- express personal opinions;
- value self, abilities and qualities.

Intervention strategies

- positive-thinking skills;
- set achievable targets;
- relaxation activities;
- exercise;
- record positive events/activities.

It is not difficult to see how close we are to making explicit an 'emotional and behavioural curriculum'. Just as we have a differentiated learning curriculum, we can no longer assume that all children enter school with similar emotional and behavioural competencies. We need to provide for children a differentiated emotional and behavioural curriculum. This will also serve to be a positive force in increasing the mental health of all children. The competencies to be developed, enhanced or achieved are those that link to the emotional needs of all pupils. As more and more teaching assistants become key staff members, they may well prove to be the staff who implement such a curriculum for many of our most challenging children. They already build relationships with them. They see them in different contexts; they see their 'brilliant corner' as well as their worst side. It makes sense then for some teaching assistants to specialise in emotional and behavioural issues and become part of a team that actively supports the inclusion of such pupils.

Group dynamics – an emotional perspective

Our analysis so far has focused very much on individuals and their emotions. However, most of the difficulties schools face in including students with emotional and behavioural difficulties stem from the challenges they present when in groups. These pupils are often very different on a one-to-one basis, where their emotional needs can be understood and managed more easily. It is how they function as a group member that gives rise to most concern. While there is much written about group dynamics, it is an applied area that needs to be further developed.

There is a natural tension when pupils function as group members. On the one hand, they have a strong desire to detach and act as individuals, while, on the other, there is the need for group identity, belonging and a sense of common purpose. Groups can therefore be seen to exist on two levels. First the group works towards the achievement of group needs and goals and, second, individuals work towards meeting their individual needs. The need to separate and attach contains both positive and negative aspects. The model shown in Figure 8.2 shows how such tensions can be seen at work within groups.

We can see much of the problem behaviour within groups as reflecting the negative end of each of the dimensions shown in Figure 8.2 (i.e. separation and attachment). This is no surprise given our previous consideration as to why many students with emotional difficulties act in ways which are challenging and inappropriate within the school context. What is happening then is that individuals' needs (which have usually been distorted through negative life experiences into negative emotional needs) lead to specific goals being sought to meet these needs. Within the group context these give rise to values that support competition rather than cooperation. These values in

| | | The need to | |
BELONG ←			→ SEPARATE
Basic individual need	Attributes	Positive behaviours	Mistaken behaviours
To belong	Relating Uniting Connecting Understanding	Making friends Joining in Sharing Trusting	Hostility Fear of rejection Suspicion Silence
Basic individual need	Attributes	Positive behaviours	Mistaken behaviours
To separate	Purposeful Independence Completing Self-control	Starting projects Leading Concentrating Problem solving	Competing Aggression Selfishness Apathy

Figure 8.2 Tensions in group identity.

turn give rise to rules that govern the roles open to individuals within the group (examples here would be the class clown, the bully, the attention seeker, the rebel). These roles lead to specific consequences which the student perceives as meeting their core emotional need to either belong or separate from the group. This cycle is represented in Figure 8.3.

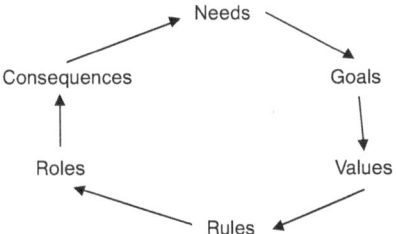

Figure 8.3 Cyclical influences on group behaviour.

We have now simplified the range of emotional needs our earlier analysis gave us into two fundamental ones which can make sense of an individual's behaviour in a group context. How can we use this information to encourage groups to work more cooperatively, be less disruptive and attention seeking?

There are many models we can apply to seek to influence group behaviour. As no model is all inclusive it is best if we take a 'best-fit' approach (see Figure 8.4). Usually with students who have emotional and behavioural difficulties it is the need to separate from the group that presents most difficulties for teachers. We can look then at existing models and techniques that can help us increase a sense of belonging to the group and working to achieve individual needs through appropriate group goals.

Only a brief account will be presented of each model, with indications as to how each can help schools manage and support pupils with emotional and behavioural difficulties. However, each of the models has significant value in helping us to engage at the group level with those whose emotional

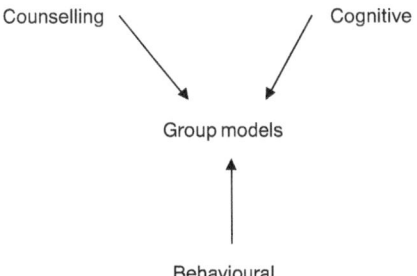

Figure 8.4 A best-fit approach to theoretical models of group behaviour.

difficulties within group settings have for a long time seemed intractable and beyond our control.

Counselling

The counselling approach is fundamental to supporting both individual and group needs as it focuses on core values and attitudes as well as communication skills. This model is probably the implicit model that is espoused by many school staff. They believe in respecting children, in valuing them for who they are, not what they could be. Communication is used to convey warmth and acceptance. Feedback is given in such a way that respects the dignity of the pupil and corrections are used as an opportunity for learning and growth to take place.

Behavioural

The behavioural approach helps to focus on the observable, the roles that students actually engage in. Using observation and collection of behaviour, this model enables us to see more clearly what triggers certain behaviours and the consequences that follow such behaviours. This ABC analysis (antecedents, behaviour and consequences) has much to recommend it as it can enable the teacher and support staff to modify a group's environment to help them change their behaviour. It is especially applicable to young children, as the best way to alter their behaviour is often for the adults to change the way in which they respond to them. This model need not be seen as antithetical to the counselling model but more as offering a range of techniques that can help us achieve our long-term goals. In essence, the behavioural approach provides the techniques to make the law of effect a key guiding principle. Namely, students are motivated to behave as they do because of the effects their behaviour have for them, and in the terms of this chapter, their behaviour meets key emotional needs.

Cognitive

This model, which is more appropriate for older students who are able to understand and reflect more on their behaviour, seeks to challenge their internal perceptions of their behaviour. Through discussion at either a group or individual level the motives for disruptive behaviour is explained to students. The core aim is to show them the consequences of inappropriate behaviour and help them develop alternative ways of getting their needs met. It tries to clarify any hidden agendas and teach pupils new ways of functioning as a group, in an open and democratic manner.

Conclusion: pragmatism versus theory

To include pupils with emotional and behavioural difficulties continues to be a real challenge for most schools. Often the perceived need is for more and more techniques – a pragmatic approach. While this is understandable without models to make sense of the challenging behaviour, techniques alone will not work. We have for many years now been familiar with a 'functional assessment of behaviour'. The theoretical model for this came from behaviourism and it continues to provide a framework from which testable hypotheses can be generated. What has been lacking is a model that incorporates an understanding of the emotional side of children's lives. The model presented above is not totally dissimilar to the behavioural one. What is being proposed is a way of interpreting behaviour as an attempt by the child to meet certain emotional needs. In so doing, their behaviour is a way of communicating such needs. Because of the complex difficulties experienced by many of our pupils, we need to be more and more prepared to take an emotional perspective when it comes to making sense of challenging behaviour.

References

Ainsworth, M. D. S. (1967) *Infancy in Uganda*, Baltimore: Johns Hopkins Press.
Maslow, A. H. (1970) *Motivation and Personality*, 2nd edn, New York: Harper Row.

9 Dealing with anger and aggression

Adrian Faupel

Introduction

There are currently a number of competing tensions around the issue of school exclusions. For some people, the numbers of exclusions are far too high. For example, the Government has set LEAs (local education authorities) and schools the target of reducing the level of permanent and fixed-term exclusions by one-third by 2002. For others (e.g. some teaching unions), they are not high enough and more children should be educated other than in mainstream settings. Hard facts in contentious issues are notoriously difficult to come by, but it is clear that permanent exclusions rose extremely rapidly in the 1990s. It is also increasingly apparent that pupils, who are permanently excluded from school, experience both short-term and longer term negative effects and that the consequences of their exclusion have a wider impact on society at large.

Those who argue that *more* pupils should be excluded do so on the grounds that the physical and emotional safety of other pupils and their educational attainments are put at risk, and, as regards the teaching unions, that teachers are prevented from teaching as they would wish and their levels of stress increased. Individual badly behaved pupils in the last resort have to be 'sacrificed' for the good of the community.

This ethical and moral dilemma which pits the rights and welfare of individual pupils against the 'common good' of the vast majority of pupils would vanish if there were no 'bad' behaviour in schools in the first place. The real 'needs' of *both* parties to the conflict or dilemma outlined above would have been met. The argument of this chapter is that most behaviour in schools of the sort that threatens the physical and emotional safety of pupils, which disrupts the learning of others and increases stress in teachers, stems directly or indirectly from feelings of anger. *If* we could reduce the levels of anger experienced by both pupils *and* staff, there would be less problem behaviour and less need for exclusion from mainstream schools. The 'management' of anger can be construed, therefore, as perhaps one of the most important items on the school agenda at the beginning of the twenty-first century.

What evidence is there for the assertion that many exclusions happen because of high levels of anger – and for the even wider claim that most difficult behaviour in schools is 'emotional' in origin?

Anecdotally at least, when teachers are asked to identify the immediate trigger for the last permanent exclusion with which they have been involved, the vast majority acknowledge the presence of anger. Less anecdotally, reasons officially provided by schools for permanent exclusion in one large LEA (Imich 1994, cited in Cabinet Office 1998), indicate that physical aggression is the most common reason given, with verbal abuse to staff and other pupils also being highly significant. Together, these categories accounted for some 60% of all permanent exclusions and there is clearly an intimate connection between physical and verbal aggression and anger. The second most common ground for permanent exclusion is the catch-all 'generally disruptive/unacceptable behaviour'. There is also a small, though perhaps increasing minority for drug offences, with further very small numbers for vandalism, arson and theft. These latter categories are also highly likely to contain elements of anger.

However, the understanding of difficult behaviour which is being proposed here actually makes the wider claim that the vast majority of all difficult behaviour is emotional in origin. Not only has there been a serious neglect of the emotional and affective aspect of child development within education, but it is only relatively recently that emotions have returned to the forefront within academic psychology.

> Psychology has had a hard time with emotion. Although popular opinion considers psychologists to be experts on affect, many of them have studiously overlooked and even openly denied the existence or the importance of this phenomenon ... It may be the multifaceted nature of emotion is responsible for our difficulties in explaining and conceptualising it.
>
> (Scherer 1987)

The roots of anger and aggression

Emotions are undeniably an important aspect of our consciousness. It has become increasingly clear that they have important evolutionary functions, with a very significant involvement of the limbic structures, which form part of the 'primitive' brain. (Goleman 1995). The activation of these structures in the presence of some external triggers, which are usually related to physical threat or to reproduction, has obvious survival mechanisms. It is not without significance that the 'drive' or 'pull' to action (what we loosely label as *mot*ivation) has exactly the same root as the subjective feeling of being driven or pulled to action (which we loosely label as e*mot*ion). The relationship between the primitive, instinctive responses focusing on immediate action and the more measured, rational, longer term view are encapsulated by relationships between limbic structures and the higher cortical functions in the brain.

As a social animal (and some would argue, a spiritual one as well), relationships are inevitably a 'core' aspect of our functioning – and relationships are essentially emotional. In fact, some would argue that it is not possible to separate social development from emotional development.

> Our relationships influence our emotions and our emotions reciprocally influence our relationships.
>
> (Saarni 1999)

There are a number of psychologists who have, over the last 50 years, highlighted the need for social relationships as perhaps *the* fundamental need of human beings. Maslow (1970), for example, identified a hierarchy of needs, including the need to belong. Adler construed the fundamental need as the need for power. This was interpreted by Dreikurs (1972) and Balson (1982) as the need to belong. More recently, a variety of constructs such as self-efficacy (Bandura 1997), self-worth, self-esteem (Harter 1990) have come into vogue (for an excellent overview of this area of psychological research, see Dweck 2000).

In the presence of a perceived physical threat (e.g. somebody coming at us with an axe), it is likely that we would physiologically and automatically respond with more rapid breathing, increased heart rate, 'butterflies' in the stomach, dilated pupils and increased sweating. At the same time, we would experience a subjective emotional state (possibly fear, possibly anger), which would result – in this case involving violent physical action – either in our running away as fast as possible or fighting as hard as we could.

Any emotional episode is likely therefore to have four components, as follows (in reality, these are not separate, but reciprocally interact with each other):

- a *thinking* aspect (particularly the 'appraisal' of the emotion);
- a *feeling* component (fear, anxiety, anger, panic, rage);
- a *physiological* dimension (increased heart and breathing rates);
- *behavioural* activity (running away, fighting).

There will also in most cases be a *social* dimension (the impact our behaviour has on other people).

However, we have seen above that our basic human needs are not simply physical. Anything which is perceived as seriously threatening our *psychological* survival will provoke the same kind of response as a physical threat. The 'psychological' threats are those perceived situations in which our sense of belonging, our self-worth, our self-efficacy, even our 'lovableness', are being challenged and called into question. The emotional, physiological and behavioural responses follow 'automatically' from such a *perceived* attack on our sense of belonging and value. It is not necessary that there is objective evidence for such an attack – it is the *perception* of such alone that is significant for an emotional episode. A teacher asking a child to read aloud may have no intention at all of belittling, devaluing a pupil, but if the pupil sees this request to read as exposing them as incompetent, the emotional, physiological and behavioural response to threat is likely to be triggered. The way the situation is perceived or appraised becomes crucial to the level and type of emotional response that is likely to follow (Lazarus 1991).

In order to develop the usefulness and application of this model of understanding difficult behaviour, a distinction between positive and negative emotions is necessary. As a general principle, positive emotions are those we like to experience: we feel good about ourselves and we enjoy the feeling. Positive emotions relate to those situations where our sense of belonging, self-worth, self-competence, self-esteem, are enhanced. Interestingly, we have affection (and affect is a synonym for emotion) for those people or activities that enhance our sense of self-worth. The people in our lives for whom we have affection are those who, in one way or another, confirm our sense of worth, our lovableness, those people who protect us, nourish us, value us. Typically, they are family and friends. We have affection for and enjoy (take joy in) activities that confirm our sense of self-efficacy and self-competence. We don't enjoy (except as time fillers) activities we have mastered and which have become so easy that they are now boring (or those activities which are so far beyond our capabilities as to be totally frustrating). We have affection for and like those activities that challenge us.

Disaffected pupils are those without affection for schools – either for their teachers, because they do not feel valued by them, or for the 'system' which adversely compares them with others, or for the tasks which they find either boring, irrelevant or frustrating and certainly not challenging. Disaffected pupils are those who perceive themselves as being put at risk by psychological threats to their sense of worth, value and lovableness – and their reaction is likely to be highly emotional.

Jumping ahead a bit perhaps from later aspects of the model, one strategy to cope with 'negative' feeling is to attack and destroy the perceived 'aggressor'. American high schools are reported to typically value academically successful pupils ('jerks') and/or good athletes ('jocks'). It is not without significance that the motivation for the targeted students in the shootings at Columbine High School, Denver, Colorado, in April 1999 was that they were considered as 'jerks, jocks and blacks'[1]. This most aggressive incident in the history of schooling, in which twelve students and one staff member were shot dead by two pupils, not to mention the twenty-six

---

1 History shows that ethnic minority groups can be devalued as scapegoats to enhance other people's self-worth: there were less than 3% ethnic minority pupils at Columbine.

wounded with gunshot wounds, seems to have been motivated by feelings of anger at being devalued by the school system.

Disaffected pupils have negative rather than positive feelings towards schooling. 'Negative' emotions are those emotions which we do not like, we do not enjoy. By describing such emotions as negative there is no intention to imply that they are always 'bad' or 'wrong' and to be avoided. This view would be clearly mistaken; while we may not like many such emotions (e.g. fear, sadness, frustration), they have clear survival value and impel us to take necessary action to avoid danger or cope with loss.

When confronted with physical danger or threat there are three primitive biological responses – fight, flight, and when either of these is impossible, playing dead. The psychological correlates for these are the emotions of anxiety, anger or depression. We experience these three classic negative emotions as extremely aversive. We have seen that 'psychological' threats, dangers or attacks are things that threaten our sense of belonging, self-worth and self-competence. In the presence of somebody doing something which is perceived as 'attacking' us in this way, the same biological responses to physical attack, with their physiological and emotional dimensions 'automatically' come into play. The particular biological option we spontaneously experience – fighting (anger), running away (anxiety) or playing dead (depression) – is dependent on a host of interacting factors, such as the nature of the threat, who is making it, the 'models' of reacting to such threats presented to us in our childhood (particularly by parents), our perceived resources and what is culturally acceptable. Each of the three emotions experienced in the face of such attacks on our self-worth are extremely aversive and we make strenuous efforts to get rid of them.

At this point it is relevant to distinguish between adaptive and maladaptive strategies that can be adopted to remove the aversive feelings of anger, anxiety and depression. Adaptive strategies are those in which our actions are, in the longer term, more likely to lead us to feel as though we belong, have an enhanced sense of self-worth. They are constructive, protect our own self-competence without destroying the rights of others; in short, they are assertive responses rather than aggressive or submissive responses to attack. On the other hand, maladaptive strategies are those which achieve immediate and short-term 'relief' from these aversive feelings but which do nothing to help us to feel as though we belong and which, in effect, often serve only to make matters worse. Such short-term solutions are extremely seductive; the principle of negative reinforcement, whereby a response that immediately removes an aversive stimulus becomes more and more probable, ensures that there is a strong likelihood of getting 'hooked' on these short-term maladaptive strategies. Adults and adolescents have a variety of short-term solutions which are used to get rid of these feelings: alcohol, nicotine, caffeine, prescribed drugs, illegal hard and soft drugs, sex. For younger children, who are learning to self-regulate their behaviour in the presence of emotions, they remain at the impulsive, spontaneous stage where behaviour expression is dictated by the emotion they are experiencing.

The implications of this model for difficult behaviour are profound and far reaching. Most difficult behaviours in schools are ultimately concerned with interpersonal relationships and they are mediated by the emotions being experienced. These emotions are a response to perceived attacks on self-worth, sense of value and belonging. In this chapter, we are concerned with the response to threat which involves 'fight' (aggression) with the accompanying emotion of anger. Following from the model outlined above, there appear to be a number of different approaches to reducing bad behaviour. One is by working preventatively to change the environment so that pupils are less likely to experience attacks on their self-esteem and self-worth (see also Chapter 2 by Gerv Leyden in this book). Another, when pupils perceive their self worth under threat from the school system, staff or peers, is to teach pupils more appropriate and adaptive strategies to handle their feelings of anger more effectively.

Preventive approaches

There are a variety of well-rehearsed reasons for avoiding the temptation to focus time and effort on individual pupils exhibiting extremes of difficult behaviour. If it is desirable to control fast-breeding alligators, the most effective way of doing so is to drain the swamp rather than shooting (and occasionally missing!) each one. The general principle that, the more children and young people value themselves, the less likelihood they will feel the need to violate the rights of others, should be the litmus test of everything that schools do with pupils. Anything which potentially gives the message that some pupils are more valued than others is likely to increase feelings of anger and aggression. It is worthwhile remembering that it is relative poverty rather than absolute poverty that is psychologically significant (Rutter 1991: Rutter *et al*. 1998), and that same principle applies to the messages of value and dignity that we give to pupils. Selection, streaming, banding, a culture of competition pervading the whole school system with winners and losers, all have profound implications for the likelihood that some pupils will feel devalued. However, these major systemic issues are beyond the powers of individual teachers to influence directly, so they cannot be the prime concern here.

Much more relevant are the more immediate aspects of the environment which teachers can control. Although major aggressive outbursts towards staff or peers appear sometimes to come 'out of the blue', in reality there is usually a chain of events leading up to and accounting for the precise nature of the aggression used. The 'aggression–incident model' (Davies and Frude 1993), provides a useful method of seeing aggression in this way, indicating where preventative measures can be more effectively used to break the chain.

For feelings of anger to occur, there must be a situation in which the person perceives some element of attack. This is the trigger. But the situation itself does not cause the feeling of anger.[2] The situation has to be interpreted or appraised as 'attacking'. There are two elements to this: a situation that is likely to be perceived by most people as an attack on self-worth and a personality that is hypersensitive to interpreting quite 'normal' occurrences as an attack on self-worth. Aggressive boys, for example, frequently interpret accidental or ambivalent actions by others as hostile and react aggressively (Dodge and Frame 1982). Here, however, we are more concerned with the types of situations which are likely to produce perceptions of attack rather than individual sensitivities of particular pupils. Analysing the elements of situations that frequently lead to anger, Davies and Frude (1993) distinguish between *irritants*, *costs* and *transgressions*.

The irritants which teachers often experience are the low-level disruptive activities that Wheldall, Merrett and others describe as 'TOOT' (Talking Out Of Turn) and 'HOC' (Hindering Other Children) behaviours (Wheldall *et al.* 1986). Individual teachers may well have their own pet 'irritating' pupil behaviours (e.g. pencil tapping, leaning back in the chair). From the pupil's point of view, teachers may provide them with a number of 'irritants' – and some of these are related to poor classroom organisation and management, such as 'dangles', overelaboration of instructions, material being unavailable (see Robertson 1996 for a review). Some environments are potentially more 'irritating' than others – particularly where there are crowds and crushes, which have been shown to lead to higher incidence of peer-to-peer aggression.

The second element of triggers for anger identified by Davies and Frude are where the situation involves some personal loss – loss of money or equipment, loss of face, loss of status. Much peer-to-peer anger and aggression revolves around these issues – the pupil angrily tearing up his or her own work may be to do with potential loss of status among peers, for example. Some teachers too are particularly prone to becoming angry when their own competence is under attack and they are laughed at for things they do not find funny.

Finally, there is frequently an element of *transgression* in anger-provoking situations. Here another person is considered to be breaking a rule or doing something that is out of order. There is usually some perceived violation of the moral order such as not betraying your friends, stealing, vandalism or spreading untrue rumour.

It is a useful exercise for teachers to try to identify, from the point of view of their pupils, what are the triggers for angry outbursts that have one, two or even all three of these different elements.

---

2 A contribution of cognitive–behavioural approaches has been to highlight the essential part that perception or appraisal plays in this process.

Angry outbursts from pupils towards staff depend partly on the extent that staff convey value and respect to pupils. This is not to deny, of course, that some pupils have such fragile sense of their own worth and self-esteem as to interpret well-intentioned actions and remarks as a further attack and react with anger and aggressiveness. However, there are some attitudes which are not helpful. Even then, in the face of such teachers, the vast majority of pupils do not react aggressively. But the 'hypersensitive' may well do so. The contribution of the staff member to the angry outburst is often not acknowledged and the angry outburst is construed as a within-child problem. The listing of these unhelpful attitudes is not to contribute to a blame culture, but is an important contribution to seeing an angry aggressive outburst as a pupil response to a perceived attack. Some members of staff may convey attitudes that do not help vulnerable pupils with fragile self-worth. Such attitudes tend to be 'authoritarian' – teachers are still powerful people, able to use their power quite capriciously, using power games such as 'Because I say so, that's why', 'Because of the actions of one we all have to suffer' or 'Thank you, Jason, for yet another magnificently brilliant, insightful and completely wrong answer' (Kreidler 1990). A lack of flexibility, assuming that 'I always know best' and 'I must have the last word' and, perhaps most of all, the need to win every battle, are teacher attitudes that provide fertile ground for confrontation.

At the other end of the scale are those teachers who do convey value and respect, even with the most difficult and confrontational of pupils. At heart, they convey respect and value by listening – listening is the fundamental first step in communication and communication is the only mechanism by which community can be established. Community is about belonging, becoming one (*unity*) with (*com*). Without listening, there can be no respect, no valuing. Such listening embraces a fundamentally non-judgemental attitude, an ability to distinguish between the behaviour (which may be completely unacceptable) and the person (who is uniquely valuable). It recognises that given their *current* understanding and skills, their behaviour makes sense and are attempts to meet legitimate needs. That need may be for attention, for choice, for stimulation, for resources – all of which are legitimate and, therefore, praiseworthy. The *strategies* employed to meet such needs will, however, be inappropriate to the extent that they violate the rights of other people and are not in the real long-term interests of the person him/herself. The teacher's role is to teach alternative strategies and replacement behaviours that effectively achieve the same end. This 'functional assessment of behaviour' as it is called (Wise 2000), involves the ability to decipher the meaning or motivation of difficult behaviour. Such behaviour is construed as trying to meet, inappropriately, legitimate ends. It is a crucial skill in effective behaviour management, at the heart of an assessment process which is not about labelling pupils, but designed to lead to interventions based on sound psychological principles. The ability to reframe intentions as being good and not deliberately harming seems to be the key to conveying a sense of value (Tyler 1998; Tyler and Jones 1998, 2000).

Dealing with angry pupils

Where emotions are concerned, pupils are not compartmentalised into home and school – emotions spill over from one to the other. So, however successful a school is in building up an ethos in which pupils are sincerely valued, both in rhetoric and reality, and however skilled individual members of staff are in being empathetic and understanding the needs of pupils, there will inevitably be some youngsters who for a variety of reasons will respond 'unreasonably' to perceived threats and there will be peers who provoke and devalue each other. This section begins by briefly considering the process of defusing confrontation, then outlines some approaches to working with individual pupils and finally considers some aspects of physical restraint.

1   Defusing confrontation

We have seen that a perceived attack on self-worth is likely to result in feelings of anger, with accompanying physiological arousal. The arousal cycle outlined by Breakwell (1997) has proved extremely useful in working with teachers and schools. The fundamental premise is that there is an inverse relationship between physiological arousal and degrees of rationality. The latter is defined as being able to take the longer term view and foresee and evaluate the pros and cons of acting in a certain way. As levels of physiological arousal increase, the immediate here and now becomes more and more dominating, so that at the point of crisis, the person is so physiologically driven as to be unable to consider future implications of what they are doing.

The arousal cycle assumes that we all have a baseline or resting level of arousal. This level will vary from individual to individual, but generally speaking normal behaviour is non-aggressive. When the person begins to appraise the situation as threatening their self-worth, or as unjust or unfair, this 'triggers' the fight response and physiological arousal begins to rise. At this early stage, pupils are not exclusively focused upon the issue. They are open to all sorts of tactics which nip the problem in the bud, they can be diverted, compromise may be reached and pupils are generally rational. However, if 'provocation' continues, or efforts to remove the perceived threat are unsuccessful, the level of arousal escalates, perhaps culminating in an outburst of rage or violence. It can be at this point that self-control is lost and control has to be provided by someone else. This is the essential rationale for physical restraint (see p. 123). The very high level of physiological arousal at the time of the outburst takes some considerable time (up to 90 minutes for an adult) to return to normal after a long plateau period. It is important therefore that school systems are in place which give pupils space and time after a violent outburst to enable them to return to levels of arousal that allow rationality to begin to operate. Intervening too soon to spell out consequences or to examine the cause of the outburst will be likely to provoke yet another outburst.

An outline of the strategies usefully employed at the various stages in the assault cycle is to be found in Paterson and Leadbetter (1999), and in the excellent material in *Preventing Face to Face Violence* (Davies and Frude, 1993). These include verbal and non-verbal calming and problem-solving strategies. The overall message is one of intervening as early as possible in ways that do not add to the sense of attack, injustice, unfairness, to recognise the increasing irrationality at the time of outburst and to give plenty of time and space before tackling the issue and consequences of the outburst. The neglect of some of these principles in schools has led to inevitable escalation, with successively higher levels of the school's management structure becoming involved and an increasing risk of physical confrontation and permanent exclusion.

2   *Working with vulnerable pupils*

The school curriculum is not just about academic learning. Just as pupils have academic learning difficulties, so they have learning difficulties in other aspects of the curriculum. The same principles of inclusion and differentiation apply to emotional and interpersonal learning difficulties as to academic learning, with the same tensions and dilemmas about how to match the demands of a common curriculum to the needs of the individual pupil, how to ensure inclusion, how to meet specific needs without labelling or giving negative messages about competence and worth. We have seen how important these messages are to increasing or decreasing levels of anger.

The emotional and social curriculum is formally delivered in the Personal, Social, Health and Emotional Curriculum. What is emerging clearly from work in the USA is that this 'emotional and interpersonal' curriculum needs to be taught explicitly to all pupils and a variety of curricular materials have been developed to deliver this. The PATHS (Promoting Alternative Thinking Strategies) curriculum (Greenberg and Kusche 1998) has been extensively evaluated and has formed an important component in a major large-scale initiative to prevent behaviour problems (Bierman *et al.* 1992; see also Webster-Stratton 1999). In the UK, the work of Deborah Waters is breaking new ground in developing attainment targets and programmes of study for a behaviour curriculum (Waters 1997; see also Moss *et al.* 1997).

The dramatic increase in levels and intensity of violence in the USA has resulted in a major focus on the need to develop conflict-resolution skills, which clearly have implications for preventing and helping to control feelings of anger. The development in the UK of peer mediation and peer counselling are examples of school-wide and systems-based initiatives all designed to help students manage conflict and to develop important interpersonal skills. An area not yet widely recognised in this country is the importance of moral education in relation to anger management (Goldstein *et al.* 1998).

For those pupils whose emotional learning difficulties are causing major concern, more targeted interventions may be necessary. These may take place in small-group contexts. Southampton provides one example of an authority-wide initiative which is currently being evaluated (Sharp and Herrick 2000). At the level of individual counselling, the 'Firework' model (Feindler and Ecton 1986; Faupel *et al.* 1998) combines environmental, cognitive and physiological (relaxation) approaches. While not undervaluing the contribution of psychodynamic interventions and their applications (e.g. art therapy) to very angry pupils, the cognitive–behavioural approaches are rather more easily assimilated into school settings and more easily taught to teachers and counsellors (Wilde 1992; Ellis and Bernard 1983; Bernard and Cartwright 1995).

Teachers in the present climate often question whether small group and individual work with pupils exhibiting intense anger and aggressive behaviour is really part of their role. It clearly is. Education is concerned with the development and growth of the whole child. It is the misplaced exclusive emphasis on narrow academic standards that needs to change. There needs to be a serious attempt to reconcile the contradictory messages being given between academic standards and social inclusion; a contradiction which lies at the heart of government policy at the present time (see Chapter 13 by Peter Gray in this book).

3   Physical restraint

When pupils 'explode' with anger, at the crisis phase of the assault cycle, their capability of reasoning disappears. We use the expression 'blind with rage' to signify that they have become as if physically unable to see beyond the immediate here and now. They have lost control. It is at this point that responsibility for control may pass to another person(s) and, in order to prevent significant harm, it may be necessary to use physical force intentionally to restrict the pupil's movement against his or her will (Hampshire LEA 1999). The DfEE guidance on physical force to control and restrain pupils was published as Circular 10/98 and attempted to clarify the powers of teachers and other staff in this area (DfEE 1998). 'Each head teacher should draw up a policy setting out guidelines about the use of force to control or restrain pupils' (DfEE 1998: 3, §6). Clearly such policies need to be understood and assimilated by all adults working in schools.

The DfEE guidance indicates that physical restraint should only be used to prevent pupils injuring themselves or others, damaging property or when a pupil is 'engaging in any behaviour prejudicial to maintaining good order and discipline' (DfEE 1998: 4, §9). The aim of intervening with force in the last of these is always to obtain good order, and restraint must always facilitate this outcome. Where restraint would not actually achieve this, or would exacerbate the problem, it could clearly not be justified on the grounds of being necessary to establish good order and discipline.

Physical force can never be used as a punishment, and can be justified only as far as, and, as long as, the pupil has not regained control of his or her own behaviour. LEAs need to provide guidance as to which methods of restraint are recommended for use in schools in those quite exceptional cases in which it is found to be necessary.

Conclusions

There is a major overlap between pupils experiencing high levels of anger and those exhibiting difficult behaviour both at school and in the wider community. The long-term prognosis for some such pupils is extremely poor (Rutter 1991; Rutter *et al.* 1998). The pressures on schools to raise narrowly conceived academic standards can divert schools away from their real task of creating learning communities. Learning is not, and never has been, just about academic learning but, increasingly, aspects of development which do not fit into a narrowly academic curriculum are seen as marginal, peripheral and not the real task of schooling. However, a core task of education should be to help pupils to learn how to live with others, preserving their own sense of self-worth and feelings of competence and, at the same time, maintaining the self-esteem and competence of others. The ability to manage conflict and cope with feelings of anger is an essential part of that core task. The usefulness of all other aspects of schooling, including academic attainment, pales into insignificance if pupils are not taught the values and attitudes and competencies of creating and maintaining a sense of community.

References

Balson, M. (1982) *Understanding Classroom Behaviour*, Hawthorne, Victoria. Australia: The Australian Council for Educational Research.

Bandura, A. (1997) *Self-Efficacy in Changing Societies*, Cambridge: Cambridge University Press.

Bernard, M. E. and Cartwright, R. (1995) *Programme Achieve*, Brighton: Anglo-Scholarship Group.

Bierman, K. L., Coie, J. D., Dodge, K. A., Greenberg, M. T., Lochman, J. E., and McMahon, R. J. (1992) 'A developmental and clinical model for prevention of conduct disorder: The FAST Track Program', *Devel. Psychpathol* 4: 509–27.

Breakwell, G. M. (1997) *Coping with Aggressive Behaviour*, Leicester: British Psychological Society.

Cabinet Office, S.E.U. (1998) *Truancy and School Exclusion Report by the Social Exclusion Unit*, London: The Stationery Office.

Davies, W. and Frude, N. (1993) *Preventing Face to Face Violence: Dealing with Anger and Aggression*. Leicester: Association for Psychological Therapies.

DfEE (1998) Circular 10/98: *The Use of Force to Control or Restrain Pupils*, London: Department for Education and Employment.

Dodge, K. A., and Frame, C. L. (1982) 'Social cognitive biases and deficits in aggressive boys', *Child Development* 51: 162–70.

Dreikurs, R. and Cassel, P. (1972) *Discipline without Tears: What to Do with Children Who Misbehave*, New York: Hawthorn Books.

Dweck, C. (2000) *Self-Theories. Their Role in Motivation, Personality and Development*, Philadelphia, PA: Psychology Press.

Ellis, A. and Bernard, M. E. (eds) (1983) *Rational-Emotive Approaches to the Problems of Childhood*, New York: Plenum Press.

Faupel, A., Herrick, E. and Sharp, P. (1998) *Anger Mangement. A Practical Guide*, London: David Fulton.

Feindler, E. L. and Ecton, R. B. (1986) *Adolescent Anger Control. Cognitive Behavioural Techniques*, New York: Pergamon Press.

Goldstein, A. P., Gibbs, J. C. and Glick, B. (1998) *Agression Replacement Training: A Comprehensive Intervention for Aggressive Youth*, Champaign, IL: Research Press.

Goleman, D. (1995) *Emotional Intelligence*, New York: Bantam Books.

Greenberg, M. T. and Kusche, C. A. (1998) *Promoting Alternative Thinking Strategies. Colorado*, Boulder, Colorado Institute of Behavioral Sciences, University of Colorado.

Hampshire LEA (1999) *Guidelines for the Use of Physical Restraint in Schools Maintained by Hampshire County Council*, Winchester, Hants: Hampshire County Council Education.

Harter, S. (1990) 'Causes, correlates and functional role of global self-worth: A life-span perspective', in R. Sternberg and J. Kolligian (eds) *Competence Considered*, New Haven, CO: Yale University Press.

Kreidler, W. J. (1990) *Creative Conflict Resolution: More than 200 Activities for Keeping Peace in the Classroom*, Millwood, NY: Kraus International Publications.

Lazarus, R. S. (1991) *Emotion and adaptation*, New York: Oxford University Press.

Maslow, A. (1970) *Motivation and Personality*, 2nd edn, New York: Harper and Row.

Moss, G., Came, F. and Webster, A. (1997) *Behaviour Education: Teaching Positive Behaviour in the Primary School*, Bristol: Avec Designs Ltd.

Paterson, B. and Leadbetter, D. (1999) 'De-escalation in the management of aggression and violence: Towards evidence-based practice', in J. Turnbull and B. Paterson (eds) *Aggression and Violence*, Basingstoke, Hants: MacMillan.

Robertson, J. (1996) *Effective Classroom Control*, 3rd edn, London: Hodder and Stoughton.

Rutter, M. (1991) 'Services for children with emotional disorders: Needs, accomplishments and future developments', *Young Minds Newsletter* 9: 1–5.

Rutter, M., Giller, H. and Hagell, A. (1998) *Antisocial Behavior by Young People*, Cambridge: Cambridge University Press.

Saarni, C. (1999) *The Development of Emotional Competence*, New York: Guilford Press.

Scherer, K. R. (1987) *The Component Process Model of Affective States: Toward A Dynamic Theory of Emotion*.

Sharp, P. and Herrick, E. (2000) 'Promoting emotional literacy: Anger management groups', in N. Barwick (ed.) *Clinical Counselling in Schools*, London: Routledge.

Tyler, K. and Jones, B. D. (1998) 'Using the ecosystemic approach to change chronic behaviour in primary schools', *Pastoral Care in Education* **16**(4): 11–20.

Tyler, K. (1998) 'A comparison of the no blame approach to bullying and the ecosystemic approach to changing problem behaviour in schools', *Pastoral Care in Education* **March**, 26–32.

Tyler, K. and Jones, B. D. (2000) 'Implementing the ecosystemic approach', *Educational Psychology* **20**(1): 85–98.

Waters, D. (1997) *The Behaviour Curriculum*, Carlisle: Cumbria County Psychological Service.

Webster-Stratton, C. (1999) *How To Promote Children's Social and Emotional Competence*, London: Paul Chapman Publishing.

Wheldall, K., Merrett, F. and Glynn, T. (eds) (1986) *Behaviour Analysis in Educational Psychology*, London: Croom Helm.

Wilde, J. (1992) *Rational Counseling with School-Aged Populations: A Practical Guide*, Muncie, IN: Accelerated Development Inc.

Wise, S. (2000) 'Colorado's response to the behaviour challenge', *Emotional and Behavioural Difficulties* **5**(1): 19–29.

Part IV
Supportive systems

10 Developing teacher-support groups to deal with challenging child behaviour

The Staff Sharing Scheme

Jey Monsen and Beverley Graham

> Despite a climate of competition and market forces, many staff ... are committed to working together and supporting each other.
>
> (Lacey 1996: 67)

Introduction

This chapter is primarily written for teachers, though parts of it will be of relevance to other agencies working with schools (i.e. educational psychologists, education welfare officers and social workers). It does not purport to be a 'how-to' manual in setting up and running staff-support groups, as such material is available in other publications (Gersch and Rawkins 1987; Gill and Monsen 1996; Hanko 1987, 1995). Instead, it aims to raise teachers' and others' awareness that INSET (in-service education and training) alone is an inadequate means of helping staff manage the increasingly complex and ill-defined problems they are expected to work with. The chapter stresses that some of the ways in which teachers make sense of these complex problems need to be challenged (e.g. the reliance upon 'within-child' causes). It suggests that teaching can be an isolating activity and that teachers therefore need structure and support to help each other in such an environment. Finally, the *Staff Sharing Scheme* is offered as one example of a staff-support group, which uses training as a precursor to setting up a structured school-based problem-solving group.

Difficult behaviour in schools

At an anecdotal level, many teachers and school-based staff perceive that the behaviour of children and young people has become more challenging. Statistics on the frequency, level and trend of behaviour problems in schools since the Second World War are difficult to interpret. All that can be commented on are indirect indicators, such as exclusion rates and teacher report. Research by Parsons (2000) on trends in exclusions indicates that during the 1990s the numbers of pupils permanently excluded from school grew five times.

Table 10.1 Percentage of primary teachers reporting that they had to deal with difficult types of pupil behaviour during the course of their classroom teaching the previous week (N = 1,050; adapted from Elton Report 1989).

Type of pupil behaviour	At least once during week (%)	At least daily (%)
Talking out of turn (calling out, distracting others)	97	69
Hindering other pupils (distracting them, interfering with equipment)	90	42
Making unnecessary noise	85	42
Physical aggression towards other pupils (by pushing, punching, striking)	74	17
Getting out of seat without permission	73	34
Work-avoidance strategies	67	21
General rowdiness, horseplay or mucking about	60	14
Verbal abuse towards other pupils	55	10
Not being punctual (being late to school or lessons)	53	11
Persistently infringing class (or school) rules	50	13
Cheeky or impertinent remarks or responses	41	6
Physical destructiveness (breaking objects, furniture)	16	1
Verbal abuse towards you	7	1
Physical aggression towards you	2.1	0

With regard to reports from teachers, research collected as part of the Elton enquiry into school discipline (DES 1989) showed primary-school teachers describing high daily levels of disruptive pupil behaviour (see Table 10.1). One feature of these findings was that the majority of the disruptive behaviour reported is best managed through whole class/school programmes (Herbert 1987). On a more positive note the findings suggested that the level of extreme aggression and disruption was low. Nonetheless, such findings support the perception that school staff are being presented with more complex and difficult problems to manage.

Over the years successive governments have pursued policies that have seen schools take on a much greater role in terms of accountability and responsibility for pupil achievement and behaviour. This delegation is often set against periods when there has been no significant increase in funding for education. As a result, government policies have encouraged schools to re-examine their use and management of existing resources, to develop new skills and reduce the need to involve outside agencies. Often schools interpret such directives within the 'one-off-gee-whiz' training framework (i.e. in-service training). Staff may well have had a 'good time' but generalisation of new skills and attitudes back to the classroom is highly unlikely to occur unless this has been systematically planned for (Day 1997; Guzzo and Dickson 1996; Eraut 1996).

Over the years, successive governments have had heated debates around how best to meet the needs of children and young people who are presenting schools with challenging behaviour. Although the terminology has changed, emotional and behavioural difficulties, as a particular category of special educational need, have remained prominent in both debates and policy. The various solutions and responses to dealing with such issues have also been a constant source of friction within educational circles.

Teachers thinking about complex and ill-defined problems

Teachers are cut off, then, from the possibility of reflecting and building on their own know-how and from the confusions that could serve them as springboards to new ways of seeing things.

(Schön 1992: 119; cited in Day 1997)

Traditionally, emotional and behavioural difficulties have tended to be interpreted largely as the product of either 'within-child' (e.g. limited ability, mental illness, delinquency, wilfulness) or 'home-based' factors (e.g. poor parenting, lack of parental control, poverty) with little attention being paid to the role that school staff and the school environment (including the curriculum) may play in maintaining such problems. In simple terms, such children and young people with such difficulties have been perceived as being either 'mad or bad' with interventions, strategies and plans reflecting one or other of these assumptions about the causes underlying the behaviour.

Contemporary debates can be seen as a mixture of the 'mad or bad' hypothesis and increasing attempts at more sophisticated interactional views of the causes of a young person's difficulties. It is now becoming more common for educationalists to refer to the complex interaction of both internal and external factors in helping to explain challenging behaviour and inform intervention planning. The ways teachers go about thinking through problem situations and the attributions they use to understand challenging behaviour are therefore important cornerstones in any school-based programme which aims to improve teachers' skill in managing such difficulties (Adelman and Taylor 2000; Miller 1996; Monsen *et al.* 1998).

Wagner (1987) was able to identify some of the 'knots' that occur in teachers' thinking around complex and ill-defined problems. Their problem solving was often characterised by circular thinking and an inability to move the problem situation forward. Other tendencies included a tendency to jump from one issue to another without being able to make any meaningful connections or links.

In addition, Wagner (1987) observed that often teachers' thought processes were embedded with much irrationality and emotion. Teachers got:

angry about students, were overawed by colleagues and sometimes identified with one of the students or had a strong desire to reach certain goals and were disappointed when they were not achieved.

(Wagner 1987: 161)

Such emotional reactions can be seen to result from teachers' vain attempts to resolve dilemmas. Such emotional thinking is likely to reduce the efficacy of problem solving and ultimately the success of interventions. Wagner (1987) noted that, in many of the discussions teachers had about the problem situations they were dealing with, the following cycle of emotional thinking was observed:

- complex and ill-defined problems usually generated much tension;
- this tension was usually experienced as anger, anxiety, hurt, aggression or depression;
- this tension affected the teacher's outward behaviour, which tended to become more tense, hurried and rigid;
- the more the teacher tried to resist the conflict, the worse it became;
- the teacher perceived the problem situation and the resultant conflict as unresolvable;
- the problem situation remained unresolvable until the teacher's thinking about the problem situation was altered.

The types of causal attributions teachers make about the nature of behaviour difficulties

In 1985, Croll and Moses undertook one of the most extensive surveys in the UK of teachers' attitudes, knowledge and practice around the area of special educational needs. They surveyed 428 junior-class teachers in 61 schools across 10 LEAs. Croll and Moses asked the teachers to explain the reasons for the special needs of children within their classes. Causal factors such as intelligence, attitude and concentration were grouped under the heading 'within-child' factors. Parental attitudes, standard of living and social or emotional conditions were grouped under 'home factors'. Table 10.2 summarises Croll and Moses's findings for teachers' causal attributions for behaviour and discipline problems.

In about 66% of cases, behaviour and discipline problems in children were perceived to be due to 'home' based factors, with about 31% of behaviour problems and about 39% of discipline problems being identified with 'within-child' factors (excluding health issues). Only about 3% of causal factors were attributed to 'school' or 'teacher' factors for behaviour problems, and about 4% for discipline problems (Croll and Moses 1985).

Miller's (1996) study was not on the same scale as Croll and Moses's research because it had a rather different purpose. He wanted to probe in much greater detail the basis of teacher attributions. He did this by

Table 10.2 Summary of causal factors identified by teachers (from Miller 1996, adapted from Croll and Moses 1985: 46)

	Type of difficulty	
	Behaviour/ emotional problem $(N = 872)(\%)$	*Discipline problem* $(N = 500)(\%)$
Any within-child (not including health)	30.8	38.8
Home	65.8	65.6
Any school/teacher	2.5	3.8
Any health/absence	2.6	1.6
Any 'within-child' or home factors	80.3	82.4

Note: Teachers were able to select more than one causal factor, as a result the columns do not add up to 100 per cent (Miller 1996: 137).

examining the attributions teachers made for positive changes that occurred within real-life interventions for children with behaviour difficulties in their classrooms.

Miller's study involved a national survey of educational psychologists, in which he explored what interventions educational psychologists used with pupils who exhibited challenging behaviour. He then conducted in-depth interviews with twenty-four teachers to try to identify the factors associated with successful behavioural interventions. He argued that schools not only have the responsibility for delivering the national curriculum, but are charged with keeping order and discipline within classrooms and the playgrounds.

He observed that, although parents were still identified as being significant in causing pupil difficulties, teachers were more likely, in his study at least, to identify causal factors which they could *alter* or at least *modify* (e.g. providing appropriate and stimulating work, providing structure to lessons and classroom life, holding fair and reasonable expectations and being consistent, firm and positive). By focusing upon such environmental and organisational factors rather than 'within-child' or 'within-home' factors, they were more likely to implement successful interventions.

This study obtained results which differed from those of Croll and Moses, who reported a much greater proportion of the responsibility for pupil difficulties being attributed to 'home' and 'within-pupil' factors. Clearly, such a contrast may reflect the different samples used. Miller's group consisted of teachers who perceived that they had successfully resolved a behaviour difficulty. Different results may have been obtained with teachers who perceived that they had not been so successful in managing behavioural difficulties and attributions to home/within-child factors may be stronger in such cases. When teachers frame problem situations as being largely caused by within-child or home factors, it is difficult to alter such features. As a result, there is a tendency for teachers to distance themselves from taking responsibility for actively attempting to analyse and manage the problem situation.

Miller's research provides a rich and extensive list of the causal attributions teachers use when they try to understand pupils they are finding difficult to manage. The most frequent 'within-child' factors identified are those to do with health and physical causes, a need for praise, a lack of acceptance of social norms and temperament or personality issues. To parents, teachers generally attributed punitive or violent home circumstances, inadequate child management, an absent father and a lack of attention. Teachers attributed the following factors to themselves as contributing to problems – setting insufficiently interesting work and having unrealistic expectations of the pupil.

The government guidelines for teachers on the national curriculum are stated in fairly prescriptive terms. In contrast, Miller observed that the guidance given regarding the management of challenging child behaviour (DfE Circular 8/1994) was usually stated in more general terms:

- manage pupil behaviour effectively;
- encourage a whole-school approach to behaviour and discipline;
- promote respect for others among young people;
- promote firm action against all forms of bullying;
- reduce the level of truancy from school;
- reduce the poor behaviour, which can lead to pupils being excluded either temporarily or permanently.

It is likely that teachers and school administrators, when attempting to deal with challenging behaviour, will be left to try and implement these vague and ill-focused guidelines. There is the assumption that school staff know what such guidelines mean and have the necessary skills and attitudes to implement them effectively.

Teaching can be an isolating activity

For the most part, teaching can be a solitary activity with staff working alone within the constraints of a single classroom. In Miller's research, staff reported feeling a sense of isolation. Research by Lieberman and Miller (1990) conducted within the USA highlights some of the unintended consequences of this isolation:

> By following the privacy rule teachers forfeit the opportunity to display their success; but also they gain. They gain the security of not having to face their failures publicly and losing face.

The following list has been adapted and extended from one first compiled by

Miller (1996) and identifies a number of factors which could contribute to teachers' sense of isolation:

- the physical structure of most schools with their focus upon single classrooms;
- the ecology of most schools which see responsibility for child behaviour as being the class teacher's and not a shared task;
- the lack of a shared language and framework which teachers can use to discuss their work with each other in an objective, open and straightforward manner;
- a culture which stresses face-saving, unilateral protection of self, giving advice and judging others;
- the lack of a commonly agreed standard by which teachers can measure their competency, leading to a lack of confidence, defensiveness and an inability to judge their own worth;
- the high value placed upon keeping their class 'under control' leading to a wariness of being observed and defensiveness.

The development of staff-support groups

> Only by staff working together to agree ways of doing things, which are consistent throughout the school and have the general support of all staff, can progress be made.
>
> (Rutter *et al.* 1979)

School responses to staff development have tended to focus upon either direct feedback to a colleague following an observation of a lesson (usually by a senior colleague), or through the provision of 'one-off' INSET. Research suggests that INSET is not a particularly effective way of developing staff competence in dealing with emotional and behavioural difficulties (Harland and Kinder 1997; Lacey 1996). Day (1997) summarises the findings of several investigations into the efficacy of INSET and concludes that:

> ... the most popular means of promoting professional development – school-provided INSET – may not properly be able to promote the necessary range of outcomes essential to continuing high quality professional developments, since they are predominantly limited to information, awareness ...

However, at an anecdotal level, the impression gained is that INSET is often seen as being an adequate solution to many, if not all, school-based problems by senior management, advisers, educational psychologists and others. If school administrators and outside agencies are serious about developing staff then they need to realise that structural and technical changes *also* require behavioural changes (i.e. the ways that teachers think and perceive problem situations) which are not produced 'by a simple process of exposing people to new truths' (Bell 1979).

Zairnik and Bernstein (1982) suggest that while INSET may alter the behaviour of participants for a brief period, there is limited evidence to suggest that changes are maintained over time. Zairnik and Bernstein (1982) argue that it is too simplistic to assume that a sole reliance upon staff training (INSET) is able to improve performance and then sustain it.

Within the educational literature there has been a growing realisation that teachers can be a useful resource to each other if encouraged to do so (Gill and Monsen 1996; Hanko 1995). School staff bring experiences, practices, perspectives, insights and anxieties about the complex nature of their work, which can be shared and built upon in moving problems forward (Dadds 1997). Staff-support groups are created for the purpose of supporting the generation and implementation of solutions to problems. However, Lacey (1996) cautions that for such groups to be effective staff need first of all support and training in *how* to operate within such groups. Lacey notes that many teachers:

> feel particularly vulnerable when they are asked to work alongside colleagues as often the demands of the relationship mean that conflict and resistance are endemic.

Unfortunately, organisational and social structures within many schools do not allow for the development of such dialogues about the real and pressing problems faced by teachers. In most cases, dialogue between staff is limited to anecdotal exchanges of advice, moaning or complaining or the sharing of techniques. Argyris and Schön (1974, 1996) have characterised this normal world of learning as 'single loop'. Such practices encourage staff to design actions that are consistent with their current (often implicit and untested) view of the world.

Single-loop learning is prevalent in most organisations (including schools) which discourage systematic self and peer review of thinking, planning and practice. Within this culture the sharing of problems is perceived as an indication of 'weakness'. Argyris and Schön (1974) advocate the need for school staff to move towards more 'double-loop learning' dialogues if they truly want to resolve difficult and intransigent problems. Double-loop learning involves the systematic exploration of a teacher's intentions and practices which are made explicit and open to testing. An important aim of staff-support groups is to encourage a relationship where teachers are able to clearly talk about their theories (of why they did what they did) and their practices (or what they actually did and how they did it). If within such groups staff can systematically explore the match or mismatch between intentions and actions and then generate new actions, transfer of knowledge from one context to another is likely to occur (Eraut 1996).

Table 10.3 Factors leading to effective INSET in schools (adapted from OFSTED 1993).

- Training needs are identified at school level.
- More than one teacher attends from each school.
- Heads/senior managers are fully aware of the purpose of the training and expected outcome.
- The training forms part of a coherent programme and is not a 'one-off'.
- The training requires preparatory work by teachers.
- The training is sufficiently extensive to allow work in school between sessions, reflections and consolidation.
- The training is targeted to the identified needs of participants and sufficiently differentiated to take account of their varying levels of expertise.
- Training is followed up by some form of support in school.

Table 10.4 Less effective INSET arrangements (adapted from OFSTED 1993).

- One-off sessions without procedures for follow-up are less likely to affect the teachers' work with pupils.
- Course patterns which offer little flexibility in delivery and assignment, or are not sufficiently differentiated for the varied needs of participants.
- Self-selected teachers who are without school or departmental support are least able to influence their fellow teachers.
- Structure of provision is unbalanced when considered against need.
- Twilight sessions show less consistent attendance rates and are too parochial.

Tables 10.3 and 10.4 summarise the findings of Ofsted's (1993) research into the factors that lead to effective and ineffective staff training. Ofsted's findings highlight that, for staff training to be effective, it needs to be based upon:

- an accurate analysis of needs which have been identified at a whole-school level;
- the active involvement of *all* staff who can *support* each other outside of the formal training sessions;
- a coherent programme and not a series of 'one-off' sessions;
- training sessions need to be developmental and linked to organisational structures within the school.

Conclusions from research

School staff are operating within increasingly accountable and stressful working environments. Anecdotal evidence and research on exclusions provides some support for the view that teachers are being expected to manage more complex and challenging child behaviour. Additional research suggests that teaching can be a very isolating activity. The efficacy of 'one-off' INSET as being adequate to support and develop staff in dealing more effectively with such complex problem situations is questioned.

Clearly, INSET can be an appropriate solution to addressing many school-based issues such as sharing information, raising awareness of issues, debating ideas and practices. However, school staff and trainers need to be clear about what their rationales are for choosing this approach. If it is the intention of school staff (or outside agencies) to develop staff skill and competence in managing emotional and behavioural difficulties, then INSET alone will not be an adequate solution. Other approaches are needed (such as those which set up supportive organisational structures within a school).

In thinking how best to support school staff in managing the complex and ill-defined problems they are confronted with, a number of key principles are identified. First, for effective interventions to be planned and implemented staff need to have access to *relevant and accurate information*. For this to develop, school staff need a shared language and problem-solving frame-work to guide their thinking, which, as Wagner (1987) has pointed out, tends to be 'descriptive, emotional and contradictory'. Second, the ways in which teachers perceive and interpret challenging behaviour is crucial to the success or failure of both problem analysis and the planning and delivery of interventions. The types of attributions teachers make about pupils with emotional and behavioural difficulties need to be 'challenged' (i.e. encourag-ing 'double-loop learning') and modified, if more effective interventions are to be implemented. As Miller (1996) concludes, this can only occur if teachers are given a clear understanding of the principles that underlie interventions and approaches and the ways in which practice has evolved to support the contributions made by school-based personnel. Third, such 'challenge' needs to occur within a supportive yet focused group context that develops skills and builds upon staff strengths. Finally, there is clear evidence (Guzzo and Dickson 1996) that team-developed interventions can have very powerful effects on complex problems.

The Staff Sharing Scheme

This section provides an overview of the Staff Sharing Scheme, which is offered as one example of a comprehensive staff-support group based upon the principles outlined in previous sections (for a more detailed discussion and presentation of the approach, see Gill and Monsen 1996). After a period of skills-based training, the Staff Sharing Group helps teachers (and other school staff) to manage the complex emotions generated when working with the challenging behaviour of children and young people.

Underpinning the consultative basis of the Scheme is the problem-analysis framework which staff use to gain emotional distance and a shared language to explore the problem situations they are concerned about so that they can:

clarify the important aspects of the problem situation (including their role); look for patterns and links, understand possible causal factors; and plan and evaluate their actions and interventions more objectively (Monsen *et al.* 1998). The Staff Sharing Group meets regularly to analyse, suggest, devise and evaluate interventions and aims to:

1   establish within a school (after a period of training) a supportive network of staff who act as resources to each other;
2   Provide a forum for more effectively utilising external support staff (e.g. educational psychologists, social workers and advisors);
3   provide regular structured sessions for staff to assist each other in solving problems, using a structured problem-analysis framework;
4   train staff in Behaviour Observation, Analysis and Management as processes for measuring and modifying problem situations and behaviour (including their own);
5   increase staff competence in communication with children, colleagues, parents and carers;
6   encourage staff to be more rational and objective in their perceptions of problem situations, thus reducing stress and anxiety;
7   encourage greater school responsibility for managing difficulties, thus reducing the need for extensive outside input.

Background and rationale to the Scheme's development

The Scheme originated in New Zealand during the 1980s when there was a pressing need to find more effective ways for educational psychologists to work with schools which presented large numbers of referrals. The Scheme was piloted and set up in England in the mid-1990s where similar conditions prevailed. In both countries, referrals to the school's link psychologist reflected in part teachers' own anxieties and emotional issues around how to manage the complex school-based challenges they were faced with on a daily basis.

It was recognised that, due to various constraints affecting the community (e.g. unemployment, lack of suitable childcare facilities, abuse, ineffective parenting, poverty, truancy, cultural differences), many children and young people were presenting schools with increasingly complex sets of needs. These problems required a greater degree of management than the single classroom teacher was often able to provide. It was thought possible that when resources within the school and the wider community were 'pooled' there would be a greater chance of having some positive effect.

A major focus of the Scheme was the need to assist school staff to take more responsibility for developing their own problem-solving networks. Part of this process involved challenging some of the existing belief systems of staff about the causes of child behaviour. Schools often believed that a referral to the link psychologist (or other outside agency) would result in some 'magical cure', or at least the psychologist would take responsibility for the 'problem child'. Many staff appeared to be searching for something wrong within the child that could be identified, diagnosed, labelled and 'fixed' through the involvement of the psychologist (often leading to an assessment and report or culminating in a statutory assessment).

This internal-attribution model of describing pupil problems does not recognise the many complex factors affecting children's behaviour (Christenson *et al.* 1983). Such a view is a disservice, both to the child, in assuming that the problem resides solely within him or her, and to teachers, in not giving them enough credit for being able to work effectively with diverse groups of children, when given appropriate support.

Prior to the Scheme's implementation, many school staff reported that they did not know how to implement interventions, and, in any case, 'that was the job of specialists'. They had doubts about their own abilities to solve problems and regarded problems as 'things to be feared'. Especially difficult was the 'unsolved problem' that reflected teachers' own feelings of anxiety and incompetence. Hence defensiveness and an attachment to the internal attribution model is hardly surprising. Part of this self-doubt about solving problems comes from the ways teachers go about thinking and responding to complex and ill-defined problems.

A collaborative-based approach as the basis of staff support

Before the development of the Staff Sharing Scheme, target schools had been used to a psychologist responding to a referral, 'seeing' a child and then writing a 'full psychological report'. This process is often referred to as the 'traditional model'. The report usually recommended what, in the psychologist's view, would be in the child's best interests. Often the recommendations in these reports were stated in terms which Argyris (1993) calls 'applicable knowledge'.

Applicable knowledge refers to general ideas and principles which have been found to be effective in other similar situations. However, applicable knowledge says very little about *how* and *what* actually to do. *Actionable* knowledge, on the other hand, specifies how applicable knowledge can be implemented in everyday life. It specifies the actual behaviour or actions that must be produced if the desired changes are to happen (Argyris 1993). Having recommendations stated in prescriptive applicable knowledge terms does not usually provide teachers with the level of clarity and specificity they need to develop effective interventions.

Writing reports in such a manner assumes that school staff have the necessary skills, understandings and ownership to carry out the suggestions being made (e.g. 'Richard requires a differentiated curriculum, social skills and self-esteem training', or 'Rachael needs a multi-sensory programme of differentiated work'). In Argyris's view, such recommendations lack the 'actionable knowledge' element and therefore most of the suggestions cannot be implemented effectively (i.e. *how do you* differentiate and *how do you* run a social skills/self-esteem group or set up a multi-sensory approach – whatever that may mean). Although an assessment and report had been completed and there was a tangible sign that something had been done, in most cases no significant change had actually taken place.

Bardon (1980) has argued that 'people ask for services they do not really want, often because they do not know how else to get services. They make assumptions about the responsibilities of psychologists (and others) that are not always warranted'. In Bardon's view 'the educational psychologist must find ways to try to increase the impact of services offered. In short, educational psychologists (and related practitioners) must work towards offering a wider range of focused and strategic services (e.g. consultation with educators and parents, in-service education and coordination of the service of others and support at a systems level).

Most development work in schools involves one or two training sessions in which information is shared. Participants often report a 'feel-good' factor after attending such sessions; the assumption being that staff behaviour will change and 'things will get better'. The Staff Sharing Scheme is rather different and assumes that generalisation of understandings or skills to the classroom is rare unless this is planned and supported by some ongoing supportive developmental process. The Staff Sharing Scheme provides participants with both a conceptual framework and the practical skills to make the Scheme work.

The elements necessary for working a consultation model are emphasised by Gordon *et al.* (1985) and more recently by Argyris (1993) and Wagner (1995a). They note several assumptions which underlie a consultation model and which are essential to its success. The first is the assumption that consultation involves shared ownership and collaborative problem solving. The consultant is viewed as being a resource to the consultee. A second underlying assumption is that, for most referrals, the indirect involvement of outside specialists with a pupil is more efficient than their direct support. The next section describes the consultation approach used to develop the Staff Sharing Scheme in schools.

Developing the Staff Sharing Scheme: consultation steps

Phase I   Assessing existing school processes for managing complex problem situations

1   TESTING THE NEED FOR A CHANGE IN MODEL OF SERVICE DELIVERY

This step involves the consultant openly testing out their inferences (attributions and assumptions) about the efficacy of current ways of working and school systems in a way that encourages school staff to enquire and challenge; the result being a clearer understanding of the issues involved.

2   ENTERING INTO THE SCHOOL SYSTEM AND PRELIMINARY CONTRACT WITH
THE SCHOOL

Most schools approached are prepared to try a new way of working and then review its effectiveness. The key factors for the consultant are to have the rationale and framework of the model clear before meeting with senior management (and later school staff) and to clarify any inferences being made. It is essential to have the agreement of the senior management team before going any further.

3   DATA GATHERING AND ASSESSMENT OF EXISTING PROCESSES AND RESOURCES

This step involves undertaking a needs analysis of the school's existing processes and resources for managing complex problem situations. This is carried out using a range of both qualitative and quantitative methods (e.g. questionnaires administered to all staff who work within the school; focus-group interviews with teachers, learning-support assistants, pupils, parents; interviews with selected staff and senior management members, classroom observations and a review of school documentation (e.g. policy documents, specific cases). All staff groups need to be involved in this process, including caretaker, governors, secretaries and dinner staff.

4   ANALYSIS, FEEDBACK AND RECONTRACTING

The emphasis at this stage is on trying to clarify and present the differences between what staff (as a group) say they are doing (their 'espoused theories', e.g. 'As a staff we help each other with problems') and what the evidence collected tells us is actually happening (their 'theories in action', e.g.'In fact most staff reported feeling isolated and dealt with problems on their own for fear of being seen as being incompetent').

At this stage, it is important to assist staff in taking a 'snapshot' of what they currently observe and experience, rather than what they think might be happening. For example, in many of the schools visited in the original project, it was reported by senior management that staff 'worked in teams and shared problems'. Yet when this assumption was tested out, very often the headteacher managed staff as individuals and staff reported feeling deskilled, defensive and isolated.

Following discussions and feedback of the needs analysis, school staff are presented with a model of how to operate a staff-support group within their school. The following components are central in negotiating a school's commitment to and acceptance of working in a more collaborative and rational way:

a   presenting an operational model of the Staff Sharing Scheme;
b   discussing the traditional versus consultative models of working with complex-problem situations;

c   presenting the aims of the Scheme, the rationale for the problem-analysis model, the skills-development sessions, which underpin the workings of the Scheme;

d   outlining the content of the training sessions and the logistics of running the Scheme;

e   outlining how the Staff Sharing Scheme runs, once training is completed (for detail of these aspects, see Gill and Monsen 1996).

Phase II   Skills-development sessions

5   ACTION STEPS

The skill-development sessions are introduced to enable school staff to formulate interventions following careful observation and analysis of problem situations. Training gives permission to staff to consult with others in a supportive team atmosphere rather than merely providing or receiving advice. It ensures that staff have equivalent understanding of problem analysis, consultation and management skills, and do not feel threatened or isolated. The approach adopted encourages staff to see their link psychologist and other support people as resources and collaborators rather than as 'rescuers' or 'gate-keepers'.

6   THE STAFF SHARING SCHEME IS UNDERPINNED BY A PROBLEM-ANALYSIS FRAMEWORK

The Scheme is underpinned by a problem-analysis model which guides staff in structuring both their thinking and emotional responses to managing complex-problem situations. Initial work with teachers highlighted that, before training, staff had difficulties in thinking about complex and ill-defined problems. They tended not to make sufficient use of the information available to them (i.e. from parents or carers, assessments, observations, school files, outside agencies); based their interpretations of the information they had on untested inferences; tended to be distracted by irrelevant lines of inquiry; often failed to link pieces of information, see patterns and trends; and usually did not recognise their own emotions and agendas in the problems they were working with.

Phase III   The Staff Sharing Scheme in operation

7   EVALUATION OF ACTIONS TAKEN AND THE SETTING UP OF THE STAFF
     SHARING SCHEME

The Staff Sharing Scheme establishes within a school, after a period of training, a problem-solving network which meets regularly to systematically manage school-based issues. The consultant (the person responsible for setting up the scheme) is one member of this team and all his or her work with the school stems as a result of decisions made at the Staff Sharing Meeting. The Scheme is based upon the following underlying principles:

a no one person within a school has sole responsibility for the well-being and learning of a child;
b problem ownership is a responsibility of staff, pupils and parents/carers;
c staff in schools have personal resources which are not always collectively utilised for the benefit of other staff members and/or pupils;
d staff in schools are welcoming of continuing education in the form of school-based training as a means of increasing their effectiveness in the management of children;
e school staff are motivated to find ways of reducing job stress.

Specific strategies from the counselling literature (e.g. Rational–Emotive Behaviour Therapy: Ellis and Harper 1997; Neenan and Dryden 2000) and work from the fields of interpersonal effectiveness and creative problem solving (e.g. critical dialogue skills: Argyris and Schön 1974; Cameron and Monsen 1998; Robinson, 1993) have been useful in enabling staff to develop greater emotional objectivity and rationality. The following sections highlight some of the strategies which have been used to support the development of a collaborative rationally based staff-support group.

Strategies from critical dialogue

Central to the Staff Sharing relationship is the fostering of trust. To enable this dimension to grow and develop, school staff have to learn to view 'critique' as valuable and constructive feedback. To this end, the technique of critical dialogue has proved particularly helpful in encouraging more 'critical understanding and guided reflection'.

Critical dialogue, as outlined by Robinson (1993), is based upon the models I and II framework proposed by Argyris and Schön (1974). In its simplest form, this framework outlines three key principles which can be used to inform and enhance interpersonal communication: increasing valid information for all; promoting freedom of informed choice; and enhancing commitment and responsibility for implementing agreed plans.

By employing these principles, the Staff Sharing group aim to be open about their views (including their reasons for them and the possibility that they may have got it wrong), to publicly test out the adequacy of their views so a shared understanding is developed and to manage bilaterally the process and content of this interaction (including the management of emotionally difficult issues). Within a typical Staff Sharing meeting, participants will employ critical dialogue skills to enhance problem understanding and, ultimately, problem management.

Robinson has summarised the process of critical dialogue as follows:

being clear and saying exactly what you think; making the reasoning and evidence base explicit which led you to think in these terms; and fully checking out possible faulty premises, based upon over generalisation, unsupported assumption or inappropriate attribution.

Robinson has suggested that critical dialogue should be focused (as far as possible) on concrete events and evidence (e.g. 'When you declared that there was absolutely no provision for extra reading support, did you mean that support provided by the parent helpers was also inappropriate or ineffective?'). Such a reality-based approach reduces discussion at the more commonly observed philosophical, abstract or emotional levels where the chances of resolving difficulties are reduced and the likelihood of unhelpful emotional argument and heated debate increases. Critical dialogue therefore aims to enhance interpersonal communication by making thinking and reasoning as explicit and accessible to Scheme members as possible.

The rationale that underpins this approach is that the Staff Sharing members require full and accurate information upon which to base their resolution of a complex-problem situation. The positive consequences observed for Staff Sharing members is that the effectiveness of joint problem solving increases as a result of greater availability of data, higher quality information, better management of emotionally sensitive and personal issues and a commitment to a personally meaningful form of development which impacts directly on tough and intransigent problem situations.

Strategies from rational–emotive behaviour therapy (REBT)

Within rational–emotive theory, Ellis emphasises that people in large part create and sustain their own emotional difficulties through irrational thinking and self-reinforcing talk (Ellis and Harper 1997 (see also Fell, Chapter 5, this volume)). People are born with an innate tendency to be both rational and irrational. However, the culture we operate in, our families, peers, colleagues and the media itself tend to foster irrational ways of thinking and viewing the world.

REBT proposes a simple *ABCDE framework*, with *A* being the *activating event* which 'caused' our distress (i.e. Nigel, an 8-year-old boy, doesn't complete his work), *B* being the *belief* or *beliefs* about the activating event (i.e. Nigel is deliberately trying to upset me and the other children; he has emotional problems) and *C* being the *consequences* both emotionally and physically of holding such a belief or beliefs (i.e. I'm feeling irritated, tired and angry).

Ellis saw that where beliefs are irrational they obscure the reality of the activating event and thus the consequences can be highly inappropriate for the individual. Ellis lists twelve major irrational idea or beliefs relating to how we, others and the environment should or must be. The characteristics of irrational beliefs include: demandingness (i.e. everyone should/must like me, 'All children should be well behaved all of the time') overgeneralisation (i.e. because one person dislikes me everyone does, 'All parents are difficult and unsupportive so it's no point in trying to work with them'), self-rating (i.e. 'I'm not as good as the teacher in the next room to me: I'm a totally useless teacher'), awfulising (i.e. 'Because I'm not as good as them I can't stand it and can't cope'), attribution errors (i.e. because the headteacher ignored me from the other side of the playground I must have annoyed him/her in some way'), anti-empirical (i.e. avoiding checking out own assumptions and attributions) and repetition (i.e. going over and over the same untested conclusions).

Within the context of the Staff Sharing Group, staff are encouraged to help each other identify and label possible irrational ideas or beliefs which may be limiting thinking about a problem. In other cases, staff are helped to devise ways to test out assumptions they have made about themselves, others or the environment. In the authors' experience this can become a humorous exchange with staff *detecting and disputing* (i.e. D) such beliefs to produce *E*, a new *effect* or consequence. Such an approach helps staff acquire a more realistic view of themselves, colleagues, parent or carers and most importantly the children and young people they work with (see Neenam and Dryden 2000 for more detail on these strategies).

Summary and conclusion

The Staff Sharing Scheme assists teachers to enhance their competence by modifying some of their beliefs about problem situations and their role within them. Westera (1985), in evaluating the Staff Sharing Scheme in New Zealand, found that training in the problem-analysis framework, and in learning specific content skills, resulted in teachers reporting less stress and more confidence in their ability in managing children's behaviour. Monsen (1994) found very similar results in his evaluation of staff perceptions using pre–post measures in two schools in a large shire county. School staff within these schools reported 'a more business-like approach to dealing with problems', 'more clarity as to roles and responsibilities' and 'a sense of shared comradeship'. In addition, and, as a by-product, the number of statutory assessments generated by one of these schools went from a median of twelve (1992–1993) to one per year (1993–1994). This trend continued with increases noted only in the last 18 months.

In evaluating the efficacy of the Staff Sharing Scheme one of the most robust findings was that individual teachers positively changed the way they perceived their students, themselves and their colleagues. School staff reported that they felt 'more in control', 'discussions are more focused and businesslike', 'things don't seem so impossible' and 'there is hope'. Collaborative problem solving meant teachers needed to learn and apply the skills of observing, gathering data, generating hypotheses and solutions, so that they could then explain their understandings to their colleagues in a way that was helpful.

School staff learned that, in order to receive assistance, they needed to provide specific data or rational arguments upon which colleagues could make valid assessments. The traditional model which encourages teachers to complain about students, see problems as solely residing within individuals and to make many untested assumptions and attributions, would not work within the structure of the Staff Sharing meetings. The group expectation, following training, was that more specific objective information was required before assistance could be planned.

Experience in England and New Zealand highlighted that school staff were welcoming of receiving collaborative assistance. During evaluation sessions staff reported liking the idea that they did not have to 'go it alone' with any particular problem, and that the responsibility was being shared with their colleagues. This resulted in a perception that something practical and real would be/could be done to help in what were often initially seen as 'hopeless situations'.

It appears that many schools are presented with increasing numbers of challenging young people and little likelihood of further significant resourcing. School staff often say 'What can we do?' This Scheme reflects one way of working with schools differently and creatively and may well address this question. Hopefully, it emphasises the positive professional relationship which can form between outside agencies, schools and young people.

Perhaps the last words should be left to the Elton Report (1989) which was one of the most comprehensive investigations into the state of school discipline within the UK.

> We conclude that the central problem of disruption could be significantly reduced by helping teachers to become more effective classroom managers. We see the role of initial and in-service training as crucial to the process. This leads us to make two key recommendations. The first is that all initial teacher training courses should include specific training in ways of motivating and managing groups of pupils, and of dealing with those who challenge authority. The second is that similar in-service training should be provided through *school based groups*. These groups should aim not only to refine classroom management skills, but also to develop patterns of mutual support among colleagues.

References

Adelman, H, S. and Taylor, L. (2000) 'Shaping the future of mental health in schools', *Psychology in the Schools* 37(1): 49–60.

Argyris, C. (1993) *Knowledge for Action: A Guide to Overcoming Barriers to Organisational Change*, San Francisco: Jossey-Bass.

Argyris, C. and Schön, D. A. (1996) *Organisational Learning II: Theory, Method, and Practice*, New York: Addison-Wiley.

Argyris, C. and Schön, D. A. (1974) *Theory in Practice*, San Francisco: Jossey-Bass.

Bardon, J. (1980) *The New Zealand Educational Psychologist – A Comparative Analysis*, pp. 21–4. Wellington: New Zealand Council for Educational Research.

Bell, L. A. (1979) 'A discussion of some of the implications of using consultants in schools', *British Educational Research Journal* **5**(1): 55–62.

Cameron, R. J. and Monsen, J. J. (1998) 'Coaching and critical dialogue in educational psychology practice', *Educational and Child Psychology* **15**(4): 112–26.

Christenson, S., Yesseldyke, J. E., Wang, J. J. and Algozzine, B. (1983) 'Teacher attributions for problems that result in referral for psycho-educational evaluation', *Journal of Educational Research* **76**: 174–80.

Croll, P. and Moses, D. (1985) *One in Five. The Assessment and Incidence of Special Educational Needs*, London: Routledge & Kegan Paul.

Dadds, M. (1997) 'Continuing professional development: nurturing the expert within', *British Journal of In-Service Education* **23**(1): 31–8.

Day, C. (1997) 'In-service teacher education in Europe: Conditions and themes for development in the 21st century', *British Journal of In-Service Education* **23**(1): 39–54.

Department for Education (1994) *Pupil Behaviour and Discipline*, Circular 8/94, London: DFE.

Department of Education and Science (1989) *Discipline in Schools (The Elton Report)*, London: HMSO.

Ellis, A. and Harper, R. (1997) *A Guide to Rational Living*, 3rd edn, Hollywood: Melvin Powers Wiltshire Book Company.

Eraut, M. (1996) *Developing Professional Knowledge and Competence*, Washington, DC: The Falmer Press.

Gersch, I, S. and Rawkins, P. (1987) 'A teacher support group in school', *Educational and Child Psychology* **4**, 3–4: 74–81.

Gill, D. and Monsen, J. J. (1996) 'The staff sharing scheme: A school based management system for working with challenging child behaviour', in E. Blyth, and J. Milner (eds) *Exclusion from School: Inter-professional Issues for Policy and Practice*, London: Routledge.

Gordon, J. L., Casey, A. and Christenson, S. L. (1985) 'Implementing a re-referral intervention system: Part I the model', *Exceptional Children* **51**(5): 377–84.

Guzzo, R. A. and Dickson, M. W. (1996) 'Teams in organisations: Recent research on performance and effectiveness', *Annual Review of Psychology* **47**: 307–38.

Harland, J. and Kinder, K. (1997) 'Teachers' continuing professional development: Framing a model of outcomes', *British Journal of In-Service Education* **23**(1): 71–84.

Hanko, G. (1995) *Special Needs in Ordinary Classrooms: From Staff Support to Staff Development*, London: David Fulton.

Hanko, G. (1987) 'Group consultation with mainstream teachers', *Educational and Child Psychology* **4**(3–4): 123–30.

Herbert, M. (1987) *Conduct disorders of Childhood and Adolescence: A Social learning Perspective*, 2nd, edn, Chichester: John Wiley.

Lappan, G. (1997) 'The challenges of implementation: supporting teachers', *American Journal of Education* **106**, November: 207–39.

Lacey, P. (1996) 'Training for collaboration', *British Journal of In-Service Education* **22**(1): 67–80.

Lieberman, A. and Miller, L (1990) 'The social realities of teaching', in A. Lieberman (ed.) *Schools as Collaborative Cultures*, Basingstoke: Falmer.

Miller, A. (1996) *Pupil Behaviour and Teacher Culture*, London: Cassell.

Monsen, J., Graham, B., Frederickson, N. and Cameron, R. J. (1998) 'Problem analysis and professional training in educational psychology: An accountable model of practice', *Educational Psychology in Practice* 13(4): 234–49.

Monsen, J. J. (1994) 'Evaluation of the staff sharing scheme', unpublished research project, Kent Psychology Service, Kent County Council.

Neenan, M. and Dryden, W. (2000) *Essential Rational Emotive Behaviour Therapy*, London and Philadelphia: Whurr.

Ofsted (1993) *The Management and Provision if In-Service Training Funded by the Grant for Education Support and Training (GEST)*, Office for the Standards in Education, London: HMSO.

Parsons, C. (2000) 'The third way to educational and social exclusion', in G. Walraven, C. Day., C. Parsons. and D. van Venn (eds) *Combating Social Exclusion Through Education*, Leuven: Garant.

Robinson, V. (1993) *Problem Based Methodology: Research for the Improvement of Practice*, Oxford: Pergamon Press.

Rutter, M., Maughan, B., Mortimore, P. and Ouston, J. (1979) *Fifteen Thousand Hours*, Wells: Open Books.

Wagner, P. (1995a) *School Consultation: Frameworks for the Practising Educational Psychologists*, London: Kensington and Chelsea Educational Psychology Service.

Wagner, P. (1995b) 'A consultation approach to the educational psychologist's work in schools', *Educational and Child Psychology* 12(3): 22–8.

Wagner, A. C. (1987) 'Knots in teacher's thinking', in J. Calderhead (ed.) *Exploring Teachers Thinking*, London: Cassell.

Westera, J. (1985) 'Evaluation of the Staff Sharing Scheme', unpublished diploma in educational psychology report, University of Auckland, New Zealand.

Zairnik, J. P. and Bernstein, G. S. (1982) 'A critical examination of the effect of in-service training on staff performance', *Mental Retardation* 20(3): 109–14.

11 Supporting and developing teachers' management of difficult and challenging pupils through coaching

Jey Monsen and R. J. (Sean) Cameron

> History provides us with many examples of successful coaching relationships – Socrates and Plato, Freud and Jung and Haydn and Beethoven. Each provided something unique to assist the other learn, develop and above all fulfil their potential.

Introduction

Like most professional groups, teachers recognise the value of receiving constructive feedback on their practice and being supported in finding new solutions to deal with work-related problems. Often, however, observable changes resulting from such feedback can be difficult to achieve and even more difficult to maintain. Teachers, like other groups, are not immune from the constraints imposed by 'professional inflexibility'.

Coaching is an individual (or group based) approach aimed at helping teachers and others to deal more constructively with their emotions and to think differently about the problem situations they work with. In so doing, teachers can gain insight into the consequences of their emotional responses, their practices and ways of thinking. They are then able to use this personally meaningful information to improve their skills and knowledge and apply these in their day-to-day practice.

Although this chapter is primarily written for teachers, the possibility of using *coaching* to supplement more traditional approaches to supervision (e.g. appraisal) is relevant to other groups working in the public sector including educational and clinical psychologists, education welfare officers, social workers and special-needs officers. The chapter describes and provides guidance on both the process of coaching and its practical possibilities.

Changing practice in organisations

Changing institutional practices is a complex undertaking. It requires more than in-service training (INSET) or altering policy statements about processes, it 'depends upon the will of school communities and, particularly, teachers' (Day 1997; Millwater *et al.* 1996). The importance of the 'people factor' in achieving organisational success has long been recognised, yet it is only relatively recently that theories of management have moved away from an overconcern with structural and process aspects to considering the 'development through people' perspective (Pedler *et al.* 1997).

In 3rd Millennium organisations, employees are less likely to be perceived as 'cogs in a machine' but rather as groups of learners who have the capacity to generate new knowledge and solutions to meet the needs of an ever-changing world. These 'soft variables' – experience, judgement, emotions, intuition, beliefs and core guiding principles – are now recognised as being of considerable importance in enabling organisations to become effective and responsive to client needs (Arygris 1982; Cameron 1995; Hawkins and Shohet 2000; Wright *et al.* 1995).

There is growing evidence that people-focused thinking has begun to penetrate the traditionally conservative world of education and some schools have begun to implement increasingly sophisticated appraisal and continuing professional development programmes. However, most of these initiatives seek to support only structural and process change. It is often difficult to point to observable outcomes that have resulted from these initiatives. Even with carefully considered feedback on strengths and poss-ible areas for improvement, changes in teacher practice seem to occur relatively slowly and only tend to be maintained when new behaviours are grounded in school norms and shared principles. Indeed, even where proposed changes are in accord with these, a considerable input of energy from the system is necessary to maintain change over time (Csikszentmihalyi 1993).

Unguided thinking

The ways in which teachers think about complex work-related problems are central to the successful management of these. Wagner (1987) has identified some of the 'knots' that can occur in teachers' thinking when they are left to their own devices. She suggests that, when teachers' problem solving is characterised by circular thinking (e.g. *'With pupils from such family backgrounds, the school can only have a minimal impact so how can I expect to achieve any real change?'*), this results in an inability to move the problem situation forward. Other blockages to understanding the nature of problems in school include jumping from one issue to another without being able to make meaningful connections or links (*'Vanessa is not happy in school, she has no friends and therefore her self-esteem is low'*) and a tendency for thinking to be embedded in emotional and irrational responses (*'I refuse to treat any child in my class differently from the rest – it's just not fair on all the good children'*). Such constructs may result from teachers' previous attempts to resolve difficulties, but unguided thinking is likely to reduce the efficacy of teachers' problem solving.

There is little evidence to suggest that the reasoning and problem-management skills of staff in the field necessarily improve with experience. Lichtenberg (1997) argues that, for improvement to occur, two requirements must be in place:

1   a clear *judgement* about what constitutes an incorrect response (or error in judgement); and
2   immediate, unambiguous and consistent *feedback* on ways to improve.

Unless these factors are in place, Lichtenberg predicts an inevitable growth of practitioner bias and self-fulfilling beliefs relating to self, others, practice and the world. He proposes a 'model of expertise' that consists of three interrelated factors:

1   *cognitive structures* (these are metaphors for the organisational systems used within the brain which contain the practitioners' knowledge, beliefs and assumptions about themselves, others, their practice and the world);
2   *cognitive processes* (these are the routine ways in which incoming information is combined with existing knowledge to inform judgements); and finally
3   *cognitive products* (these are the results of information processing, i.e. the outcomes generated by practitioners as a consequence of their cognitive structures and information processing).

To illustrate the interaction of these three factors, consider the following example. If teachers operate on the basis of biased or faulty cognitive structures (e.g. *'most pupils with challenging behaviour are bright under-achievers'*), they are more likely to engage in ineffective cognitive processing (e.g. *'IQ is therefore the best indicator in identifying and helping such pupils'*), ultimately producing inaccurate cognitive products (e.g. *'therefore, I must always request that the educational psychologist carry out an IQ test with pupils who present with emotional and behavioural difficulties'*). Even if cognitive structures are not biased, errors in reasoning may still produce inaccurate judgements (e.g. *'therefore, only schools which specialise in EBD [emotional and behavioural difficulties] are appropriate placements for such pupils'*).

In their sobering article about the development of expertise, Frensch and Steinberg (1989) have suggested that, as they become more 'expert', practitioners may experience increased *inflexibility* within their information processing systems. For example, faced with a problem situation, many experienced teachers may seek confirmation of their existing knowledge and beliefs rather than actively considering new possibilities. In failing to understand the need for lifelong learning and personal/professional development, practitioners are ignoring the well-established psychological principle, recognised for almost a century and summarised in Dewey's observation that '*The most important attitude that can be formed is the desire to go on learning*'.

Supervision

Most teachers are encouraged to consider critically their professional effectiveness through regular appraisals. This is often seen within a hierarchical system of supervision which supports management-related functions such as monitoring and appraising staff performance rather than focusing upon learning or development. Within the public sector there appears to be a lack of consensus about how supervision (and staff support) should be carried out. Some managers assume that learning and support functions can be combined with management appraisal functions, others see these activities as being more discrete. The dilemma for school administrators and teachers is to sort out clearly the purpose and functions of the various supervision frameworks (Hawkins and Shohet 2000).

While it may seem reasonable to include appraisal as part of an array of supportive activities contributing to teachers' development, many teachers only experience a management-linked form of supervision (Pomerantz 1993). In addition, other support mechanisms such as team meetings, training and informal peer discussions, though popular, may not address crucial issues because they tend to be public, lack structure and are usually focused upon group needs and activities. There is little evidence that classroom practice is significantly altered.

Teachers need regular opportunities for supported reflection on their practice. This may occur through discussions where work issues are opened up for scrutiny by a 'critical friend'. However, anecdotal evidence suggests that such sessions, if unstructured, can result in a monologue of problems where the listener is overwhelmed by detail and unsure or confused as to their role. It is not surprising then that the 'critical friend' can end up either positively reframing the problem list ('*Treat your difficulties with Stewart as a normal part of working in an EBD unit*') or giving off-the-cuff advice ('*Have you tried happy faces? I find they really work*').

Dissatisfaction with the effectiveness of some of the existing approaches to supervision have led to the development of frameworks based more on partnership. These attempt to separate management functions from learning and support and to provide greater structure for the supportive relationship. *Coaching* is such a framework and requires the teacher and the coach (a peer, a senior colleague, or external support person such as an educational psychologist, or in some cases a group of colleagues) to approach work-related problems together. Frameworks such as coaching (and mentoring) rest upon the assumption that a teacher's practice can only be developed by providing direct feedback on aspects of practice that are of concern to that teacher, rather than items on an evaluation forms or aspects which are the particular concerns of the coach (Reavis 1976). When used in conjunction with other approaches, coaching can be a useful tool in supporting teachers to think more objectively when they are managing work-related problems, rather than being overwhelmed by irrational ways of thinking and emotional themes.

The coaching process

A teacher in an EBD unit starts to discuss the frustration he is feeling as a result of trying to work with a disturbed boy. Through the coaching process the coach helps him separate out his unhelpful emotional needs (i.e. 'I have to be successful with every EBD boy I work with') by getting him to notice the complex system he and the boy are in and the different expectations placed on them ... by parents, headteacher, social worker and others. At the end, he says he is clearer about his needs and role.

Despite the level of formal organisational support which may be available to teachers, some of the problem situations they encounter may be long-standing, complex or recurring. Coaching provides a framework which enables the class or subject teacher to step back from complex problems, examine these more objectively and generate new ways of thinking.

Coaching is a dynamic developmental opportunity where one member of staff (a consultee/coachee) works with a peer or other work colleague (the consultant/coach) to explore, in depth, the factors underlying a problem that the consultee has encountered. Such explorations will include a closer examination, not only of the *problem context* (e.g. people, constraints and opportunities) but also of the consultee's personal *attitudes and perspectives* and the extent to which these can reduce, maintain or exacerbate problems.

In its simplest form, the coaching sequence involves the following steps (Melrose 1994):

1   spotting opportunities and/or problems;
2   considering individuals' strengths or weaknesses;
3   explaining what needs to be done to enhance strengths and develop weaknesses;
4   modelling or role-playing developmental tasks;
5   encouraging the coachee to try them out and practice them;
6   reviewing outcomes.

Melrose's six steps closely resemble the model of coaching which has long been used in a variety of sports and adapted for the business context (Howe 1993; Graham *et al.* 1994). However, a more comprehensive approach is needed for 'caring professionals' which focuses less on skill development and more on systemic and personal issues. Such a framework is outlined below. This draws on a range of different concepts and approaches:

1 *understanding the problem situation*
  - obtaining a rich picture through open questions
  - paraphrasing sections of the problem
  - reflecting emotions and feelings
  - clarifying the problem with closed questions;
2 *summarising the problem situation;*
3 *examining systemic aspects;*
  - inviting comments on organisational factors which support or reduce the problem
  - identifying organisational changes required;
4 *developing cultural understanding*
  - checking the coherence, relevance, internal consistency and external validity of the coachee's actions/thoughts about the problem
  - agreeing an action plan;
5 *considering underlying personal dimensions*
  - suggesting connections/themes
  - highlighting mismatches
  - unpacking apparently hidden agendas
  - pointing out personal/professional gaps in expertise
  - identifying key conflict areas
  - attempting 'long-shot' explanations
  - inviting possible dimensions from the coachee;
6 *exploring selected dimensions*
  - reflecting on the problem dimensions list
  - selecting one/two dimensions for discussion;
7 *creating an action menu*
  - creating action possibilities menu from the coachee
  - offering additional possibilities;
8 *planning action*
  - discussing a plan of action
  - carrying out a cost–benefit analysis of the plan
  - considering possible pitfalls
  - role playing/rehearsing/scripting
  - discussing outcome and process measures;
9 *evaluating outcomes/processes*
  - discussing what went well with the action carried out
  - considering what was learned
  - considering what to do differently next time
  - reflecting on any personal/professional development needs for the coachee emerging from this action;
10 *carrying out a meta-evaluation*
  - identifying assets of coaching sessions
  - identifying areas for improvement to coaching session
  - reviewing coaching arrangements
  - reflecting on any personal/professional development needs for the coach emerging from the coaching session.

This kind of framework allows the coachee to gain additional insight into the nature of such problems, enables a consideration of the controlling factors and promotes the generation of strategies which can then be turned into an action plan. Such a plan can enable the classroom teacher to manage a persistent or complex problem situation more successfully. For both coach and coachee, learning can take place at both a *micro-level* (e.g. better strategies for managing a particularly challenging child, parent or colleague) and at a *macro-level* (e.g. reflecting on insights into beliefs, attitudes and constructs which may have emerged from the coaching process)

Let us provide an illustrative example of this model in action, in the form of a 'coaching record', written in the first person by the coachee. The focus of the example is on a teacher working in a unit for pupils with behavioural difficulties based in a secondary mainstream school in a large shire county (the names used are fictitious).

CONFIDENTIAL

Coaching Record

Name: Nigel Southern (teacher)
Coach: Philip Clark (educational psychologist linked to the EBD unit)
Date: 6 December 2000   Time taken: 45 minutes

Problem summary

I am currently working as a teacher in an EBD unit attached to a large secondary school. I only transferred into this position from my job as a PE teacher late last year, because there was a shortage of staff. The contract runs for another year. My headteacher and the head of the unit thought I would be excellent for the job – and indicated that, if it worked out, the job could be mine. In terms of salary it would represent a real promotion. I guess I was flattered and though I had some doubts I 'jumped in head first'. I have been becoming increasingly frustrated and depressed because I don't seem to be able to get across to all the pupils – one boy in particular (Stewart). When I was a PE teacher I never had any difficulties motivating or managing the kids. I enjoyed the reputation I had with staff and pupils and was seen as one of the 'better' teachers in the school ... Now I find I've started to shout at the pupils and I don't feel in control. I feel I've let the school down and sometimes I feel I don't even want to come here any more.

Brief notes on the main problem dimensions discussed

1 My main problem I guess is the feelings I have of failure and being out of my depth. I really miss my previous position as PE teacher.

*2 Related to this is my frustration at not being able to work effectively with some of the boys in the unit, especially Stewart who seems angry with the world. I have tried everything but nothing works. I now find myself blaming Stewart for my problems and would like him removed because I think then the unit would work better and I could get on with the 'real job of teaching'. I feel bad even thinking these things but find myself doing so more and more. I have even found myself avoiding him or being overly hard on him. Sometimes I have even tried the 'nice approach' hoping that if I am nice to him he will do the same back! Listening to myself this is really pathetic as it never works and I only feel even more frustrated and dishonest (a bit of a wimp really).

*3 I also feel really disappointed with the headteacher and head of the unit because they promised me so much and flattered me. But now that I'm in the job they are too busy to do much and I sense they are disappointed in me. I've had no training and am expected to just 'get on with it'.

4 I am concerned about what my colleagues are thinking of me. I had a great send-off in the PE department and everyone was really happy for me. Now I feel really embarrassed and a real failure.

*An * indicates the problem dimensions chosen for further analysis.*

Brief notes on problem dimension(s) chosen for discussion

Dimension 1   How to deal more effectively with a challenging adolescent

- Stewart is a 14-year-old and appears angry at the whole world.
- I have tried everything but nothing works (i.e. ignore or avoid, firm, nice).
- I now find myself blaming Stewart for my problems and would like him out.
- I think then the unit would be a happier place and I could then get on with teaching.
- I feel bad saying these things but find myself doing so more and more.
- I feel disappointed and a bit of a failure.

Dimension 2   How to obtain appropriate support and backup from senior management

- I feel angry and disappointed with the headteacher and head of the unit.
- But I have never told them how I feel.
- They promised me so much, flattered me just so I would help them out.
- Now that I'm in the job they are too busy to do much to help me.
- I sense they are disappointed in me.
- I've had no training and am expected just to 'get on with it'.

Possible actions resulting from discussions

Dimension 1   How to deal more effectively with a challenging adolescent

1 I realise I need to get some emotional distance between Stewart and myself so that I can gain some objectivity (detachment). I think you were right about 'whose needs were not being met' (need for a sense of competence, need to be liked). This made me think that I was behaving like a victim – to use your words. I guess I wanted everyone to think that I was the best EBD teacher there ever was. I really liked the attention I got when in the PE department. It is rather embarrassing to admit how much I have let Stewart get under my skin and how much my ego has got in the way (i.e. by not asking for or expecting assistance or being clearer about my role). This isn't helpful either to Stewart, the class or to me. I didn't even know that this was what I was doing until hearing myself talk to you today.

2 I will make an attempt to try and focus on the times when Stewart is OK and quietly let him know (we talked about a tally system on my watchstrap – I'll think about that one!). What really struck me talking with you was how inconsistent I have been with Stewart (and others), one minute being 'nice' (but not honest) and the next minute firm and shouting. I need to be a lot more honest and consistent with Stewart and the class in general – also, as you said, with other teachers and the senior management team – a good point.

3 I will think about your idea of interviewing Stewart (using the student report) so that I can get a clearer picture of how he is making sense of things and maybe gain some insight into how to motivate him – your idea of building on my strengths (i.e. sports is a good one and one I hadn't thought of). I guess I thought I had moved away from PE but can see how it could be used effectively

with these pupils (i.e. sense of achievement, working together, burning up energy and building on an area of personal strength and so on).

Dimension 2   How to obtain appropriate support and back-up from senior management

1 I need to organise a three-way meeting between myself, the head-teacher and head of the unit to take control of the situation and not act like a victim. I will update them on my work, tell them about the difficulties I am experiencing and explore with them some practical solutions which will assist me.

2 I liked your point that, before this meeting, I need to have thought about some concrete ideas myself. This is important so that the meeting isn't seen as me dumping problems onto them but rather using them to help me identify one or two practical things that they can do/organise, which should help me.

Action plan with completion and review dates

Dimension 1: How to deal more effectively with a challenging adolescent

1 Develop more objectivity by:
  a focusing more on times when Stewart is OK and acknowledge and rewarding this;
  b interview Stewart (using the student report);
  c using PE as a way to motivate and positively challenge the students.

I will start in the new term and review progress with you at our next coaching meeting 23 March 2001. I will ring if I get stuck.

Dimension 2: How to obtain appropriate support and back-up from senior management

1 Organise a three-way meeting with the headteacher and head of the unit.
2 Prepare for this meeting.

Before the end of this term I'll set a date for an early January meeting and spend some of the Christmas break sorting out the issues in my head and trying to focus on a few positive ways they could assist me (i.e. regular prep time, supervision, training, learning-support assistant).

Evaluation, comments and practice development opportunities

1 Through the coaching process I feel I was able to identify some of the issues which I was not acknowledging to myself (i.e. my need to be seen as the best EBD teacher in the world, my lack of consistency, some of my unmet needs). I guess I had allowed myself to be overwhelmed and as a consequence had lost my objectivity. It was hard for me to hear some of your reflections but I'm glad I stuck with it.

2 I have also become a lot more aware of the complex system I operate in and the different expectations placed on me by myself, headteacher, head of unit, other staff and pupils. In the end I feel clearer about what my needs are and what my role is.

3 While I'm in the EBD unit I now feel motivated to give it my best shot (with realism and support from senior management). I guess the biggest issue for me now is to really take stock and think about whether I want to carry on in the EBD unit at the end of the contract or return to teaching PE. This is a big decision and one which I would like to discuss at one of our coaching sessions nearer the time.

Influencing skills

Effective coaching not only involves a *reflective* component (where there is an opportunity to consider and evaluate past and present practice) but should also include a dimension of *challenge*. Constructive challenge and confrontation by a coaching partner may be required to enable a coachee to understand his/her particular part in the problem scenario and the extent to which some perspectives and attitudes may be contributing to (or maintaining) the problem situation (Monsen *et al.* 1998). Part of the task of the coach may be to create a disturbance in current thinking to allow a change of perception by the coachee to occur (Wagner 1995a, b).

If the new perspective is not to be resisted or rejected, it has to possess (as Wagner points out) 'a minimum level of congruence with the colleague's existing beliefs, perceptions or constructs'. This process may involve offering alternative interpretations of events from those taken by the coachee and encouraging new ways of perceiving the situation. Wagner has argued that if the coach can offer an interpretation that is viewed as 'insightful', the coachee's perception of the problem may change and this shift can encourage a search for strategies that can lead to longer term changes in the coachee's personal as well as professional effectiveness.

As Wagner (1995a, b) has noted, this process of acquiring insight has long been recognised across the field of theoretical and applied psychology and has been referred to in a variety of different ways including: a cognitive shift, a reframing of the problem, a reconstruction of the event, a new hypothesis or the employment of a new model. At an everyday level, it is a phenomenon which will be immediately recognisable to many people who find themselves helping to change the perspective of others. One example might be where a teacher attempts to persuade a parent to consider that their son, who constantly demands reassurance about the quality of his work, may require comments that enhance self-acceptance rather than admonishments to 'Just grow up!'.

In a coaching session, the use (or overuse) by the coachee of vague/general criticism, uncompromising statements or labels and stereotypes might invite some degree of challenge by the coach. Similarly, the emergence of self-defeating thought patterns or behaviour (suggesting the existence of unrealistic inner rules) may also require a gentle challenge, which may aid later reflection and insight. Ellis and Harper (1997) list seven major and frequently occurring irrational ideas or beliefs that relate to how individuals believe that they, others and the environment *should* or *must* be. The characteristics of irrational beliefs include:

- *demandingness* (i.e. everyone should/must like me);
- *overgeneralisation* (i.e. because one person dislikes me everyone does);
- *self-rating* (i.e. I'm not as good as them);
- *awfulising* (i.e. things can only get worse);
- *attribution errors* (i.e. because my colleague/ friend ignored me, I must have annoyed them);
- *anti-empirical* (i.e. my grandfather smoked 40 cigarettes a day and lived until 84);
- *repetition* (i.e. I must check my front door five times, as someday I could leave it unlocked).

Teachers are not immune from such beliefs. A number of them are listed in Pauline Fell's chapter on teacher emotions (Chapter 5 in this book).

Challenging the perspectives of coachees can provide them with opportunities to reconsider (or even change) their attributions, which may be hindering their personal and professional development. In particular, this process can help teachers to recognise that some of their behaviour may be less effective than originally perceived. Understanding this cause-and-effect relationship can enable coachees to take responsibility for their own feelings and perspectives without having to blame others. Helping colleagues to focus on self-defeating thought patterns, which led to ineffective behaviour, can be a powerful medium for change, as William James noted nearly a century ago: '*The greatest discovery of my generation is that human beings can alter their lives by altering their attitude of mind*'.

A successful coaching contract

As well as having a process framework that is both explicit and transparent, a number of other important variables in the coaching relationship need to be considered (Kearney 1994). It is important to recognise issues which are outside the competence (or professional comfort zone) of the coach: avoid the development of co-dependency; maintain confidentiality; discuss the appropriate level of self-disclosure; manage the expression of strong emotions; maintain the support-versus-challenge balance in coaching sessions; agree ownership of any notes taken during the coaching session, decide on the type of coaching arrangement (e.g. hierarchical versus peer and/or group) and the time commitment required.

As the coaching relationship evolves, it will be necessary to revisit some of the issues listed in the last paragraph. Therefore, a termly or yearly evaluation should be built in to the coaching process. Evaluation issues should include:

- feedback from consultee to coach on the benefits/drawbacks of the coach's style;
- a revision of the contract terms (using the issues list from the previous paragraph);
- a short feedback session on how coaching advice was used/adapted in practice;
- the implications of the above for the coach and coachee's practice development.

The technique of coaching, and the critical dialogue which underpins it, typically tend to have a personal (and often private) effect. Some thought may therefore need to be given to identifying demonstrable outcomes. First of all, the coachee may be encouraged to articulate subtle shifts that have taken place in his or her belief system. For example, a support worker, following coaching, might say '*I used to think that, if my professional advice was good enough, then colleagues and parents should take it on board and implement it; whereas now I tend to spend more time helping people to arrive at ways of managing their own problems*'. Such qualitative data is important since it can provide evidence of the impact of a coaching session on an individual.

At a more quantitative level, observable change can also be identified. For example, the support worker described above might be able to highlight the changes in practice which have accompanied his or her cognitive shift, by noting that more time is now spent building on the ideas of others, checking our organisational obstacles to change and getting colleagues or parent commitment to implement agreed action. Clearly, these are behaviours that can be measured.

The possibility for double-loop learning within coaching

Argyris and Schön (1974, 1996) investigated the ways in which people went about learning and solving problems within a wide range of groups, including teachers. They found that, within the normal world of work, most complex problems are routinely processed in a 'single-loop' way. Single-loop learning refers to the observation that most people strive to solve problems by trying to maintain the status quo and designing solutions that relate to existing and often problematic factors. In most cases, this process means that the underlying causes of problems (and our ways of thinking about them) remain unaltered and new actions can therefore be ineffective. Interestingly, most people are totally unaware that this is what they are doing.

Let us consider an example of a single-loop learning approach in a school situation: a school working group is set up to consider the increasing problem of disruptive and antisocial behaviour in the playground. The school uses untrained support staff to supervise play times. The working group is made up of teaching staff and spends considerable time reworking policy documents, focusing on improving the present system for managing support staff and by considering more effective sanctions for pupils who misbehave. There is no consideration of broader issues such as why untrained support staff are used for this activity, why younger and older children are mixed together or why playtimes do not involve more organised games.

Argyris and Schön (1974, 1996) stress that sometimes people need to move towards more double-loop learning processes in which intentions and practices are raised to an explicit and publicly accessible level. A double-loop learning approach to the playground management example might be for staff (including support assistants) to consider other possible mediating variables including the promotion of prosocial behaviour within the school, the availability of alternative play resources in the playground, the role models provided by staff and the use of trained peer mediators.

In summary, single-loop approaches aim to improve existing solutions to problems. These kinds of solutions tend to be ineffective. Staff core beliefs and practices are not challenged or raised to an explicit level. On the other hand, a double-loop learning approach aims to stand back and question the very basis for the design of the original set of solutions. This is achieved by clarifying what the problem is and what is it that people want to achieve (i.e. how to improve and effectively manage playground behaviour). As a result, staff beliefs about the problem and their subsequent practices are opened up to question and challenge. Within the coaching process opportunities for double-loop learning are actively encouraged. This is achieved by both the coach and the coachee engaging in a 'critical dialogue'.

The critical dialogue

Central to the coaching relationships is the fostering of trust, openness and opportunities for double-loop learning. To enable these dimensions to establish themselves, the coachee has to learn to view criticism as valuable and constructive feedback. To this end, we have found the process of *critical dialogue* helpful in encouraging the development of 'critical understanding' (Cameron and Monsen 1998; Monsen *et al.* 1998; Robinson 1993). Critical dialogue, as outlined by Robinson, is based upon the framework proposed by Argyris and Schön (1974, 1996). In its simplest form, this framework outlines three key principles which can be used to inform and enhance communications – increasing the availability of valid information for all; promoting free and informed choice within the dialogue; and enhancing commitment and responsibility for double-loop learning.

A coach who actively works with the coachee, to achieve a shared understanding of the problem, avoids many of the intended and unintended consequences which can follow if judgements (i.e. attributions and evaluations) are not checked out (Argyris 1982; 1993). Coaching sessions that are comprised largely of unilateral and unchecked assumptions and judgements are more likely to increase misunderstandings and defensiveness in both participants (Argyris, 1982, 1993). It is likely that involving the coachee will improve the overall understanding of the problem by both parties. Argyris suggests that, 'the best way to achieve this is to state our views in ways that allow them to be publicly tested and falsified. To do so, we must make our reasoning explicit, and organise it in such a way that it is testable.

Within this process of making one's thinking accessible to others, Argyris stresses the importance of both parties giving and receiving valid feedback on the accuracy and validity of their views and practices. In discussing feedback the importance of not only cognitive but also interpersonal processes is again stressed: 'feedback must have at least two features: it must contain valid information, and it must be communicated in a way that does not make the receiver defensive and hence unlikely to hear the information' (Argyris 1982). Critical dialogue is one way of enabling the coach and coachee to gain such feedback, and thus lead potentially to greater understanding and clarity about problems.

Robinson (1993) has summarised the process of critical dialogue as follows: being clear and saying what you think, making the reasoning and evidence base for your thoughts explicit and fully checking out any faulty premises (based on overgeneralisation, unsupported assumption or inappropriate attribution). Robinson also suggests that critical dialogue should as far as possible be focused on concrete events and evidence. Such a reality-based approach reduces discussion at the (more commonly observed) philosophical or abstract levels where the chances of resolving difficulties are low and there is a higher likelihood of emotional argument and heated debate.

Critical dialogue therefore aims to enhance communication by making thinking and reasoning as explicit and accessible as possible. The rationale underpinning this approach is that the coach and coachee require full and accurate information on which to base their resolution of a personal/ professional problem. The positive consequences for both coach and coachee are that the effectiveness of joint problem solving increases as a result of the greater availability of data, higher quality information, better management of emotionally sensitive and personal issues and a commitment to a personally-meaningful form of practice development which impacts directly on the tough and apparently intransigent problems with which teachers work.

Coaching and counselling

Counselling and coaching often appear to share common objectives. Counselling has been described as 'helping people to assume more responsibility for their own lives' (Nelson-Jones 1984), especially when they are 'involved in problem situations which they are not handling well' (Egan 1990), and wishing to become more effective at 'solving personal, social, emotional and decision problems' (Faupel 1990). In addition, there is the implicit assumption within both counselling and coaching processes that the counsellor/coach is working to improve the client's/coachee's understanding of their problem. In fact, in a survey of counsellors, the most frequently cited reason for undertaking counselling was to help 'the client's self-understanding and self-awareness', and for those who sought counselling it was 'the desire for greater understanding of feelings and behaviour' (Hansen *et al.* 1986). Clearly, as we have seen, some of the coaching aspirations and outcomes closely resemble those of counselling.

However, it is in the means for achieving such objectives that major differences begin to appear. In particular, the coaching framework is more detailed, the role of the coach is more directive, the focus of coaching is on work-related issues and the action plan is likely to be more structured than in the case of a counselling session. The relationship between coach and coachee also appears to be less hierarchical than in counselling encounters. In short, the coachee retains a high level of control over the content of the coaching session, the exploration of particular problem dimensions and any actions chosen.

Final comments

The focus of this chapter has been on the value of coaching as a systematic and effective way of supporting teachers and others who work with pupils with challenging behaviour. We have argued that coaching is more likely to achieve real changes in practice than one-off in-service training, staff meetings or less formal counselling. The ideas underpinning the coaching process draw heavily on recent developments in psychology, which also have a relevance to the development of organisations as well as the individuals who work within them.

Pearn Kandola (1995) and others refer to the growth and development of *learning organisations*. The major characteristics of these are that staff take on a shared responsibility for their own learning and for the learning of colleagues. Building on these concepts, Senge *et al.* (1994) point out that, to be truly proactive, staff need to understand *how they* contribute to their own problem situations rather than mistakenly focusing only upon external causes. By offering a framework which enables teachers to examine both the systemic and the personal variables involved in managing complex work-related problems, coaching encourages the growth of both insight and guided critical reflection and opens the way to more meaningful and ongoing personal and practice development.

Note: This chapter represents a substantial reworking of an earlier paper written for educational psychologists (Cameron and Monsen 1998). Permission has been obtained from the publishers to include elements of this paper in the current chapter.

References

Argyris, C. (1993) *Knowledge for Action: A Guide to Overcoming Barriers to Organisational Change*, San Francisco: Jossey-Bass.

Argyris, C. (1982) *Reasoning, Learning and Action*, San Francisco: Jossey-Bass.

Argyris, C. and Schön, D. A. (1996) *Organisational Learning II: Theory, Method, and Practice*, New York: Addison-Wiley.

Argyris, C. and Schön, D. A. (1974) *Theory in Practice*, San Francisco: Jossey-Bass.

Cameron, R. J. and Monsen, J. J. (1998) 'Coaching and critical dialogue in educational psychology practice', *Educational and Child Psychology* 15(4): 112–26.

Cameron, R. J. (1995) 'Management in educational psychology: The people factor', *Educational Psychology in Practice* (Special Issue: Management): 44–52.

Csikszentmihalyi, M. (1993) *The Evolving Self: A Psychology for the Third Millennium*. New York: Harper Collins.

Day, C. (1997) 'In-service teacher education in Europe: Conditions and themes for development in the 21st century', *British Journal of In-Service Education* 23(1): 39–54.

Egan, G. (1990) *The Skilled Helper: A Systematic Approach to Effective Helping*, 4th edn, Pacific Grove, CA: Brooks/Cole.

Ellis, A. and Harper, R. (1997) *A Guide to Rational Living*, 3rd edn, Hollywood: Melvin Powers Wiltshire Book Company.

Faupel, A. W. (1990) 'Does portage need counselling?', paper given at Portage National Conference, Yeovil, Somerset: National Portage Association.

Frensch, R. A. and Steinberg R. J. (1989) 'Expertise and intelligent thinking: When is it Worse to Know Better?', in R. J. Steinberg (ed.) *Advances in the Psychology of Human Intelligence*, Hillside, NJ: Erlbaum.

Graham, S., Wedman J. F. and Gawin-Kester B. (1994) 'Manager coaching skills: What makes a good coach?', *Performance Improvement Quarterly* 7(2) 81–94.

Hansen, J. C., Stevic, R. R. and Warner, R. W. (1986) *Counselling: Theory and Process*, 4th edn, Newton, MA: Allyn and Bacon.

Hawkins, P. Shohet, R. (2000) *Supervision in the Helping Professions*, 2nd edn, Buckingham: Open University Press.

Howe, B. (1993) 'Psychological skills and coaching', *Sports Science Review* 2(2): 30–47.

Kearney, D. (1994) *Coaching*, Yeovil, Somerset: Organisational and Personal Development Consultants.

Lichtenberg, J. W. (1997) 'Expertise in counselling psychology: A concept in search of support', *Educational Psychology Review* 9(3): 221–38.

Melrose (1994) *The Coach* (video pack and Trainer's guide), London: Melrose Learning Resources.

Millwater, J., Wilkinson, M. and Yarrow, A. (1996) 'Facilitating professional development through the study of supervision and institutional change', *British Journal of in-service Education* 22(1): 41–54.

Monsen, J., Graham, B., Frederickson, N. and Cameron, R. J. (1998) Problem analysis and professional training in educational psychology: An accountable model of practice, *Educational Psychology in Practice* 13(4): 234–49.

Nelson-Jones, R. (1984) *Personal Responsibility, Counselling and Therapy: An Inter-cognitive Approach*, London: Harper and Row.

Pedlar, M., Burgoyne, J. and Boydell, T. (1997) *The Learning Company; A Strategy for Sustainable Development*, London: McGraw-Hill.

Pearn Kandola (1995) *Tools for a Learning Organisation*, Oxford: Pearn Kandola.

Pomerantz, M. (1993) 'The value and purpose of supervision for educational psychologists', *Educational Psychology in Practice* (Special Edition: Supervision), 10(2): 31–4.

Reavis, C. A. (1976) 'Clinical supervision: A timely approach', *Educational Leadership* 33: 306–63.

Robinson, V. (1993) *Problem Based Methodology: Research for the Improvement of Practice*, Oxford: Pergamon Press.

Senge, P. M., Roberts, C., Ross, R. B., Smith, B. J. and Kleiner, A. (1994) *The Fifth Discipline Fieldbook*, London: Brealy.

Wagner, P. (1995a) *School Consultation: Frameworks for the Practising Educational Psychologists*, London: Kensington and Chelsea Educational Psychology Service.

Wagner, P. (1995b) 'A consultation approach to the educational psychologist's work in schools', *Educational and Child Psychology* 12(3): 22–28.

Wagner, A. C. (1987) 'Knots in teacher's thinking', in J. Calderhead (ed.) *Exploring Teachers Thinking*, London: Cassell.

Wright, A., Cameron, R. J., Gallagher, S. and Falkner, J. (1995) 'Plus ça change, plus ce n'est pas la même chose: Quality psychology in practice', *Educational Psychology in Practice* (Special Issue: Management), April: 6–15.

12 A systemic approach to emotional factors in dealing with behaviour difficulties

The Birmingham Framework for Intervention

Hugh Williams and Amanda Daniels

Introduction

High levels of emotion are often experienced by adults working with children with behaviour difficulties. All those who work with families will know that parents often show more emotional stress and disturbance than the 'problem child' – especially where the behaviour causing concern is perceived by others to be extreme 'naughtiness'. Society is understandably intolerant of what it considers to be bad behaviour in children, and people often look to blame parents and carers on the assumption that they are at fault. It is not surprising that diagnoses like Oppositional Defiance Disorder (ODD) and Attention Deficit Hyperactivity Disorder (ADHD) (American Psychiatric Association, 1994), which imply that the child's behaviour has a biological basis, tend to be very popular with parents. In many cases, they feel that the label reduces the level of blame that tends to be ascribed to them (Miller 1999).

A related phenomenon exists in classrooms. Whatever the level and quality of their training in this area, teachers are expected to be able to keep good order. When it breaks down, most teachers find it hard to attribute the cause to any lack of techniques or skills. For teachers already feeling under threat, there is a fear that such an 'admission' would be taken as a sign of professional incompetence. Again, it is more professionally acceptable to cite causes that relate to within-child problems (e.g. bad upbringing or medical or quasi-medical conditions). Miller (1996) has shown that these latter attributions are very common among teachers.

This leads to a problem for those developing policy in the field. Attributions such as these inevitably lead to a 'referrals culture', where children are passed on to the 'experts' with the assumption that they are the only people who can meet their needs. Non-expert action in schools is often seen by the staff as a 'hoop' that has to be gone through to get the 'real' help. In such a context, attempts to deal with any perceived underlying limitations in staff skills or knowledge can be highly contentious.

This chapter describes the Framework for Intervention project that has been operating across schools in Birmingham for the past few years. This is designed to help schools and teachers look at factors in schools and classrooms that can contribute to difficult pupil behaviour, without attributing blame to a group of professionals who feel increasingly criticised.

A systemic approach to dealing with emotions

The Framework for Intervention approach is primarily concerned with creating optimal environments for children in schools, and the use of environmental manipulation to target specific areas of concern. In this it would fall clearly into the category of 'systemic behavioural approaches' described by Miller (1996). However, it differs from the few examples that Miller gives which fall into this category (reality therapy, assertive discipline, decisive discipline) in that all the others focus directly on the behaviour of children. In fact, the Framework has more in common with general school improvement processes than with other more specific approaches to behaviour.

The Framework approach can best be put in context by an analysis of its relationship to the factors that influence behaviour (see Figure 12.1). Table 12.1 classifies a number of approaches according to the extent to which they concern themselves with various causalities and outcomes. Of particular note is the dual approach, within the Framework model, to the problem

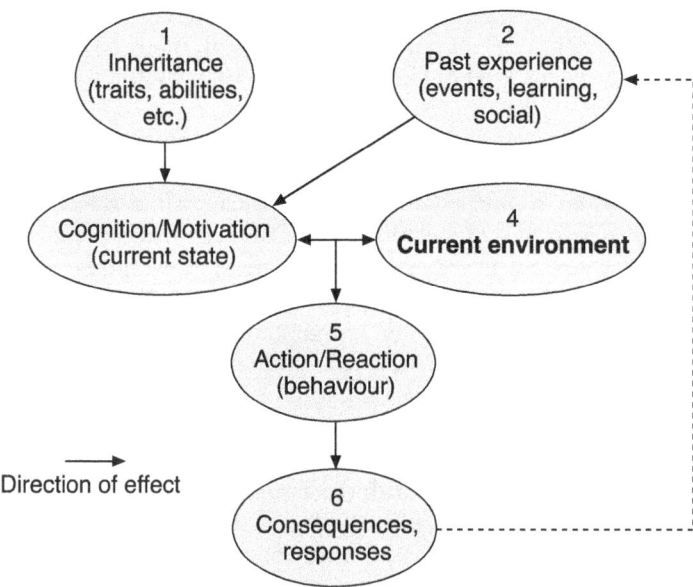

Figure 12.1 Causes of behaviour.

Table 12.1 Elements addressed in various approaches to behaviour difficulties

Intervention	Elements addressed (focus in italics)
Psychometrics	1. *Inheritance* 3. Cognition/Motivation (current internal 'state')
Psychodynamic approaches	2. *Past experience* 3. Cognition/Motivation (current internal 'state')
Behavioural approaches	4. Current environment (limited aspects) 5. *Action/Reaction* 6. *Consequences*
Cognitive therapy/Brief therapy	3. *Cognition/Motivation (current internal 'state')* 5. Action/reaction 6. Consequences
Personal construct psychology	2. Past experience 3. *Cognition/Motivation (current internal 'state')*
Environmental intervention (Framework Level 1)	Pupils: 4. *Current environment* 5. *Action/Reaction* 6. Consequences Teacher: 2. *Past experience* 3. Cognition/Motivation (current internal 'state') 4. *Current environment* 5. *Action/Reaction* 6. *Consequences*

raiser (the teacher) and the focus of the problem (the child). While there are elements of this in other problem-solving approaches (solution-focused brief therapy, in particular), we believe that this aspect makes the 'Framework approach' stand out from all others.

This aspect, we believe, is crucial to working with children exhibiting behaviour difficulties. Children are not the only 'actors' in schools and they are not the only ones who have needs. The perceptions of the children's behaviour by the adults will, themselves, be affected by the same factors as described in Figure 12.1. In short, the responses of adults to children are adult behaviour, affected by similar considerations of experience, logic and emotion. Any approach that does not take this into account is working, therefore, with only one-half of the potential sources of variation in any situation.

What does this mean to the people involved? In traditional systems for dealing with pupil behaviour, teachers are either expected to learn new skills and operate new techniques (Canter and Canter 1992) or resign themselves to the fact that the pupil behaviour is of such an order that only specialist provision (i.e. provision beyond their skills and knowledge) will meet the child's needs. Both approaches have failed to take into account the teacher's reality and to utilise their knowledge and skills.

Developing the Framework as a 'no-blame' environmental approach

In 1996, one of the authors was asked by Birmingham City Council Education Department to conduct a review ('New Outlooks') of all aspects of the local education authority's approach and provision for children with behaviour difficulties in school, and to propose a way forward. Such a review was of course not novel; illustrious predecessors had occurred since schooling began. Probably the best British example was the 'Elton Report' (DES 1989) which by 1996 was doubly notable for the general recognition of its great quality and almost complete lack of implementation.

The reason for the latter was plain to see. Elton had reported at a time before the effects of the Education Reform Act (ERA) of 1989 had started to take hold in English schools and many of its recommendations were based on a system in which LEAs still governed schools. In addition, the pace of change that followed ERA, particularly in school governance and the introduction of the National Curriculum, probably diverted attention from behaviour in schools in the earlier years of the 1990s.

This is not to say that there were no problems. Between 1992 and 1996 numbers of excluded pupils quintupled (Parsons *et. al.* 1996). This appeared to be linked in part to the development of greater self-governance in schools (which had gained a large measure of control over the exclusion process) and the increasing sense of competition between them (particularly following the introduction of academic league tables). There was some evidence too of a steep rise in the number of pupils put forward for statements of Special Educational Need (SEN) on the basis of emotional and behavioural difficulties (EBD), a condition first officially recognised in 1994 (DfE 1994).

Those involved in New Outlooks were not short of ready-made solutions for behaviour problems. The field offered a variety of whole-school and individual approaches to behaviour (e.g. Wheldall and Merrett 1984; Canter 1990, Cheeseman and Watts 1985). However, the rising numbers of exclusions and statements meant in practice that most attention centred on responses to children with significant behaviour problems rather than preventive measures. In 1997, when the government gave guidance to LEAs on writing their behaviour support plans (DfEE 1997), the examples of good practice contained eleven which were reactive, while six had some elements of prevention. None addressed more systemic issues.

Therefore, the New Outlooks team headed into largely uncharted territory when it decided that the first task would *not* be to devise new ways of 'pulling the bodies out of the water', but to seek a systemic way of reducing the numbers being thrown in.

The solution devised had a tight specification. It would need to be a system that all involved could understand and follow: schools, support agencies, parents and pupils. It would have to be practical and involve minimal bureaucracy. It would need to be credible to all and thus based on sound and tested approaches. Last, and most difficult, was the requirement that it would address problems from the earliest signs in the classrooms and corridors.

In the view of the review team (who all had practical and current experience of working in schools in behaviour problems) this last factor was crucial. Their experience suggested that teachers only referred problems (even within their schools) once the situation had become very difficult. There was a general expectation that they would try their own solutions first before contacting busy colleagues for help. This had the perverse effect that the 'niggling' problems (which teachers reported to Elton to be by far the most common, disruptive and demoralising type) had to become worse before help could be sought. This undoubtedly led to teachers feeling it necessary to emphasise or even exaggerate the problems they were experiencing.

Fortunately, the team had access to a recent and relatively successful model in the national Special Educational Needs Code of Practice (DfE 1994). This structured approach to dealing with SEN went much of the way to fulfilling the team's criteria:

- it was understood by most involved;
- it was not excessively bureaucratic (apart from the existing statementing process);
- it was based on existing good practice and it had achieved a measure of credibility;
- it had an initial stage that formalised the early work of class teachers.

The team wrote a general guidance document entitled *Behaviour in Schools: Framework for Intervention* (Ali *et al.* 1997). There were chapters drawing on the excellent information already available on whole-school factors, classroom management and relationships with parents and the wider community. But the core of the document concerned dealing with individual problems and had a structure that unashamedly drew on the Code.

The Framework for Intervention suggested three school-based stages (like the Code), but these were entitled 'levels' to avoid confusion. There were increasing degrees of intervention leading to a Level 3 which involved individual behaviour plans (IBPs), support from external agencies and services and close contact with parents.

But at Level 1 the focus was quite different. The pupil or pupils whose behaviour caused concern were the catalyst, and their improvement was the benchmark for progress, but the intervention centred on their *environment* rather than through individual programmes.

Classroom teachers (or any other staff in the school) were encouraged to tell the 'behaviour coordinator' (BeCo) (a role that the Framework encouraged schools to establish), as soon as they had any concern that 'normal' behavioural procedures were not dealing with a problem. Furthermore, schools were asked to make it clear to staff that '*Raising a concern shows strength, not weakness*'. (A poster with this wording has proved to be extremely popular with schools.)

The response to raising a concern was the use of the Behavioural Environment Checklist (BEC) (Ali *et al.* 1997). The checklist was a taxonomy of aspects of the whole-school and classroom environment that might affect behaviour. The list was devised by a multi-disciplinary team of professionals working with children in school in consultation with school staff, but was based on information that had already appeared in various 'behaviour packages' (e.g. Moss *et al.* 1997; Luton *et al.* 1991).

The 'concerned teacher' (or any other member of staff) would be asked to complete the checklist by the BeCo. They became the 'lead person' at Level 1 and, at a later meeting, would be helped by the BeCo to produce a 'behavioural environment plan'. The content of the plan could be related to any area of the checklist where the lead person had indicated there was room for improvement. A 'baseline' measure of the level of behaviour causing concern would be taken at this time.

The following example demonstrates the process up to this point:

Annette Jeavons teaches Class 5AJ at Grove Avenue JI School. In October, after utilising the regular behaviour system with the new class for over a month, she is concerned about two boys, Neil Johnson and Hardev Baines. She feels that they are taking far too long to settle down, that they disrupt the class through constant arguing and leaving their seats for spurious reasons, and while out of their seats interfere with others' possessions and distract them from work. It can take up to three-quarters of an hour on bad days to settle the class to Annette's satisfaction.

The school is a Framework for Intervention school and the poster in the staffroom reminds Annette that in this circumstance she should talk to Steve Watford, the school's BeCo. Steve gives her the Behavioural Environment Checklist to complete, and, although it is long, she finds it interesting to complete, with items like 'There is collective responsibility for behaviour management in the school' giving her considerable pause for thought.

She discusses several items with Steve where she feels there are problems. In the end, she focuses on 'Routines for movement around the school site are clear' and 'A pupil's good behaviour is "named" and reflected back' as being areas where she thinks there could be substantial improvement. Both these could be related to the problem behaviour. She constructs a plan with Steve's help to:

- work with colleagues to produce a better plan for the pupils to come back to the classroom after breaks;
- utilise 'fair pairs' – a system of reinforcing appropriate behaviour exhibited by others in a way specifically targeted to improve the behaviour of others.

(Williams 1990)

Once the Behavioural Environment Plan is formulated, Steve and Annette decide which particular behaviours are going to be counted as a baseline measure of the two boys' behaviour. They decide that Annette will note the number of occasions that they are out of their seats during two morning and two afternoon sessions. The baseline check is carried out before any plans are put into effect.

Annette automatically becomes the lead teacher on both tasks and sets up a meeting with two other class teachers to set up and carry out the 'return from break' plan. At the same time, she starts to implement the 'fair-pairs' system in class. Steve informs Jo Carter, the head teacher, of Annette's plans.

Thus a relatively simple early response is instituted with the class teacher taking the lead. At no time is there any suggestion of fault or blame – it is an entirely positive process. The object of the action is a small-scale example of school improvement carried out by a teacher who has been empowered by the process.

The plan and its execution are reviewed after about 6 weeks. There are two measures of success. The first is a repetition of the observations used at the baseline stage to determine what change there might have been in the target behaviours. In practice, however, the most important measure is any change in the teacher's view of the problem.

Piloting and implementation

A short trial of the basic processes of Framework for Intervention was carried out in 1997 with twenty schools taking part (Daniels 1997). In general, the results were good, especially in the shift in opinion among staff towards feelings of greater ownership of behaviour problems (this question has been examined more closely by Williams 2000). The process worked efficiently in schools, with supporting professionals (educational psychologists and behaviour support teachers) reporting that the system widened the range of solutions which could be discussed. Several examples of successful interventions were cited including within-class and playground strategies. Every school completing the trial reported favourably on the process.

Since 1998, the Framework has been introduced to over 200 schools in Birmingham across the whole age range. Behaviour coordinators in each of the schools attend a 5-day training programme carried out over three terms. This training introduces them to the basic structure and tasks involved in supporting staff at the different levels. In addition, they receive a small amount of training on traditional methods for working with children with behavioural difficulties.

However, most of the course is taken up with methods for developing the process in their schools through training, meetings and linking in with the school development plan; and on methods for working with individual members of staff to reduce their anxieties, elicit their true concerns and to convert the feelings and ideas presented by their colleagues into workable plans. A core construct of this area is the notion of 'ARC' (acceptance, respect and change). The terms here have a somewhat specialist meaning:

- *Acceptance*: that all people (children included, of course) start from where they are – there is no point in thinking that they should have a completely different pattern of behaviour or thought, just because they 'ought' to!
- *Respect*: that people do what they do for a reason. It may not make sense to others, but it almost certainly makes sense (maybe unconsciously) to them. What's more, however, they are judged by others, few people consciously see their own behaviour as wrong.
- *Change*: despite all the factors above, people can and do change even in the most unlikely circumstances. Never give up hope.

Readers may note how similar these components might be to a course on counselling; indeed, much of the training material comes or is adapted from such courses.

The techniques included in the training depended on a judgement of their compatibility with the principles of the Framework. Given the emphasis on 'no blame' and 'empowerment' it should be no surprise that solution-focussed methodologies (De Shazer 1985) have provided a sub-stantial component.

Relationship of training to management theory

A rather more curious influence on training are the works of the American statistician, W. Edwards Deming, who was credited with being the adviser who lifted Japanese industry from the ruins of the Second World War to its recent strength. Deming's work in the field of management (Deming 1982, 1994), especially with regard to employees, provided a strong basis for advice to behaviour coordinators on the introduction of the Framework into the school, and how to incorporate it into the personnel-management processes of the school.

In many ways the message is revolutionary. There is, of course, a need for central planning in the management procedures of schools and there will always be 'do it this way' edicts coming from head teachers or committees set up for the purpose. In fact, schools have to have policies covering many areas, behaviour being one. 'Framework thinking' would agree that this is essential for setting up the procedures of schools, and necessary to avoid anarchy. However, it is in the field of evaluation, maintenance and repair that the Framework, influenced by Deming, states that those at the 'work face' know their jobs best, know what the problems are and, most importantly, can usually offer the best solutions (though they may need help and techniques to formulate them). Therefore, in this crucial area of maintenance and troubleshooting, the contribution of staff should be seminal. We do not just empower because we think that it is a good thing to do. The main reason for doing it is that it is the crux of the most effective school improvement – and therefore best for the pupils.

Thus the training moves from 'how to complete a behavioural environ-ment plan' to fundamental discussion of the basis of good management of schools. (For a more detailed discussion of the theoretical foundations of Framework for Intervention see Williams and Daniels 2000.)

The results of the work on Framework suggest that there is change which reflects this core component (Daniels 1997; Cole 2000), though there is undoubtedly some way to go in fully establishing this view in Framework schools (Williams 2000).

A whole-school approach to empowerment for all?

It is clear that traditional approaches to behaviour concerns may well contribute to a sense of inadequacy and powerlessness among teachers at the chalkface (e.g. Lovey 1992). It hardly needs stating that the degree to which teachers feel able to handle behaviour in class, and indeed their perceptions of that behaviour, will be affected by their emotional state including their professional self-image. Since, as we have seen, behaviour in classrooms is always a very emotive issue (DES 1989) the very schemes presented to reduce behaviour difficulties may well contribute to future behavioural problems by undermining the teacher's sense of being in control.

Whether Framework for Intervention can change this process by its focus on empowerment, and thus improve the emotional state of teachers experiencing difficulties, remains to be proved. The evidence so far points that way, but there are still concerns about the extent to which schools have incorporated the approach into their core constructs. After all, there is likely to be little effect if the highly respectful Framework message of empower-ment is undermined by teachers' experience of continuing daily top-down and deskilling events.

The answer to this problem could come from the seemingly universal applicability of the first principle of the Framework – first deal with the environment. In the current educational context of increasing self-govern-ance of schools, head teachers cannot be forced to change the personnel ethos of their schools. However, national and local policies could be adapted to provide an environment where the 'no blame', 'problem-solving' and 'empowering' approaches to school management are fostered – rather than undermined, as seems often to be the case at present.

We believe that the benefits of this would extend far beyond better approaches to behaviour problems. In some ways, the argument comes full circle at this point as the influences of Deming come once again to the fore. Schools managed on a Deming/Framework basis may well be more productive institutions; there is good reason to believe that all measures of school effectiveness would benefit (see Mt Edgcumbe School 2000 and Holt 2000). The implicit recognition of emotional and 'self-image' needs of the teachers, and the focus on effective and responsive environments at every level, should also lead to happier and more fulfilled staff groups.

There is no doubt that a small start has been made through the Framework, and that, with incorporation of the same principles from policy level to classroom operations, the final goal of empowering pupils through the same processes may be possible in the foreseeable future.

References

Ali, D., Best, C., Bonathan, M., Bower, D., Cardwell, A., Craik, N., Daniels, A., Dooner, J., Holland, M., Holmes, W., Kingsley, A., Lake, D., McLauchlin, A., Martin, N., Peatfield, C., Snowden, W., Vickery, L. and Williams, H. (1997) *Behaviour in Schools: A Framework for Intervention*, Birmingham Education Department.

American Psychiatric Association. (1994) *Diagnostic and Statistical Manual of Mental Disorders*, 4th edn, (DSM IV), Washington: APA.

Canter, L. and Canter, M. (1992) *Assertive Discipline*, Santa Monica, CA: Canter and Associates.

Canter, L. (1990) 'Assertive discipline', in M. Scherer, I. Gersch, and L. Fry, (eds) *Meeting Disruptive Behaviour*, London: Macmillan.

Cheeseman P. L. and Watts, P. E. (1985) *Positive Behaviour Management*, London: Croom Helm.

Cole, T. (2000) *Evaluation of Framework for Intervention*, unpublished report, University of Birmingham.

Daniels, A. (1997) *Framework for Intervention Trial Scheme: Final Report*, Birmingham: New Outlooks, Birmingham City Council.

De Shazer, S. (1985) *Keys to Solutions in Brief Therapy*, New York: W. W. Norton & Co.

Deming, W. E. (1982) *Out of the Crisis*, Cambridge, MA: MIT Press.

Deming, W. E. (1994) *The New Economics for Industry, Government, Education*, Cambridge, MA: MIT Press.

DES (Department for Education and Science and the Welsh Office) (1989) *Discipline in Schools: Report of the Committee of Enquiry chaired by Lord Elton*, London: HMSO.

DfE (Department for Education) (1994) *The Code of Practice for the Assessment and Identification of Special Educational Needs*, London: HMSO.

DfEE (Department for Education and Employment). (1997) *Guidance on the Writing of behaviour support plans*. London: HMSO.

Holt, M. (2000) 'The concept of quality in education', in C. Hoy, C. Bayne-Jardine and M. Wood, (eds) *Improving Quality in Education*, London: Falmer Press.

Lovey, J. (1992) *Treating Troubled and Troublesome Adolescents*, London: David Fulton.

Luton, K., Booth, G., Leadbetter, J., Tee, G. and Wallace, F. (1991) *Positive Strategies for Behaviour Management*. Windsor: NFER Nelson.

Miller, A. (1996) *Pupil Behaviour and Teacher Culture*, Cassell: London.

Miller, A. (1999) 'Squaring the triangle: Pupil behaviour, teachers and parents and psychology', *Educational Psychology in Practice* 15: 75–9.

Moss, G., Came, F. and Webster, A. (1997) *Behaviour Education*, Bristol: Avec Designs.

Mount Edgecumbe School (2000) Online at: www.mehs.educ.state.ak.us Alaska, USA.

Parsons, C., Castle, F., Howlett, K. and Worrall, J. (1996) *Exclusion from School: The Public Cost*, London: Campaign for Racial Equality.

Wheldall, K. and Merrett, F. (1984) *Positive Teaching: The Behavioural Approach*, London: Allen and Unwin.

Williams, G. (2000) An evaluation of the Birmingham Framework for Intervention Programme in terms of attribution, unpublished dissertation, University of Birmingham.

Williams, H. (1990) *Fair Pairs: They Know What I Like*, Birmingham: Birmingham City Council Psychological Service.

Williams, H. and Daniels, A. (2000) 'Framework for Intervention Part II: The road to total quality behaviour?', *Educational Psychology in Practice* 15(4): 228–36.

Part V
Provision issues

13 Policy and provision for behaviour
The challenges of an emotive area

Peter Gray

Introduction

Most of the chapters in this book have concentrated on the emotions experienced by pupils presenting behavioural difficulties and those who are in daily contact with them. However, emotions have a bearing too at the policy level. Those in a policy-making role, whether they be managers in schools, local authority officers, civil servants, local or national politicians, can feel under considerable pressure to find a 'robust response' to problems experienced at the chalkface. English teaching unions, which have lost influence over some of the broader areas of educational policy, have increasingly focused their energies on concerns about teaching conditions, and, in particular, the effects of difficult pupil behaviour on teacher stress. The issue of pupil behaviour has also acquired a more significant political status, with major media interest and the two major UK political parties battling it out to prove that they are the most able to maintain or restore proper standards of behaviour in schools.

In this context, policy-makers themselves are drawn to some 'unhelpful beliefs', such as 'there must be an answer to this problem that (a) satisfies everybody and (b) has minimal additional financial cost (as long as we look hard enough)' or 'it is possible to achieve this without any impact on other policy areas we hold dear'. Inevitably, such beliefs lead to rather simplistic solutions. A current example is the emphasis on early intervention at the preschool and primary stage. There is evidence (e.g. from the High Scope Project in the USA) that focused early inputs can prevent the need for costly services at a later stage. However, there are a number of factors that mean problems will still occur (e.g. life experiences, family crises, adolescence pressures, influence of secondary-school pressures and demands). Services for young people, schools and families at this stage still need to be provided and early intervention, despite its impact, is no substitute for them.

In an earlier paper (Gray 1997), I outlined some features of the area of policy and provision for pupils with emotional and behavioural difficulties that present particular challenges to policy-makers. A particular issue is that politicians and officers (and, at a more local level, managers in schools) tend to be presented with partial information, both in the sense that is incomplete and also that it is subjective and thematic. The context is usually emotive and pressure based. It can be difficult to get beyond descriptions and formulations that are anecdotal or linked to personal prejudice.

As a consequence, national and local policy in the area of emotional and behavioural difficulties is characterised by inconsistency, with a range of underlying tensions typically being addressed by a series of short-term pragmatic 'solutions', rather than being adequately addressed and resolved. In this chapter, some of these underlying tensions will be considered in detail and examples given of policy inconsistencies (for further details, see Gray and Noakes 1998). Reference will then be made to two 'solutions' currently favoured: the use of projects and the expansion (and regulation) of off-site provision. It will be argued that these are an inadequate alternative to addressing more fundamental issues relating to the true value accorded to social and educational inclusion. A number of elements are then identified that are more likely to ensure progress towards a more coherent framework for developing effective behaviour-support provision.

Underlying tensions

Individual pupils'/parents' versus teachers' rights

Over the last 20 years, in line with international trends, there has been an increasing focus on children's rights. In this country, there have been particular issues around the need for better procedures for child protection, arising from some notable cases of significant abuse. The emphasis has been on proper planning for children at risk, both in terms of their care and education, as opposed to crisis responses that are reactive and ill considered. It is not enough to respond to the needs of adults; the key issue has to be what is in the best interests of the child.

With regard to behaviour difficulties in schools, there has been increasing awareness of the rights of minority groups and concerns about how far these are adequately addressed. For example, there has been evidence over time (e.g. Osler 1997) that boys of African–Caribbean origin and those of mixed heritage are excluded at a higher rate than pupils from other ethnic groups. This concern has extended to pupils from other vulnerable groups (e.g. those in public care and those with statements of need). On a different level, the inclusion of emotional and behavioural difficulties within the broader definition of special educational needs has led to recognition of their rights of access, wherever possible, to a mainstream education and to properly planned individual educational programmes (IEPs).

At the same time, there has been an increasing recognition of the rights of parents. This has been partly linked to the growth of consumerism and partly to greater awareness of the key role played by parents in the development of their children. The rights of parents, since the Children

Act (1993), continue to be recognised even when a child enters the public care system. For children with emotional or behavioural difficulties, legislation on both pupil exclusions and special educational needs has significantly increased parental rights to a proper consideration of their child's circumstances.

Many teachers would argue that, during this same period, there has been a significant increase in their range of responsibilities, not just for implementing curricular and other educational innovations, but also in terms of the requirement to address pupil issues (such as risk and vulnerability) and to have reference to expected procedures. Over the last few years, in particular, as pressures on teachers have mounted (and, some would say, in the absence of appropriate recognition of their efforts), there has been an increasing trend towards the assertion of *teacher* rights. A particular focus has been on the demands placed on them by pupils who are challenging in the classroom.

There are examples of this trend on a number of fronts: first, schools have actively espoused approaches to managing pupil behaviour such as assertive discipline (Canter and Canter 1992), which include a strong message about the teacher's right to teach (and other pupils' right to learn). Second, teaching unions have fought hard to retain the power to exclude (and to change the balance between their rights and those of the individual pupils they find troublesome). Third, schools have pushed for legislation that outlines the responsibilities (as well as rights) of parents, which has led to the requirement in England for parents to sign home–school contracts.

Reconciling the increasing tension between the rights of individual pupils and their parents, on the one hand, and those of teachers (and other pupils), on the other, is a major issue for policy-makers and managers. There are plenty of examples of where this has gone badly wrong. For example, in some notable cases, teacher unions have advocated their members' 'right' to choose not to teach a pupil who is legally entitled to access his/her current school. The tension has been particularly acute where governors (or appeals panels) have gone against head teachers' decisions to permanently exclude. In many such cases, teachers have argued that they have had to put up with unacceptable behaviour from the pupil over a significant period of time. While it is reasonable to expect limits on what teachers should have to endure, schools should also be expected to work conscientiously and professionally to try and overcome problems, making positive use of external support where appropriate (see Gray and Panter 2000). Unresolved problems are not good for teachers; however, research shows that they are also bad for pupils, their parents and for society at large.

Punishment versus welfare

The dominant tradition in Britain, at least since the Second World War, has been that children and young people presenting difficult behaviour need welfare rather than punishment. While a range of sanctions have been applied in school settings, this has not extended to any broader notions of children having criminal responsibility (see Gerv Leyden's Chapter 2 in this book for a comparative view). However, policy-makers and managers are under continuing pressure to differentiate those young people who are intentionally disruptive from those who are not in control of their own actions (because of home circumstances, lack of skill or emotional 'disturbance'). At school level, there are often dilemmas about whether the appropriate response is support or discipline, as well as ongoing practical issues about how far these can meaningfully be separated (see Gray 1998).

There is an increasing trend towards more punitive measures, fuelled by media coverage and strong public reaction to events such as the murder of the 2-year-old, Jamie Bulger, by two 10-year-old boys, and by police concern about young serial offenders. Measures introduced by central government over the last few years include curfews imposed in certain areas for young people below a certain age, as well as the creation of detention centres for younger offenders. These tend to be introduced with little research evidence of their effectiveness, and again reflect a political drive for 'something to be done' rather than a coherent strategy.

In schools, there has been increased use of exclusions, with numbers of permanent exclusions rising fivefold during the 1990s. This rise has occurred in special schools as well as mainstream. There has been increased use of unit provision, both within mainstream schools and off-site. However, it is not always clear how far this is seen as a punitive or supportive measure.

Policy-makers and managers continually have to balance competing demands: that young people who break established rules should be seen to be punished (and not 'get away with it'), against the need for more positive and humane responses which have more chance of achieving effective and lasting change. At a national level, this is exemplified by the inconsistency in the government's stance on exclusions: on the one hand, an emphasis on the need for access to mainstream schools for pupils with emotional and behavioural difficulties (in line with other groups of children with special educational needs), with properly planned programmes of intervention; on the other, the philosophy of 'two strikes and you're out' and the right to exclude pupils who are 'persistently disruptive', with no qualification in terms of the nature of the school's response.

Standards for the majority or excellence for all

The government's Green Paper *Excellence for All Children* (1997) emphasised the need for high expectations and greater rights of access for pupils with special educational needs, including those with emotional and behavioural difficulties. However, there has been some reticence about setting achievement targets for vulnerable groups in the same way as they have been set for 'the majority'. Targets have been set for reducing the number of permanent exclusions in England and Wales. However, these have been set for *local education authorities* (LEAs), which now have no direct control over schools' use of this sanction. In addition, there is an acceptance that permanent exclusions will still need to be used (as opposed to the national expectation that overall educational achievement will continue to rise).

The government's 'orthodoxy' is that good schools are ones that get good academic results as well as meeting the needs of their more vulnerable pupils. However, in practice, there are widespread concerns that the more limited agenda for increasing 'standards' for the majority (the '80%' defined in government documents) is being achieved in many schools at the expense of attention to (and tolerance for) pupils who present particular challenges.

For politicians, however, such a minority is not necessarily vocal; meeting the needs of the majority may be enough to satisfy the electorate's concerns about educational standards in schools and the need for enhanced skill levels for British citizens in a competitive economic climate. There are, of course, a range of lobby groups advocating the needs of particular disability groups, but these do not typically cover the range of the significant majority of pupils whose behaviour difficulties are linked to their social and economic conditions. The extent to which policy-makers and managers include these within their concerns is partly a product of the problems they cause and the degree to which they are committed to trying to achieve a fairer and more socially inclusive society.

Social inclusion has been given a high official priority within recent government initiatives, with a series of statements being made about the costs of marginalisation to the individuals concerned and to society at large. However, there is a sense in which such initiatives are being 'bolted on' to the general thrust of legislation which, some would argue, has done little to redress the balance of inequality that exists between those with adequate financial and personal resources and those who struggle on a daily basis to survive and make ends meet.

It is interesting to note the reaction of a teachers' union leader, reported at the time of the release in 1997 of the government Green Paper referred to above. He was quoted in *The Times Educational Supplement* as saying '... ministers were living in "cloud cuckoo land" if they believed more emotionally disturbed children could be integrated into mainstream class-rooms ... thousands of children had already had their education disrupted by pupils with emotional and behavioural problems ... and thousands of teachers had been driven into early retirement or ill health ... union members might be pulled out on strike as a last resort if the new influx made lessons impossible ...'.

The tenor of this reaction was emotive and unsupported by evidence: there are only small numbers of pupils in special schools for emotional and behavioural difficulties and the government has never implied that they would be reintegrated overnight. However, the quote goes on to reflect teachers' more general concerns about some of the tensions between inclusion and the government's standards agenda – 'To expect teachers to teach them (pupils with EBD) and the other children in the class *and* meet the government's targets to raise standards is living in cloud cuckoo land'.

The fundamental issue here is clearly the definition of standards and how inclusively these are framed. The tension is greater where there is an implication that standards are for some pupils, not all, or where the definition relates to narrower interpretations of desirable learning outcomes (and is limited to more traditional and normative measures of academic performance).

Competition or corporate responsibility

Margaret Thatcher's comment, 'There is no such thing as society', has come to represent the 'cult of the individual', which has been seen to be at the heart of the previous Tory government's policy. Within the field of education, a number of government reforms (particularly the 1988 Education Act in England and Wales) set out to increase the degree of autonomy held by individual schools and to promote a culture where they saw themselves as self-managing enterprises. The Conservatives continue, in opposition, to characterise local authorities as inhibiting forces that impose unnecessary political and administrative shackles on school development (see May 2000). They argue that educational standards are best improved by schools (and pupils) competing to achieve excellence.

The application of the 'free market' model to education has tended to give minimal attention to the effects of competition and selection on those schools and pupils that have less capacity for 'choice'. We have already experienced the effects of open enrolment on some schools that have found it increasingly hard to climb out of a negative downward spiral, as parents opt to send their children elsewhere. For many of these, the path has ultimately been towards closure, which only serves to move difficult problems on elsewhere.

In the area of emotional and behavioural difficulties specifically, the free-market model has encouraged schools in England to exclude. In response, local authorities have endeavoured to support parents in finding new schools for their children, only to find an increasing level of resistance towards admission. In the absence of significant additional finance, they have struggled to make satisfactory provision for the numbers of pupils concerned, and, in some urban areas, officers have felt that they are trying to push back a rising tide. It is hardly surprising therefore that surveys, such as those carried out by the Audit Commission (e.g. *Missing Out*, 1999) have found an increasing number of pupils out of school with unacceptably low levels of provision.

Over the last few years, there has been more willingness among some schools to work together, and, in collaboration with their local authority, to try and address the problem. This has been partly assisted by the government's expectation of reduced numbers of exclusions (and associated additional finance) and partly by schools' own frustrations with the 'exclusions carousel' (where problems have been moved around schools without proper assessment or planning for successful admission). In addition, there has been less divisiveness and more cooperation between schools as a result of the government's move away from encouraging schools to adopt grant-maintained status.

The legacy of the competitive model, however, is still strong and there is only weak encouragement for schools to collaborate and work together. Much of the incentive to do so comes from local authorities (although there are also examples of school-led initiatives: Evans *et al.* 1999). And yet, the future of such organisations, in England at least, remains uncertain. As will be seen in the next section, the issue of provision for pupils with emotional and behavioural difficulties can only be properly addressed if people do work together to solve problems, rather than passing on responsibility elsewhere.

'Pragmatic solutions': the call for pupil referral units

Off-site units for 'disruptive pupils' have existed for some time. They appear to have been first introduced in England in the late 1970s by the Inner London Education Authority as a result of increasing concern within mainstream schools about challenging pupil behaviour. Some authors associate this concern with broader dissatisfactions among the teaching profession at that time, and also, more specifically, with the ways in which some schools managed the abolition of corporal punishment.

Successive reviews by HMI (Her Majesty's Inspectorate) of both off-site provision and day special schools for pupils with emotional and behavioural difficulties raised issues about the breadth of curriculum provided and the lack of access to positive peer models (e.g. HMI 1989). Continuing concerns led to greater regulation of off-site provision (1993 Education Act), with a new designation of pupil referral unit (PRU). Pupils attending such a provision were given the same curriculum entitlements as pupils in schools, and PRUs became subject to Ofsted inspection. The first round of Ofsted inspections led to renewed concerns about provision quality (Ofsted 1995), with significant criticisms about levels of academic expectation, planning for reintegration and the mix of pupils attending.

Since then, Ofsted has reported an overall improvement in standards in PRUs inspected (Ofsted 2001a), particularly with regard to academic expectations and pupil attendance. However, levels of reintegration from PRUs to mainstream schools remain relatively low. There remains a continuing issue about the extent of provision made for pupils out of school following permanent exclusion, although the government has set targets for LEAs to make full-time provision for all such pupils by 2002.

Table 13.1 The economics of off-site provision – annual cost of off-site provision to mainstream schools (based on an area with seven secondary schools + feeders)

	Cost to each school in the area		
	School with 120 pupils on roll (£)	School with 300 pupils on roll (£)	School with 1,000 pupils on roll (£)
10-place PRU	950	2,376	7,920
20-place PRU	1,900	4,752	15,840
50-place PRU	4,751	11,877	39,590

The two main political parties seem to be convinced that PRUs are a significant way forward for pupils with behavioural difficulties, provided they are well managed and orientated towards high academic achievement (rather than alternative schooling or therapeutic education). In a flurry of correspondence to *The Times Educational Supplement* about the exclusions issue, Labour ministers pointed to the growth in numbers of PRUs since the last election and the numbers of pupils attending them (see Smith 2000). The Tory shadow spokesperson (May 2000) highlighted the Opposition's commitment to 'specialist high-quality progress centres' (which appear to vary little from PRUs, as currently defined[1]). The *TES* leader at the time concluded, 'As many young people will continue to invite exclusion, it is evident that more – and better – pupil referral units need to be established' (*TES*, 4 August 2000).

Interestingly, the increase in numbers of PRU/off-site unit places is typically presented as a 'no-cost solution'. As such, it is an attractive one, to teacher unions, the media and to politicians. However, 'specialist high-quality centres' inevitably do have a cost and this needs to be properly understood by all relevant stakeholders in order to judge 'value for money'. The best way to illustrate this is by looking at the potential costs to mainstream schools of setting up new off-site provision, set against the probability of schools accessing places.

The figures in Tables 13.1 and 13.2 are calculated on the basis of an overall cost per pupil of £10,000 (which takes into account staffing, materials, buildings and pupil travel). Table 13.1 also assumes that costs are spread evenly across schools, taking pupil numbers only into account.

It can be seen that the costs of a small PRU to a small mainstream school (e.g. a village primary) would be relatively low. However, costs for a larger

1 The only difference here seems to be the Labour government's aspiration for unit provision to be more school based, as reflected in the recent commitment to establish 'learning support units' in targeted mainstream secondary schools, with Excellence in Cities project funding.

Table 13.2 The economics of off-site provision – availability of provision (rate of pupil access)*

	Availability to each school in the area		
	School with 120 pupils on roll availability	*School with 300 pupils on roll availability*	*School with 1,000 pupils on roll availability*
10-place PRU	1 per 11 years	1 per 4 years	1 per year
20-place PRU	1 per 5 years	1 per 2 years	2 per year
50-place PRU	1 per 2 years	1 per year	4 per year

* Based on an assumption of 100% turnover of pupils each year (i.e. places being available for 1 year only).

establishment to a large school (e.g. a typical secondary) would be more substantial.

Many schools looking at these figures might say such costs would be a small price to pay for provision being available when needed. However, Table 13.2 shows how little access some schools would actually gain (figures are based on schools getting a 'proportionate share' of provision; clearly some schools might gain more if provision was targeted to greatest need across the area).

Access would be low even for large schools if there were less than 100% pupil turnover each year. The evidence from Ofsted and various other studies (e.g. Topping 1983) indicates that reintegration is rarely achieved for more than 25% of pupils. Access is clearly enhanced if pupils attend PRUs only on a part-time basis, but this implies that mainstream schools would, in most cases, be expected to provide for a significant amount of the pupil's timetable.

A number of PRU staff would argue that reintegration rates would be higher if pupils placed in this form of provision had less complex needs. The implication here is that a number of pupils currently attending PRUs are wrongly placed and need to be elsewhere (e.g. in day or residential special schools). Costs per place for this kind of special school provision are typically more expensive than PRUs. This kind of adjustment would therefore involve greater expenditure than the budget currently available in most LEAs. Finally, without additional finance, access to PRU provision (as a preventive resource) is likely to become even more limited, if one adds in the new requirement on LEAs to provide full-time education for excluded pupils who are out of school for longer than 15 days.

So, PRUs are by no means the answer. Unless mainstream schools are able to work with such provision in more imaginative and effective ways, it will always be a very restricted resource. Large increases to education budgets would, of course, allow more off-site places and more access. However, most mainstream schools, when given choice about how to spend, say, £10,000 extra money, would tend to want to use this to supplement their own internal provision.

Schools and LEAs in England have been sheltered from some of the real costs of alternative provision by the availability of project funds. The nearest that schools have got to financing off-site provision themselves has been the use of 'fines' for exclusion.[2] There are varying views on the effectiveness of this particular policy. However, interestingly the Conservative Opposition has proposed the abolition of such financial 'penalties' (May 2000). It is difficult to see, in the absence of such funds, how the necessary new finance would be available to fund the further expansion of off-site provision that they propose.

The problem with projects

A massive amount of new project funding has come into the area of social inclusion over recent years. Funding has been targeted at particular geographical areas with higher levels of deprivation (e.g. Single Regeneration Budget, Education Action Zones, Excellence in Cities) or at achieving particular outcomes (e.g. reducing exclusions or levels of youth offending). In many ways additional funding has been welcome. However, as a strategy for achieving sustainable and generalisable change, project funding has created as many problems as it has solved.

The key problems with this strategy is summarised in the next four subsections.

(a) Sustainability

Project funding is typically short term. The expectation is generally that, if initiatives have been successful, they will be adopted by schools or authorities and funded by them. However, even where there is evidence of success, budgets do not always allow allocation of additional long-term funds, and the lessons and achievements of projects can be wasted. A more conservative approach, assuming no continuation of funding, leads to initiatives that seek to use resources already available in more effective ways. However, where projects are evaluated on short-term pupil outcomes, the temptation is always to create additional provision, in the hope that someone somewhere will provide in future. In some cases, project-funding

2 Following the 1993 Act, LEAs in England and Wales were allowed to deduct from schools' budgets the remaining proportion of the funding linked to the pupil for the financial year (the age-weighted pupil unit). This was relatively insubstantial. In 1999, secondary schools received significant amounts of devolved funding for social inclusion (pupil retention grant). In most LEA schemes, it is now possible to deduct more substantial amounts when pupils are permanently excluded and need to be placed elsewhere.

timelines are extended and this can offer a breathing space, but this does not address the issue of sustainability in the longer term.

An example here is the use of project funds by secondary schools to create on-site units (funds have been derived from a number of sources, such as Pupil Retention Grant and Excellence in Cities (learning support units) initiatives). Whether or not such projects are successful in helping reduce permanent exclusions, there is a key issue about the stability of funding. Most secondary schools with such facilities would argue that their maintenance is totally dependent on the continuation of additional funding. If the funding is removed (and schools/authorities cannot find the funds themselves), what is the likelihood of any long-term change in practice – or the trend of reduced exclusions – being maintained?

Interestingly, the recent summary of Ofsted's first six inspections of Education Action Zones commented that, although there was evidence of improvement on the dimensions targeted, only two of the zones had given sufficient thought to sustainability of programmes beyond their lifetime (Ofsted 2001b)

(b) Generalisability

Few projects involve similar amounts of money being allocated to all schools. More typically, individual schools or authorities are targeted, on the basis of assessed need or perceived capacity to deliver. In deciding where funds should go, there are clearly issues of equality of opportunity, and equitability is not always apparent in funding distribution approaches. However, a more fundamental issue is whether it is possible for organisations with similar needs and issues to learn from those that receive additional project funds.

Again, on-site unit projects provide a good example. Secondary schools are usually interested in participating in such initiatives, *provided that* pupils involved come from their own school population. On-site units serving a broader catchment area are far less popular, at least in the secondary phase, because schools fear that such provision will create additional problems (and affect their image). On-site units are often relatively well-resourced. In this form, any generalisation of such provision to other schools (even if limited to those schools with higher levels of need) would be very expensive and unlikely to be achieved without considerable extra government resources. In this context, what can be learned by other schools from those with project funds, if they are unable to access these themselves?

A similar issue occurs at local authority level. Some have been particularly successful in accessing funds from a range of government project sources. It is often these that tend to be quoted as examples of good or innovative practice with regard to social inclusion. And yet, how can other local authorities learn from these without similar levels of additional funding?

(c) Judging effectiveness

It is rare, in the author's experience, that schools, authorities or others say that additional project funds have *not* been useful. Any additional resources are likely to be put to some good use. The critical issue is whether funds are spent to the best effect. In practice, it is difficult to judge project effectiveness for a number of reasons. First, even though specific outcome measures are used (e.g. reductions in numbers of exclusions), these cannot always be related directly to project inputs. They may be affected by other developments. Moreover, in some areas, there are a number of projects working in parallel and it can be difficult to establish which element is responsible for the positive effects achieved. Second, although funding bodies aspire to have some degree of control over the focus of individual projects, this is rarely the case in practice.

Education Action Zones are a case in point. The large amount of funds involved, together with the multiplicity of projects initiated, presents a monitoring nightmare. Centralisation of project management leads to high levels of administration and bureaucracy, whereas delegation of funds and responsibility tends to lead to practice that is parochial and where comparisons cannot easily be made.

(d) Operational issues

A more practical problem with projects, particularly with shorter term funding, is that it can be difficult to recruit staff and there is normally some delay before they can start work. This creates problems in meeting expected timescales, as well as making effective use of the finance available.

It is perhaps not surprising that some schools and local authorities have argued that the large amount of project funds which the government is retaining centrally (to achieve better control, in its view, over priority and focus) would be better spent on enhancing levels of core provision. One secondary head teacher (Sweeney 2000) comments as follows: 'In recent years, this emphasis on circumscribed funding has advanced to uncharted levels. Central government has discovered the use of influencing the educational agenda by backing its priorities with ring-fenced cash. This is designed to ensure that funding percolates to those parts perceived as most important ... Schools are required to account separately for the extra money which is restricted to particular purposes. We inevitably find ourselves justifying the use of additional funding for what should be core activities. We don't imagine that anyone is deceived in the process, but we are left with no alternative, as we are faced with a tight core budget on the one hand and an *embarras de richesses* for specified activities on the other.'

Towards a more rational policy for emotional and behavioural difficulties

In an earlier paper (Gray 1997), I suggested that some irrationality in policy with regard to emotional and behavioural difficulties is probably inevitable. In this chapter, I am arguing that this should be minimised. More careful thought needs to be given to the longer term issues presented by 'solutions' such as those described above, which may have short-term political 'capital', but are not, in the long run, a sensible or useful 'investment'. The following principles are suggested to guide developments: it is argued that these should ultimately make a difference, although they offer no magic or immediate 'solution':

1 Maximise the funding provided directly to schools for them to manage as flexibly as possible.
2 Link this funding to clear expectations about inclusive practice (which should be monitored at a school level as part of the government's measurement of standards).
3 Develop sustainable models of behaviour support, involving:
    i   long-term funding;
    ii   clarity about the need for turnover/throughput;
    iii a capacity for both prevention and substantial intervention when needed;
    iv   clearly expressed and agreed performance indicators.
4 Improve coordination across agencies, with joint accountability for all relevant outcomes at managerial level and close working links 'on the ground'.
5 Improve coordination across any new development initiatives, so that these do not work in a piecemeal way or lead to duplication. This could be achieved through more explicit area coordination, led by local authorities or other relevant agencies.
6 A more realistic and comprehensive approach to evaluation, which includes outcomes at school, pupil and family level and considers both short-term and longer term effects.

The key elements in all these principles are simplification, stability and greater coordination. Unfortunately, the history of policy in this area has tended to be very different, with successive new 'big ideas' replacing old ones which are seen to have failed. In fact, there is little new in some of the initiatives currently in progress. Schools have experienced the joys and pains of on-site units over the years. And are the latest round of home-school initiatives so different to those generated by the community liaison teachers of old? Maybe it is important to recognise that this particular policy area is not *soluble*; our response should be guided more by the lessons we have learned through experience (that can often feel like a hard struggle for all involved). As a number of authors have already indicated in this book, the solution is not to develop a further range of fragmented, incoherent and largely ineffective responses, but to work together to draw on what we already know and get the best out of what is already available.

References:

Audit Commision (1999) *Missing Out: LEA management of school attendance and exclusion*, Abingdon: Audit Commission Publications.

Canter, L. and Canter, M. (1992) *Lee Canter's Assertive Discipline: Positive Behaviour Management for Today's Classroom*, Santa Monica, CA: Canter and Associates.

DfEE (Department for Education and Employment) (1997) *Excellence for All Children: Meeting Special Educational Needs*, London: The Stationery Office.

Evans, J., Lunt, I., Wedell, K. and Dyson, A. (1999) *Collaborating for Effectiveness: Empowering Schools to be Inclusive*, Buckingham: Open University Press.

Gray, P. J., Miller, A. and Noakes, J. (eds) (1994) *Challenging Behaviour in Schools: Teacher Support, Practical Techniques and Policy Development*, London: Routledge.

Gray P. J. (1997) 'Policy in a world of emotions: Where to now with EBD?', Keynote chapter in *'Inclusion or Exclusion': Future Policy for Emotional and Behavioural Difficulties*, London University Institute of Education Policy Options Series, Tamworth: NASEN.

Gray, P. J. and Noakes, J. (1998) 'Current legislation for pupils with emotional and behavioural difficulties: A clear way forward?', *Support for Learning* 13(4): 184–7.

Gray, P. J. (1998) 'Following the patterns of behaviour', *Special!*, Autumn: 20–1.

Gray, P. J. and Panter, S. (2000) 'Exclusion or inclusion? A perspective on policy in England for pupils with emotional and behavioural difficulties', *Support for Learning* 15(1): 4–7.

Her Majesty's Inspectors of Schools (HMI) (1989) *A Survey of Provision for Pupils with Emotional/Behavioural Difficulties in Maintained Special Schools and Units*, London: Department of Education and Science.

May, T. (2000) 'Platform: Let's set schools free', *Times Educational Supplement*, 16 June 2000.

Office for Standards in Education (Ofsted) (1995) *Pupil Referral Units: The First Twelve Inspections*, London: Ofsted.

Office for Standards in Education (Ofsted) (2001a) *Standards and Quality in Education: The Annual Report of Her Majesty's Chief Inspector of Schools*, London, The Stationery Office.

Office for Standards in Education (Ofsted) (2001b) *Education Action Zones: commentary on the first six zone inspections – February 2001*, London: Ofsted.

Osler, A. (1997) *Exclusion from School and Racial Equality*, Report to the Commission for Racial Equality, London, CRE.

Smith, J. (2000) 'Exclusions policy myth': Letter to the Editor. *Times Educational Supplement*, 11 August 2000.

Sweeney, P. (2000) 'The pound in your project v core budget', *Times Educational Supplement (Scotland)*, 13th October 2000.

Topping, K.J. (1983) Educational Systems for Disruptive Adolescents. London: Croom Helm.

Index